CRAIN

THE DICTIONARY OF ADVERTISING

edited by
Laurence Urdang
Managing Editor, *Random House Dictionary
of the English Language*.

NTC Business Books
a division of National Textbook Company • Lincolnwood Illinois U.S.A.

Illustrated by Aldona Powers

1988 Printing

Copyright © by Crain Communications, Inc., an imprint of National Textbook Company, 4255 West Touhy Avenue, Lincolnwood (Chicago), Illinois 60646-1975. All rights reserved. No part of this book may be reproduced, stored in a retrieval system, or transmitted in any form, or by any means, electronic, mechanical, photocopying or otherwise, without the prior written permission of National Textbook Company.
Library of Congress Catalog Card No. 76-45506.
Manufactured in the United States of America.

8 9 0 ML 0 9 8 7 6 5 4 3 2

Dedicated to Arthur E. Tatham
and the late J. Kenneth Laird, founders of
Tatham-Laird & Kudner

PREFACE

The need for a comprehensive dictionary of advertising terms has long been evident. The intended purpose of this volume is to provide the user with the most complete, accurate, durable and convenient record available of the meanings of words and terms used by North American marketers, particularly those involved with advertising.

The vocabularies which form this glossary include those used in marketing planning, copywriting, art direction, graphic supply, print production, commercial production, program production, media planning, media research, media analysis, media buying, marketing research, consumer research, field interviewing, statistical analysis, merchandising and promotion planning, public relations counseling, data processing and advertising finance.

This first published edition incorporates over 4,000 entries—fully ten percent of the number of entries in a recent popular edition of a dictionary of the entire English language. This work is intended to serve as a supplement to such a basic English dictionary. Included are special meanings of ordinary words, words unique to a single specialty, specialized terms, names of devices, services and organizations, and extensive cross-references for abbreviations, acronyms and synonyms.

Reference has been made to the major broadcast networks, industry organizations, and syndicated research firms, since their influence on the basic terminology of the business has been pervasive. Rather than be accused of arbitrary discrimination or excessive length, reference to or the proprietary terminology of such suppliers as project-oriented research houses, advertising agencies or individual media vehicles have not been included. For such items, we refer the reader to such widely available sources as the Red Books, Green Book, Standard Rate & Data, or direct contact with the supplier in question.

Our objective has been to serve a variety of users, from secretaries concerned with spelling and grammar, to students seeking basic understanding of terms, to more experienced professionals concerned with accurately distinguishing between the meanings of one term and another.

The history of development of this volume at Tatham-Laird & Kudner extends over a decade, where progressively expanded versions have been used internally as a reference work for those in the agency's training program. To insure that only the highest standard of editorial quality and accuracy was observed in the published work, the editorial services of Mr. Laurence Urdang and his associates were retained. Mr. Urdang's many distinctions as a lexicographer are widely recognized, particularly his contributions as managing editor of the Random House Dictionary of the English language.

We recognize that while this is the most comprehensive collection of its kind prepared to date, it cannot yet be considered perfect or complete. We invite our readers' suggestions, so that our next edition may be of even more service.

C. R. Standen
Chairman of the Management Committee,
Tatham-Laird & Kudner Advertising

Chicago, Illinois
March 1, 1977

A

A.A., *author's alteration.*

A.A.A.A., *American Association of Advertising Agencies.*

AAAA spot contract, a standardized contract between an advertising agency and spot television supplier which specifies agreed-upon terms of a purchase; model format prepared by the American Association of Advertising Agencies. Cf. *television time contract.*

A.A.F., *American Advertising Federation.*

A and M, *art and mechanical.*

A.A.N.R., *American Association of Newspaper Representatives, Inc.*

A.A. rating, see *average audience rating.*

A.A.W., *Advertising Association of the West.*

A.B.A., *area-by-area allocation.*

ABC, *American Broadcasting Company.*

A.B.C., *Audit Bureau of Circulations.*

abeyance order, a spot television advertising order for commercial time which is not available at the time of purchase.

A.B.M.S., *Audit Bureau of Marketing Services.*

above-the-line cost, (in television) any budgeted expense for producers, directors, cast, or script. Cf. *below-the-line cost.*

A.B.P., *American Business Press, Inc.*

abscissa, *noun* (in statistics) the horizontal coordinate of a graph. Also *x-axis*. Cf. *ordinate.*

abstract, *adjective* (of a television stage set, the background of a photograph, or the like) purely decorative or mood-setting and without resemblance to a specific place.

abstraction, *noun* (in advertising graphics) a composition with recognizable human, animal, or inanimate figures represented as generalized or geometric forms.

Academy leader, 1. (in motion pictures) a leader stating that its film has been made to the specifications of the Academy of Motion Picture Arts and Sciences.
2. a leader of a film numbered so that its reel can begin at the proper moment; lasts eight seconds.

A.C.B., *Advertising Checking Bureau.*

acceptance, *noun* a media supplier's approval of the terms of purchase offered; typically refers to negotiations for purchase of network television time.

access, *noun* see *daypart.*

accordion fold, a zigzag, accordion-like fold in a sheet of material, permitting it to be extended to its full breadth with a single pull.

accordion insert, an insert, as in a magazine, with an accordion fold.

account, *noun* 1. a business relationship, as between an advertising agency and a client.
2. a client of an advertising agency.
3. a customer of a supplier or tradesman, as one purchasing goods or services for advertising production.

account conflict, a potential conflict of interest arising when an advertising agency accepts competing clients.

account executive, 1. an advertising agency employee primarily responsible for maintaining liaison with designated agency clients, and for development and control of advertising plans for clients. Also *account manager, contact executive.*
2. (in Canada) a person who sells media space or time.
3. a representative of a marketing organization responsible for maintaining liaison with designated clients.

account representative, see *account executive.*

account supervisor, an advertising agency employee responsible for supervising the work of account executives, and for maintaining liaison with client counterparts. Cf. *management supervisor.*

A.C.D., *associate creative director.*

acetate, *noun* 1. a thin plastic, used in clear or translucent sheet form for various purposes in advertising graphics, as for overlays and repro proofs.
2. an individually recorded phonograph disc, as opposed to one pressed to reproduce a master.

acetate proof, a printer's proof made on transparent acetate as camera-ready copy or as an overlay.

A.C.I., *Advertising Council, Inc.*

A. C. Nielsen Company, a research and marketing service firm providing such services as: the syndicated *Food Index* and *Food and Drug Index,* reporting measured consumer product purchases (in contract-specified categories) in food, drug, and mass merchandiser outlets, using bimonthly sample audits; the syndicated *Television Index* and *Station Index,* reporting measured audience size and composition for (respectively) national and local television programming; and the *Coupon Clearing House,* which processes store redeemable coupons for clients under contract.

A county, any county belonging to the twenty-five largest cities and consolidated urban areas in the United States; the designation is that of the A. C. Nielsen Co. Cf. *B county, C county, D county.*

across the board, (in television or radio) on the same station, at the same time, on every available day of the week, typically Monday through Friday.
across-the-board, *adj.*

action, *noun* 1. (in television or motion pictures) any movement intended to be transmitted or recorded.
2. a director's order to begin such movements.

action shot, 1. see *moving shot.*
2. a photograph of something or someone in motion.

ACV, *all commodity volume basis.*

A.D., 1. *assistant director.*
2. *art director.*

ad, *noun* 1. see *advertisement.*
adjective 2. see *advertising.*

Ad-A-Card, *noun, trademark* a perforated tear-off coupon attached to advertisements in selected Sunday newspaper comics and supplement sections.

Addressograph, *noun, trademark* a machine printing addresses on envelopes or the like from letterpress plates through an inked ribbon.

adequate sample, (in statistics) a sample large enough to minimize chance as a factor affecting the data obtained in an investigation.

A.D.I., *area of dominant influence.*

adjacency, *noun* 1. a television or radio program preceding or following another.

2. an interval between programs, available as commercial time.

ad lib, 1. verbal or physical action introduced by a performer without specific reference to a script, score, or the like.
2. something done by a performer in this way.

adnorm, *noun* a term used by the research firm of Daniel Starch & Associates to indicate the amount of measured readership exposure of an advertisement placed in a certain periodical, based on experience with the periodical, the size of the advertisement, the use or non-use of color, and the type of product advertised, considered as a proportion of the norm established for advertisements of the same sort. Also *adnorm score.* Cf. *noted, seen/associated, read most.*

ad-noter, *noun* a term used by the research firm of Daniel Starch & Associates to designate a reader who claims to have noticed an advertisement in a certain issue of a certain periodical. Cf. *noted score.*

adpage, *noun* (in Canada) the percentage of readers of the target area for printed advertising who have actually observed the page containing the advertising.

advance canvass, a round of visits to retailers in a territory to obtain support for a promotional campaign.

advertise, *verb* to attempt to persuade people to voluntarily produce a recommended behavior pattern by presenting them with an openly sponsored, multiply reproduced message; the message is delivered by purchased use of a medium's space or time. Public service advertising is excepted, since media do not charge for placement of such messages.

advertised price, 1. (in television or radio) a standard price for a quantity of advertising time, taking into consideration the frequency of the advertiser's commercials and the total amount of time he has purchased. Cf. *basic price.*
2. the price for a product or service as stated in an advertisement.

advertisement, *noun* an openly sponsored, multiply reproduced message, intended to persuade people to voluntarily produce a recommended behavior pattern, and presented by purchased use of a medium. Also *ad.*

advertiser, *noun* a person or organization that pays for the placement of an advertisement.

advertising, *noun* 1. a marketing process which uses advertisements directed to prospects as a means of meeting marketing objectives; as a marketing tool, advertising is uniquely able to reliably and quickly deliver consistent messages, efficiently.
2. a commercial profession or craft which seeks to develop and place advertisements in the most productive, efficient manner possible.
3. loosely, an advertisement or advertisements. Also *ad.*
advertising, *adj.*

advertising agency, an independent commercial service organization that contracts with advertisers to develop and manage their advertising, for a fee or for a commission derived from a standard media discount on the advertiser's spending. Also *agency.*

advertising allowance, a payment or service by a source of goods or his representative to a merchant for advertising a product of the source.

advertising appropriation, the amount of money budgeted by an advertiser for advertising for a specific period of time.

Advertising Association of the West, a group of West Coast advertising organizations, absorbed into the American Advertising Federation in 1967. Abbreviated *A.A.W.*

Advertising Checking Bureau, a service organization that supplies advertisers and agencies with tearsheets of advertisements run in publications and with other information, in order that client and competitor advertising impact can be assessed. Abbreviated *A.C.B.*

advertising contract, 1. an agreement between an advertiser and a communications medium for advertising space or time; usually negotiated by an advertising agency.
2. an agreement between a source of goods or his representative and a retailer that the latter will advertise the former's goods in return for stated consideration.

Advertising Council, Inc., The, a nonprofit organization, supported by the American Association of Advertising Agencies, that acts as a medium for the production of messages regarded as in the public interest, such as support of nonpartisan political causes, charities, etc. Abbreviated *A.C.I.*

Advertising Federation of America, an association of organizations representing various activities relating to advertising; now part of the American Advertising Federation. Abbreviated *A.F.A.*

advertising manager, an employee of an organization that advertises who is reponsible for review and approval of advertising plans and usually, executions of advertisements; sometimes responsible for approval of sales promotion plans. Typically reports to a marketing director.

Advertising Register, See *Standard Advertising Register.*

Advertising Research Foundation, a foundation sponsored by advertisers, advertising agencies, advertising media, and researcher associations, with the purpose of advancing advertising research methodology and maintaining research standards; when invited, it will audit and endorse those research projects which meet its standards. It publishes the *Journal of Advertising Research.* Abbreviated *A.R.F.*

advertising reserve, an advertising budget fund established without a prior specification for its use, to be used subsequently for unanticipated contingencies.

advertising weight, the number of advertising messages used in or planned for a campaign. Also *support.*

advisory board, 1. a group of retailers who advise a wholesaler on items to be stocked, merchandised, and advertised cooperatively by a voluntary association of such retailers. Also *advisory committee.*
2. a group of brokers advising a manufacturer.

A.F.A., *Advertising Federation of America.*

affidavit of performance, a notarized statement from a television or radio station that a message or program was presented as ordered.

affiliate, *noun* 1. any organization that contracts to supply goods or services, to advertise and merchandise, or in various ways to carry out the policies of a company operated in close association with it.
2. a television or radio station that contracts to make a portion of its time available to a network.
verb 3. to unite with another company as an affiliate.

affiliated chain, a regional chain of retail stores associated with other, noncompeting stores for the advantage of large-scale purchasing or for exclusive territorial rights to the marketing of certain brands.

affiliated retailer, 1. a retailer affiliated with a voluntary chain.
2. a retailer who participates with others in a cooperative wholesale purchasing operation.

affiliated wholesaler, 1. a wholesaler who sponsors a voluntary chain of affiliated retailers.
2. a wholesaler who is a member of a voluntary chain of wholesalers.

"affordable" method, a method for determining marketing budgets based on use of judgment as to what is affordable after other spending and profit goals are established.

A.F.M., *American Federation of Musicians.*

afterimage, *noun* an illusory visual image remaining with a spectator after the actual image is no longer visible.

afternoon drive, see *daypart.*

AFTRA, *noun* see *American Federation of Television and Radio Artists.*

A.F.T.R.A., *American Federation of Television and Radio Artists.*

agate line, (in periodical publishing) a unit of space calculated for advertising sales purposes; equal to 1/14 inch in depth by one standard column in width. Also *line.*

agency, *noun* see *advertising agency.*

agency commission, a commission paid by a communications medium, as a television or radio station or a periodical, to an advertising agency, usually in the form of a 15% discount on the gross advertising rate billed to a client by the agency.

agency network, see *network.*

agency of record, an agency that purchases media time or space for another agency or a group of agencies serving the same client. Abbreviated *A.O.R.*

agency-produced program, (in television or radio) a program, often a special or spectacular, assembled as a package by an advertising agency and sold to a station or network ready for presentation.

agency recognition, see *recognition.*

agency recommendation, see *recommendation.*

agent, *noun* any self-employed person who negotiates the buying and selling of goods or services without taking title to such goods or services.

A.G.M.A., *American Guild of Musical Artists.*

Agricultural Publishers Association, a nonprofit organization of publishers of periodicals edited for farmers' interests. Abbreviated *A.P.A.*

AID, 1. *Arbitron Information on Demand.*
2. *Automatic Interaction Detector.*

aided recall, a measure of recall of an advertisement or series of advertisements by a test respondent who has been aided by prompting.

air, *verb* 1. to broadcast (a television or radio commercial or program).
adjective 2. noting or pertaining to that which is broadcast.

AIR BRUSH

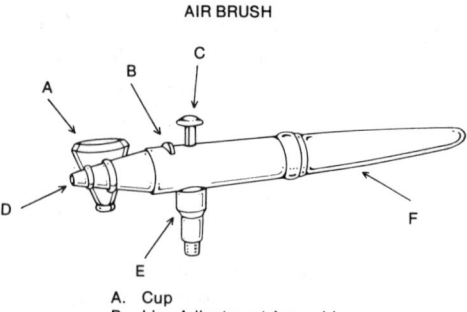

A. Cup
B. Line Adjustment Assembly
C. Finger Lever
D. Protecting Cap
E. Valve Casing
F. Handle

airbrush, *noun* 1. a device for applying paint by means of an atomizer, making possible subtle gradations of tone; used in poster work and photographic retouching. *verb* 2. to paint a surface with an airbrush.

air check, a recording of a television or radio broadcast, used by a sponsor for evaluation and record-keeping purposes.

air date, a scheduled broadcast date for a television or radio program or commercial.

all commodity volume basis, see *distribution.* Abbreviated *ACV.*

All-Inclusive Study, an A. C. Nielsen Co. report on audience data containing tabulation of four-week cumulative television audiences, used to estimate reach and frequency and to calculate gross rating points.

all-news format, see *format.*

allocation, *noun* 1. (in television and radio) the assignment of frequency and power to a station by the Federal Communications Commission.
2. (in promotion) a preassigned quantity of merchandise to be made available or sold to an individually designated prospect. Also *allotment.*

"all other" circulation, circulation outside city limits and the retail trading zone of a newspaper's market of origin, as established by the Audit Bureau of Circulations.

allotment, *noun* 1. a specific number of poster panels offered to an advertiser by an outdoor advertising company.
2. any equitable distribution of advertising space or time for which demand exceeds supply.
3. See *allocation.*

allowance, a special temporary price reduction on merchandise offered to retailers by manufacturers or their representatives; usually temporary, and often accompanied by specific cooperative terms of sale, such as that the retailer will temporarily lower his resale price to consumers. Also *temporary allowance, buying allowance.*

All Radio Marketing Study 2, a report prepared by Three Sigma Research which provides data on cross-media audience duplication as related to product usage in selected product categories; New York City and Los Angeles provide the sample bases. Abbreviated *ARMS 2.*

alternate-bundles run, (in periodical printing) a variety of split run in which different versions of an advertisement are printed in separate phases of a press run, the two versions of the advertisement being geographically co-mingled when the issues are bundled for circulation delivery.

alternate sponsorship, sponsorship of a television or radio program by two or more advertisers in turn, day by day, week by week, or program by program, within the same time slot.

alternate weeks, scheduling instructions to a medium, especially newspapers, indicating advertisements are to appear every other week.

AM, (amplitude modulation) a method of radio broadcasting, using the signal from a source (microphone, tape, record, etc.) to modulate the amplitude of the carrier wave generated by a radio transmitter to produce sound: 550 to 1600 kilohertz. Cf. *FM.*

A.M.A., *American Marketing Association.*

ambient light, (in theater, motion pictures, and television) undirected light giving general illumination to a scene.

ambient sound, (in theater, motion pictures, television, and recording) the sound reflected from interior surfaces rather than direct from a sound source.

American Advertising Federation, a national association of advertising agencies, media owners, advertisers, and others whose purposes are to promote professional and public understanding of the usefulness of advertising and to raise professional standards. Founded in 1967, it is a merger of the Advertising Federation of America and the Advertising Association of the West. Abbreviated *A.A.F.*

American Association of Advertising Agencies, a national association of independent advertising agencies, whose purpose is the promotion of advertising generally, the improvement of the advertising business, and service to member agencies and their employees. Abbreviated *A.A.A.A.* Also *Four A's, 4 A's.*

American Association of Newspaper Representatives, Inc., the former name of the National Advertising Sales Association. Abbreviated *A.A.N.R.*

American Broadcasting Company, a television and radio network founded in 1927; known until 1945 as the Blue Network. Abbreviated *ABC.*

American Business Press, Inc., an organization of business publishers founded in 1965 with a merger of Associated Business Publications and National Business Publications. Abbreviated *A.B.P.*

American Federation of Musicians, a national union of musicians. Abbreviated *A.F.M.*

American Federation of Television and Radio Artists, a union of actors, singers, announcers, and certain technicians in live television and radio broadcasting. Abbreviated *A.F.T.R.A.* Also *AFTRA.*

American Guild of Musical Artists, a union of musicians. Abbreviated *A.G.M.A.*

American Marketing Association, a national association, formed in 1937, for the promotion of improved marketing practices. It publishes the *Journal of Marketing* and the *Journal of Marketing Research.* Abbreviated *A.M.A.*

American Newspaper Publishers Association, an organization, founded in 1887, of publishers of daily newspapers in the U.S. and Canada. It has about 1000 members, for whom it maintains economic data of various kinds, including the credit ratings of some 1200 advertising agencies. Abbreviated *A.N.P.A.*

American Psychological Association, a professional organization of practicing psychologists and professors of psychology. Abbreviated *A.P.A.*

American Research Bureau, Inc., a national measurement service providing information on television and radio audience size and composition for advertisers and advertising agencies. Abbreviated *A.R.B.*

American Society of Composers, Authors and Publishers, an organization, formed in 1914, that licenses nondramatic performances of musical compositions on behalf of its members and collects royalties for them. Also *ASCAP.* Abbreviated *A.S.C.A.P.*

American Statistical Association, a national professional organization of statisticians, founded 1839, publishing the *Journal of the American Statistical Association.* Of interest to marketing and advertising researchers are two sections: that of Business and Economic Statistics, and that of Social Statistics. Abbreviated *A.S.A.*

American Television and Radio Commercials Festival, an annual competition of commercials for a gold statuette (*Clio*) awarded to the outstanding competitors.

amplifier, *noun* a device for strengthening an electronic signal. Also *amp.* Cf. *preamplifier.*

amplitude modulation, see *AM.*

A.N.A., *Association of National Advertisers.*

analysis of variance, a statistical method of determining the relative input of a number of variables on a specified outcome.

anchor, *verb* to mount (a printing plate) on a block with screws and solder.

angle shot, (in motion pictures, television, and photography) any shot from an unusual angle, e.g., from above or diagonally on the same level.

animatic, *adjective* 1. noting or pertaining to mechanical animation.
noun 2. a television commercial produced from semi-finished artwork, generally used only for test purposes. Cf. *photomatic.*

animation, *noun* (in motion pictures or television) the creation of an effect of movement, life, or human character to a representation of an object, animal, or person. This may be done by means of a series of cartoons *(cartoon animation);* a film creating a story or a repeated sequence *(cyclic animation);* the actual movement of drawings *(mechanical* or *limited animation);* or the imparting of motion to photographed objects *(live animation).*

animation camera, a camera used for photographing animations, frame by frame, as the objects photographed are moved on a table (*animation stand*) beneath.

announcement, *noun* a television or radio advertising message, especially one between programs. Cf. *occasion, commercial.*

announcer, *noun* 1. a person employed by a television or radio station to introduce programs, and to deliver information, announcements, commercials, etc.
2. a commercial spokesperson.

annual discount, a discount given by a print or broadcast medium to an advertiser who purchases fifty-two consecutive weeks of space or time. Also *annual rebate.*

A.N.P.A., *American Newspaper Publishers Association.*

answer print, a final film print of a television commercial prepared for review and approval before airing. Cf. *fine cut.*

antenna, *noun* a tall structure for the broadcasting or reception of television or radio waves.

antique finish, *noun* a relatively soft, textured paper used mainly for folders, leaflets, and the text pages of books. Also *antique paper.*

A.O.R., *agency of record.*

A.P.A., *American Psychological Association.*

A.P.O., *optical answer print.*

applause mail, mail expressing approval of or commenting favorably on a television or radio program.

apple box, *noun* (in television) a riser for a performer or prop.

Aquatone, *noun, trademark* an early form of the Optak process.

A.R.B., *American Research Bureau, Inc.*

arbitrary method, a method for determining an advertising appropriation based on an estimate of cost made in the absence of objective cost figures.

Arbitron, 1. *noun* an automatic electronic monitoring device used by the American Research Bureau to give immediate information on television viewership. Arbitrons placed in the television sets of a representative sample of area viewers furnish information on channels being viewed to a central computer for tabulation. Cf. *Audimeter.*
2. television audience measurement services of ARB based on use of the Arbitron device's data.

Arbitron Information on Demand, an Arbitron service that provides client specified custom spot television audience measurement data. Abbreviated *AID.*

arc, *verb* (of a motion picture or television camera) to move in a curve while making a shot.

arc lamp, (in photography) a brilliant lamp that uses the arc between two slightly separated electrodes and the vaporization of the electrodes as its source of illumination.

arc light, (in photography and motion pictures) a light that uses the electric arc between electrodes as a source of brilliant illumination of a scene or a set.

area-by-area allocation, a technique for assigning an advertiser's media budget on a local basis in a manner proportionate to established or potential local sales of the advertiser's product or service. Abbreviated *A.B.A., ABA.* Also *market-by-market allocation, MBM.*

area of dominant influence, a geographic market assignment made by Arbitron on a county-by-county basis, on the basis of which a home market receives the preponderance of television viewing from each county. Abbreviated *A.D.I.* Cf. *exclusive market area.*

area sample, (in statistics) a population sample selected by geographical area.

A.R.F., *Advertising Research Foundation.*

ARMS 2, *All Radio Marketing Study 2.*

arousal method, a method for testing advertising effectiveness in which a galvanometer attached to a respondent measures differences in the sweating of his palms. Cf. *galvanic skin response.*

arrears, *plural noun* subscribers whose subscriptions to a periodical have lapsed but who are retained temporarily on active subscription lists. According to Audit Bureau of Circulations, arrears must be dropped from circulation figures after three months.

art, *noun* any illustration in an advertisement that is not typeset, including photographs and hand lettering. Also *artwork.*

art and mechanical, noting or pertaining to graphic materials required for production of an advertisement: *art and mechanical costs.* Abbreviated *A and M.*

art buyer, an employee of an advertising agency or commercial studio who is responsible for commissioning art or photography for advertising reproduction.

art card, (in television) a cardboard sign, about 11" by 14", bearing light letters or designs against a black background.

art director, an employee of an advertising agency or similar organization who is responsible for developing the general design, and supervising the final artwork (and often typography) of advertisements. Abbreviated *A.D.*

art service, an independent service for the creation of advertising art.

A.S.A., 1. *American Statistical Association.*
2. *American Standards Association.*

A.S.A. rating, a measure of the speed with which a given type of film reacts to light, as indicated by the American Standards Association system.

ASCAP, *noun* see *A.S.C.A.P.*

A.S.C.A.P., *American Society of Composers, Authors and Publishers.*

ascender, *noun* (in typography) a stroke of a lower-case letter going above the x-height; b, d, f, h, k, l, and t have ascenders. Cf. *descender.*

ascending letter, (in typography) any letter that rises above the x-height, as a capital letter or a lower-case letter with an ascender.

as-it-falls method, a technique for assigning media weight to a test market which attempts to deliver the same level of weight which would be delivered into that market by the theoretical national plan to be tested. Cf. *little America method, correct increment method, translation.*

aspect ratio, the width of a motion picture or television screen in relation to its height.

assembly dailies, film footage from a day's shooting selected and spliced in proper sequence.

assessment method, a method for determining an advertising appropriation based on a specific amount per item sold in the most recent budgetary period.

assistant director, (in motion pictures or television) a person whose job it is to assist in implementing a director's instructions.

associate creative director, an advertising agency employee responsible for devising advertisements, and who reports to a creative director.

association, *noun* 1. (in statistics) the degree of measurable apparent relationship between two statistical variables as measured by co-variations in the relationship.
2. (in psychology) the joining of two ideas or of two words expressing such ideas in the mind of a subject. In *controlled association,* the subject is limited in his ideas or words by his instructions; in *free association* he is allowed to express any idea that comes spontaneously to mind, especially as a response to a stimulus, such as a word or object.

Association of National Advertisers, an association of business organizations that advertise nationally, formed to promote effective advertising and to forward the interests of its members. Abbreviated *A.N.A.*

assortment, the variety and combination of products or service offered for sale by an organization. Also *product line.*

atmospherics, *noun* the graphic identity of a corporation, as represented by the physical appearance of all of its publicly visible property, communications, and employees.

attitude intensity, (in psychology) the degree of resistance to change in an attitude.

attitude scale, (in research) a quantitative scale used to measure repondents' attitudinal response to a given stimuli.

attitude study, a survey of attitudes toward an organization, product, service, etc., as expressed in the answers of respondents to questions; often made before and after an advertising campaign or the like to determine change of attitude.

audience, *noun* 1. persons or households with persons who view or hear television or

radio programs or commercials, or who read a given print medium or advertisement, especially as expressed in a quantitative measurement.
2. see *studio audience.*

audience accumulation, the total net audience exposed to repeated periodical, outdoor, television, or radio advertising.

audience composition, see *audience profile.*

audience duplication, the degree of exposure of a television or radio audience to more than one program sponsored by an advertiser or of a potential periodical readership to the same advertising in different issues or different magazines. The number of duplicate exposures is usually expressed as a percentage of the total.

audience flow, the prior and subsequent program selections made by the audience of a television or radio program, statistically measured. Three options are possible: the same station; another station; and the set not in use.

audience-holding index, an index of the degree to which the audience of a television or radio program at its beginning continues to hear it until its end.

audience-participation program, a television or radio program in which the active cooperation of the studio audience (or at home listeners to live shows) is requested in the production of the show.

audience profile, a digest of the relevant characteristics of the typical audience of a communications medium, such as age, family size, income, or location; used to evaluate the suitability of the medium for specific kinds of advertising. Also *audience composition, percent composition.*

audilog, *noun* a log of programs seen by television viewers collaborating in a rating survey conducted by the A. C. Nielsen Company, as prepared by an Audimeter.

Audimeter, *noun, trademark* an electronic device used by the A. C. Nielsen Co. for the automatic recording of television set use and tuning by viewers collaborating in a rating survey. Cf. *Arbitron.*

audio, *noun* 1. the medium of electrically transmitted or reproduced sound, especially in the context of television, where the audio signal, supplying the sound, is contrasted with the video signal, supplying the image.

audit, *noun* 1. any official examination of accounts, statistics, or other figures kept by a business.
2. (in periodical publishing) such as an examination of circulation figures by the Audit Bureau of Circulations.

Audit Bureau of Circulations, an organization of advertising agencies, advertisers, and publishers whose purpose is to determine correct circulation figures for periodicals of publisher members and to distribute these for the benefit of the membership as a whole. A *publisher's statement,* verified by an *audit report,* is issued. Abbreviated *A.B.C.*

Audit Bureau of Marketing Services, an organization affiliated with the Audit Bureau of Circulations, established in 1966 to offer auditing services to various advertising media and marketing services not audited by the A.B.C. Abbreviated *A.B.M.S.*

audition, *noun* 1. a performance by an actor, musician, or other performer to determine his or her suitability for use in a show, program or advertising commercial.
2. a test performance of a program to determine its suitability for sponsorship.

audition record, a recording or transcription of a radio program that serves the purposes of an audition.

audit report, an annual report, printed on white paper, disclosing the results of an audit by the Audit Bureau of Circulations. Also *white audit.*

authorization, *noun* a chain headquarter's approval allowing their stores to stock or otherwise promote a designated item.

authorized item, (in retailing) an item authorized by chain headquarters for distribution or promotion at a store manager's discretion, but not carried in the chain's warehouse.

author's alteration, 1. (in proofreading) an alteration made on a proof by the author or on his behalf.
2. either such an alteration or an editorial alteration; any alteration other than one to correct printer's error. Abbreviated *A.A.* Also *author's correction.* Cf. *editorial alteration, printer's error.*

autocorrelation, (in statistics) the correlation of each error term in a regression model with a preceding error term; can bias linearity of estimates prepared by ordinary least squares estimation. Also *serial correlation.*

automatic distribution, distribution of goods by a wholesaler or by the headquarters of a chain to retailers without a specific order; usually done on a guaranteed-sale basis.

Automatic Interaction Detector, a multivariate technique used for reducing large combinations of data to determine what variables (e.g., demographic and attitudinal) and categories within these variables combine to produce the greatest discrimination in defining a dependent variable such as product or brand usage. Abbreviated *A.I.D.*

automatic merchandising, the use of vending machines as a means of retail distribution and sale.

automatic ordering, (in retailing) arrangement for a standing order to replenish a basic stock item.

automatic vending machine, see *vending machine.*

availability, *noun* (in television or radio) a period of time offered by a station or network for sponsorship. Also **avail.**

available audience, (in Canada) potential television or radio audience.

available commercial time, (in television or radio) the amount of commercial time allowed during a specific broadcast period by the code of the National Association of Radio and Television Broadcasters.

average, *noun* (in statistics) a figure accepted as the exact medium in a set of figures considered together. Also *mean.* Cf. *median, mode.*

average audience rating, (in television or radio) a rating based on the number of persons tuned in to a program compared with some basic figure, e.g., the number the program is able to reach; calculated by averaging a series of ratings made at intervals over a brief period of time. Also *AA rating.*

average frequency, the number of exposures of an average household or consumer over a specified period of time to a series of advertisements through all media carrying the advertisements.

average net paid circulation, the average circulation of a periodical per issue, established by dividing the total number of copies sold for the period being examined by the number of issues during the period.

Average Valued Impressions Delivered, (in Canada) the sum of the average gross audience for a television or radio program, time block, etc., as estimated at quarter-hour intervals. Abbreviated *AVIDS.*

A/W, *alternate weeks.*

B

baby billboard, *informal* a car card.

baby spotlight, a small theatrical spotlight. Also *dinky inkie, inky, inky dink.*

backer card, *noun* a large advertising card or poster designed to fit on the back of a display bin or on a pole.

background, *noun* 1. (in television or radio) anything supporting the primary message of a commercial, as scenery, music, or sound effects. Abbreviated *B.G.*
2. the stated context of previous occurrences, current environment, and desires for the future within which advertising and marketing plans are developed and executed.

backing, *noun* (in television) any flat visual background for a performance.

backlight, *verb* (in photography or the performing arts) to light a person or object from a position more or less behind. **backlighting,** *n.*

backload, *verb* to schedule the use of the bulk of a budget for the latter part of a planning period; serves as a precaution against overspending a budget which may be reduced. Cf. *front load.*

back of book, the section of a magazine following the main editorial section.

back room, *noun* the product storage area of a retail store, as distinguished from the sales area.

back-time, *verb* 1. to time a draft of a script backwards from fixed copy of known length at the end, to determine remaining time available.
2. to time a television performance, recording, etc. backwards to synchronize added effects.

back-to-back, two commercials or programs shown one directly after the other.

back up, 1. to print the reverse side of a sheet after printing its face. Also *backup.*
2. to solder metal to a printing plate to increase its thickness to 11 pt. for patent base printing.

back-up space, an advertisement space which must be purchased in a magazine or newspaper in order to run an insert; usually equivalent to one black and white page. Also *back-up page.*

baffle, *noun* (in motion pictures, television, and radio) a movable partition for absorbing sound or light and thus preventing undesirable reflection.

bait advertising, advertising that offers a sale item at a low price to entice buyers, although the cost of an actual purchase is intended to be higher.

balance, *noun* (in film, television, or radio) the blending of sounds, as dialogue and background music, so that they are in a proper relation when heard.

balanced, *adjective* 1. (of retail items) featured and sold together.
2. displayed together but sold separately.

balancing light, a secondary light upon a photographic subject, motion picture or television scene, etc. intended to prevent excessive light-and-shade contrast from the key light. Also *fill light, flat light.*

BALLOON

balloon, *noun* an enclosed space in a cartoon containing the dialogue or thoughts of a character.

Balopticon, *noun, trademark* 1. (in television) a machine made by Bausch & Lomb that projects still images, usually onto a reflecting surface, for tracing or for pickup by a camera.
2. a slide used with this device. Also *balop.*

B&W, *black and white.*

banner, *noun* 1. a display poster for retail advertising, especially one draped over a wire or cord so as to be readable from both sides.
2. a bold newspaper headline.

bantam store, a small food store run like a supermarket but limited in stock to food, with only certain brands and item sizes available.

B.A.P.S.A., *Broadcast Advertising Producers Society of America.*

B.A.R., *Broadcast Advertising Reports.*

bar graph, see *graph.*

barn door, *noun* (in photography) a device consisting of adjustable flaps at the sides of a floodlamp, used to keep the projected light from certain areas.

barter, *noun* (in television or radio) the furnishing of products by an advertiser as full or partial payment for spot broadcasting time or free mentions. Time so purchased is called **barter time,** and its purchase is usually arranged by a **barter broker.**

base, *noun* 1. A wooden or metal block on which a printing plate is mounted. Also *block, mount.*
2. (in statistics) the total number of items in a sample, representing the denominator in the computation of percentages.

base figure, (in statistics) a figure with which other figures are compared.

base line, (in typography) the line on which the base of all the capitals of a font and the bodies of all its lower-case letters align.

base rate, see *open rate.*

basher, *noun* see *scoop.*

basic network, the minimum group of stations belonging to a television or radio network; used as a basis for contract negotiations with an advertiser.

basic price, the standard price of a periodical, for which it is sold to its ordinary readership under normal conditions. Also *advertised price.*

basic service, (in Canada) a cable television service equivalent in range to that of a conventional VHF television set. Cf. *converter service.*

basis weight, the weight of a ream (500 sheets) of paper, the sheets being of the standard size for the specific type of paper. For writing paper the standard size is 17 by 22 inches; for book paper, 25 by 38 inches; for cover stock, 20 by 26 inches.

bastard measure, (in typography) a line not evenly measured in picas or half picas.

bastard size, any size that does not conform to standard sizes in typography, periodical make-up, or prescribed advertising space units.

battered, *noun* (in printing) damaged type

or plate not suitable for printing. Also *battered type*.

Bayesian analysis, (in statistics) a method for assigning subjective probabilities to uncertain conditions, rather than relying solely on objective data obtained from samples or populations.

B.B.M., *Bureau of Broadcast Measurement*.

BC, *back cover, outside; fourth cover:* used in ordering advertising.

B county, a county other than an A county that has more than 150,000 inhabitants in itself or that is part of a metropolitan area with more than 150,000 inhabitants; the designation is that of the A. C. Nielsen Co. Cf. *A county, C county, D county*.

B.C.P., *broken-case price*.

B.D., *brand development*.

B.D.I., *brand development index*.

bearer, *noun* 1. (in printing) a metal strip enclosing set foundry type to distribute pressure when a form is locked up.
2. type-high, dead metal left around an engraved plate during the proofing and molding operations.

beat, *noun* 1. (in acting) a pause long enough to count once.
2. (in music) a rhythm system supporting a musical work.

beauty shot, a close-up of a product advertised in a television commercial.

behaviorism, *noun* (in psychology) a psychological theory that regards actions as the consequence of measurable, conscious factors (e.g., conflict, conditioning, stimuli, reward systems).

believability, *noun* the degree of acceptance as truth of advertising's contents, especially its claims, evidenced by persons exposed to it.

bell cow, see *blue chip*.

bell-shaped curve, see *normal distribution curve*.

below-the-line cost, (in television) any cost for technical assistance, equipment and props, music, special effects, rentals, taxes, insurance, etc. Cf. *above-the-line cost*.

Ben Day process, an obsolete mechanical process for transferring textural effects, as hatching or stippling, from an inked relief film or screen to a printing plate, allowing shaded and tinted areas to be printed as line cuts rather than as halftone plates. Also *Benday process*.

best food day, a day on which a newspaper runs editorial material on food, making that day's edition the most advantageous for retail grocers' advertising and hence, for the advertising of food manufacturers; usually Wednesday evening or Thursday editions.

best time available, schedule an advertiser's commercial, at the broadcast station's discretion, in the best available commercial occasion; a scheduling instruction for television or radio advertising. Abbreviated *B.T.A.*

beta coefficient, a coefficient measuring the relative influence or effect of one variable (the independent or predictor variable) on another variable (the dependent or criteria variable).

Better Business Bureau, an agency supported by a local business community to detect and prosecute frauds and to correct misleading advertising.

bevel, *noun* (in printing) the edge of a printing plate, trimmed on an angle, by which it can be clamped to a press bed or cylinder.

B.G., *background*.

Bible paper, a fine, very lightweight book paper used especially for letterpress and gravure printing. Also *India paper.*

bicycle, *verb* to transport one set of films, engravings, or other reproduction materials from one place of use, as a television studio or printing house, to another to eliminate making duplicate material.

bid, *noun* 1. a stated offer to purchase something at a specified price, usually under circumstances where the seller has not specified a price, or where there exists the potential for the seller finding other competitive buyers for an item or service in scarce supply.
verb 2. to make such an offer.

bill, *noun* 1. see *poster.*
2. an invoice.

billback allowance, a merchandising allowance in which the discount is not given to the purchaser until he provides proof he has complied with the merchandising requirements. Also *billback.*

billboard, *noun* 1. a flat, upright structure for the display of outdoor advertising. Cf. *painted bulletin, poster panel.*
2. an outdoor advertising panel of twenty-four or thirty sheet poster size.
3. (in television and radio) a brief announcement identifying the sponsor of a program.

billing, *noun* 1. a charge made to an advertiser by an advertising agency, based on the listed or gross charges of the media from which space or time has been purchased, along with any other charges and fees incurred by the agency that are passed on to the advertiser.
2. loosely, the money spent by an advertiser through an agency.
3. the actual charge made by a medium of communication to an advertising agency; the gross charge less the agency discount.

bimodal distribution, (in statistics) a distribution of scores that tends to peak at two points rather than forming a normal distribution curve when plotted graphically.

binary system, a mathematical system or language based on the presence or absence (1 or 0) of information.

binaural sound, a two channel audio recording which provides a very close approximation of multidirectional sound sources through headphones; recorded by placing microphones in positions analogous to human ears.

binding, *noun* 1. the process of joining printed sheets into a completed book or the like.
2. the type of process used in joining a book.
3. the part of a book or the like that joins its pages or signatures.

bit, *noun* (in a dramatic performance, commercial, or the like) a single action or scene.

bite, *noun* the etching of a printing plate by an applied acid.

bite off, (in television or radio) to eliminate a scheduled part of a show without previous planning.

black and white, *adjective* 1. (of printed sheets and photographic prints) printed in only one color, typically black, on white paper.
noun 2. a black and white photographic print. Abbreviated *B&W, B/W.* Also *monotone.*

black letter, (in typography) a display type that is characterized by heavy, closely spaced, vertical strokes and imitates the effect of late medieval calligraphy. Also *Gothic.*

blackout, *noun* a ban on local broadcasting of a live event.

black week, a week of network television audience behavior not measured in detail by the A. C. Nielsen Co.; four per year. Also *dark week.*

blanket contract, a general agreement between an advertiser and a medium of communication covering all products advertised, regardless of the agencies involved. Also *master contract.*

blanket coverage, the ability of television and radio stations to reach any place within a geographical area.

blanking paper, (in outdoor advertising) unprinted paper framing a poster.

bleed, *verb* 1. to print an illustration so that it goes to the very edge of a page on one or more sides, without a border or margin.
2. (of an illustration) to extend to the edge of a page in this way.
noun 3. the arrangement of an illustration on a page by bleeding: *a bleed on two sides.*

bleed in the gutter, (in periodical publishing) to run an advertisement uninterrupted across the gutter of a spread; to bridge a gutter.

bleed poster, a poster used on a billboard without a white border.

blind, *adjective* (in printing) using no ink, so as to create a raised or sunken design, as on heavy paper or cardboard: *blind embossing, blind stamping.*
blind, *adv.*

blind offer, an offer placed inconspicuously in an advertisement: often used to measure reader attention to the advertisement. Also *buried offer, hidden offer.*

blind product test, a research test in which respondents are asked to evaluate products bearing no brand names or similar identification.

blister pack, a package consisting of a card faced with a convex plastic casing enclosing the product. Also *bubble card, skin pack.*

block, *noun* 1. any of the successive major time intervals in the daily schedule of a television or radio station.
2. any such time interval on several days of the same week; a strip.
3. see *base.*
verb 4. to mount a printing plate on a block.
5. (in motion pictures or television) to calculate a shot in terms of the camera position and other requirements.
6. to plan the action of a motion picture or television performance in terms of movement and camera shots before a dry run or rehearsal.

block city, a city on which the U.S. Bureau of the Census publishes block-by-block data.

block out, to eliminate areas from a photographic negative or print by masking or opaquing.

blocked-out time, (in television or radio) time that is not sold to advertisers.

block programming, (in television or radio) the scheduling of related programs within the same time block. Cf. *mood programming.*

blowup, *noun* an enlargement of a photograph, illustration, graph or other printed material.
blow up, *v.*

blue, *noun, informal* 1. blueline.
2. blueprint.

blue chip, a high-margin sales item that sells well. Also *bell cow.*

blueline, *noun* a proof of offset printing work, made on photosensitive paper and typically blue. Also *blue.* Cf. *vandyke.*

blueprint, *noun* 1. an inexpensive photographic print that reproduces lines and solid shapes in white on a dark blue background.
verb 2. to copy (lines or figures) on a blueprint.

17

blue sky, *(informal)* see *synectics.*

blurb, *noun, informal* a brief announcement in the editorial content of a medium.

blurmeter, *noun* an optical device for obscuring type, trademarks, and other features of an advertisement or package associated with a brand in order to test the impact of the basic design.

B.M.I., *Broadcast Music, Incorporated.*

B.N.F., *Brand Names Foundation.*

board, (in television or radio) a studio control panel.

board fade, (in television or radio) a diminution of sound created in the control room rather than in the studio. Cf. *live fade.*

body copy, (in printing) the main text of a piece of printed matter, as opposed to a headline, title, or the like. Also **body text.**

body type, type for setting text; type used for body copy. Cf. *display type.*

B. of A., *Bureau of Advertising.*

bogus work, (obsolete custom) unused typesetting of advertising copy composed at a newspaper merely to conform with a union contract; done when a matrix or plate of an advertisement was supplied ready for use.

boldface, *noun* any printing type whose strokes and serifs are thicker than those normal for its font; used to call attention to certain words without an increase in type size.
boldface, *adj.*

bond paper, a hard-surfaced, strong paper used for stationery, documents, envelopes, etc. in its better grades, and in other grades for office forms, price lists, etc.

bonus, a cash reward to an employee conferred in addition to regular earnings; as to a salesperson for extra effort or achievement.

bonus goods, goods given by a manufacturer to a retailer as a reward for a large purchase. Cf. *free goods, allowance.*

bonus pack, a specially packaged product designed to provide purchasers with extra content, at the usual price. Cf. *twin pack.*

bonus spot, a television or radio advertising occasion offered gratis by a station as a means to increase a sponsor's gross rating points or as a bonus for the purchase of a package.

bonus station, a television or radio station carrying a commercial network program free of extra charge in addition to the network stations whose time has been bought by the sponsor.

book, *noun* 1. a piece of reading matter consisting of a number of printed or hand executed pages bound together.
2. (in periodical publishing and advertising) a magazine.
3. see *book flat.*
verb 4. to schedule a program or performer for a broadcast or other public appearance.
booking, *n.*

bookend, see *endpaper.*

book flat, in theater or television, a double flat, hinged at the center so as to fold or unfold. Also *book, two-fold flat, wing flat.*

book paper, a lightly textured, rather bulky paper used for the printing of book texts, and manufactured in sheets whose basic size is 25 by 38 inches.

boom, *noun* (in television) a horizontal arm for positioning a microphone or camera over a set; its operator is a **boom man.**

boondoggle, *noun, informal* a business trip of an unusually attractive nature, paid for wholly or in part by a person's employer or client.

booster, *noun* a device for strengthening television signals received to improve reception.

borax, superficially impressive, low quality merchandise.

bottle hanger, a paper advertisement designed to hang around the neck of a bottle.

bottom line, net profits or losses, usually before taxes.
bottom-line, *adj.*

boutique, see *creative boutique.*

boxboard, *noun* a grade of heavy paper suitable for folding into boxes.

box holder, 1. a person renting a post office box.
2. a person in a rural area whose mail is delivered.

box set, a theatrical, television, or motion picture set that gives a complete illusion of an enclosed space from a fixed viewpoint.

boxtop offer, an offer to a consumer of a gift, coupon refund, or premium in return for a boxtop or label from the package of a product.

B.P.A., *Business Publications Audit of Circulations.*

B.P.I., *brand potential index.*

bracket, *noun* (in typography) a transitional feature, customarily in the form of an arc, between a serif and a principal stroke of a letter.

branch house, a warehouse for local distribution of a manufacturer or wholesaler's goods, usually containing a branch sales office.

branch store, a subsidiary of a retail store, usually smaller than the parent store.

brand, *noun* 1. a graphic symbol, a word or words, or combination of both that distinguishes a product or service of one seller from those of others.
2. a line of products or services distinguished by such means. Cf. *brand name, trademark.*

brand association, association of a specific brand with its general product category; used to measure the share of mind the brand enjoys. Cf. *share of mind.*

brand development, a measure of the concentration of a brand's consumption; typically, the units or dollars of a product consumed per thousand population.

brand development index, a measure of relative geographic concentration of a brand's sales; typically, sales per thousand population of an area indexed to the national rate. Abbreviated *B.D.I.* Cf. *brand potential index.*

brand differentiation, the degree to which a brand has succeeded in establishing an image as unique, especially when its unique attributes are perceived as beneficial.

brand extension, a line extension or flanker item marketed under a single brand name.

brand franchise, 1. a contractual arrangement between a manufacturer and a wholesaler or retail chain for exclusive distribution of a brand within a territory.
2. see *brand loyalty.*

brand image, the pattern of feelings, associations, and ideas held by the public generally in regard to a specific brand. Also *brand personality.*

brand loyalty, loyalty of a customer to a particular brand of goods.

brand manager, an employee of a manufacturer who is responsible for the marketing plans of a brand and usually for its advertising. Also *product manager.*

brand name, the verbal part of the identifying symbol of a specific brand. Cf. *trademark*.

Brand Names Foundation, an organization of manufacturers using brand names and of other groups founded to popularize the purchase of products with brand names. Abbreviated *B.N.F.*

brand personality, see *brand image*.

brand potential index, the ratio of a brand's brand development index and its category development index for a geographic area, or a brand's share of market for a geographic area as indexed to its national share of market. Abbreviated *B.P.I.* Cf. *brand development index, category development index*.

brand preference, the degree to which prospects consider a brand acceptable or unacceptable, especially relative to competitive brands.

brand share, see *share*.

B.R.C., *Broadcast Rating Council.*

break, *noun* 1. (in the performing arts) a pause in a rehearsal or performance as for rest or, in television or radio, a commercial. *verb* 2. to have such a pause.
3. (of a cameraman) to move a camera to another location.

breakage allowance, 1. a monetary allowance in a transaction between a seller and a buyer in anticipation of normal breakage.
2. a reimbursement to a buyer by a seller for breakage when the seller assumes responsibility.

breakaway, *noun* 1. a motion picture or television set or prop designed to collapse or break in a disaster scene.
adjective 2. deliberately constructed to collapse, bend, or shatter easily: *breakaway chairs for the barroom-brawl scene.*

breakdown, *noun* 1. (in motion pictures or television) an analysis of a script in terms of its requirements for casting, materials, time, cost, and other factors.
2. the roughing out or blocking of actions and camera shots in a scene or show prior to rehearsals or dry runs.

break-even point, the point, measured in dollar volume of sales or billings, at which the operating costs of a business are covered and net profits begin to appear. Also *payout*.

bridge, *noun* (in periodical publishing) to run an advertisement across the gutter of a spread.
2. a transitional passage of audio between two parts of a television or radio program.

Bristol board, any of a variety of stiff, moderately heavy papers used for ink drawings, cards, mailing pieces, pamphlets, etc. Also *Bristol, Bristol paper*.

broad, *noun* a 2000 watt, boxlike motion picture or television floodlight.

broadcast, *verb* 1. to transmit material to the public on a television or radio station. *noun* 2. material so broadcast.

Broadcast Advertising Producers Society of America, an organization of television and radio commercial producers. Abbreviated *B.A.P.S.A.*

Broadcast Advertising Reports, an organization that monitors television and radio commercial activity in selected market areas to report to subscribers on the brands advertised, schedule location, and length of all announcements. Abbreviated *B.A.R.*

broadcast calendar, a calendar used for accounting purposes in the television and radio broadcasting industry, containing months of four or five whole weeks, each month beginning on a Monday.

broadcaster, *noun* 1. the owner of a television or radio station, or a group of stations.
2. a person who uses broadcasting as a medium of advertising or for other communi-

cations goals.
3. a television or radio station performer.

Broadcast Music, Incorporated, a society of music publishers that licenses performances of music copyrighted by members. Abbreviated *B.M.I.*

Broadcast Rating Council, an organization for maintaining television and radio audience research standards. Abbreviated *B.R.C.*

broadcast spectrum, the segment of the total range of electromagnetic waves assigned to television and radio broadcasters by government authority.

broadsheet, *noun* a newspaper-size advertisement approximately 15" wide and 22" high.

broadside, *noun* a promotional piece consisting of a single printed sheet, often printed on one side only and folded for mailing.

brochure, *noun* a booklet whose appearance has been given special design attention, and that has often been bound in special cover stock.

broken-case price, a special price to a retailer for a partial box or case of goods that includes the cost of unpacking and repacking. Abbreviated *B.C.P.*

broker, *noun* an agent in the purchase or sale of goods; as the agent of a seller, especially of packaged goods, serves to extend or supplant the seller's sales force in return for a commission.

brokerage, *noun* 1. the activity of a broker.
2. a commission to a broker.

broker's warehouse, a warehouse operated by a broker in order to maintain a stock of the products he represents.

bronze, *verb* to affix bronze powder to a printed sheet with the aid of sizing in order to obtain a metallic sheen.

bronze proof, an acetate proof whose printed areas are coated with bronze powder to increase their opacity.

brute, *noun* a 10,000-watt arc motion picture or television spotlight. Also *10k.*

B.T.A., *best time available.*

bubble card, see *blister pack.*

buckeye, *noun* a visually crude, tasteless advertisement.

budget, *noun* 1. an amount of money earmarked by an organization for future expenditure in a stated time period for a designated marketing activity.
2. a consumer's household spending plans.

buffet, *noun* a single serving size of food can holding less than 10 ounces; used especially for vegetables, fruits, and juices.

bulk, *noun* the thickness of a printing paper.

bulk circulation, distribution of a periodical in quantity as opposed to single copy sales.

bulk mailing, a mailing of third-class matter, in large quantities of identical pieces at a special rate.

bulldog edition, 1. a regular edition of a newspaper sold before the date it bears. Also *predate.*
2. the earliest edition of a daily newspaper.

bullet, *noun* (in printing) a heavy dot, used to draw attention to an item of a list or to some other special feature, especially in subheads and body type.

bulletin, *noun* 1. any information sheet circulated within a trade or a business organization.
2. a late news item of special importance.
3. see *painted bulletin.*

bulletin spectacular, a semi-permanent outdoor sign, usually painted, as opposed to an outdoor board utilizing printed poster paper.

bumper, *noun* an addition to the last part of a television or radio program made to prevent it from ending too soon.

Bureau of Advertising, the promotional arm of the American Newspaper Publishers Association. Abbreviated *B. of A.*

Bureau of Broadcast Measurement, (in Canada) a service organization formed by broadcasters, advertisers, and their advertising agencies to provide periodic broadcast audience survey data on a local and national basis.

buried advertisement, *adjective* (of a periodical advertisement) surrounded by other advertising so as to be inconspicuous.

buried offer, see *blind offer.*

Burke test, a test service of Burke Marketing Research, Inc. which measures recall of an advertisement among those persons exposed to it the preceding day. Cf. *day-after recall.*

burn, *noun* an afterimage on a motion picture or television image that results from focusing on a shining object.

burnish, *verb* to rub a halftone plate in such a way as to flatten the dots and thus darken a printing area of the plate.

burst, *noun* see *flight.*

business, *noun* 1. an enterprise, or its sales.
2. those particular actions performed by an actor to establish atmosphere, outline character, or otherwise highlight the role. Also *stage business.*

business-building test, a test to determine whether a proposed change in advertising or marketing effort will produce enough new business to justify the costs involved.

business paper, a periodical directed to a particular industry, trade, profession, or occupation.

Business Publications Audit of Circulations, a nonprofit organization that audits the paid and unpaid circulations of business publications. Abbreviated *B.P.A.*

business reply mail, advertising mail that includes an envelope or card allowing the recipient to reply without paying postage.

bust shot, a photograph of a person from the middle chest upward.

busy, *adjective* (of a design or the like) excessively or chaotically detailed.

buy, *noun* 1. a motion picture or television scene approved as presented.
2. a purchase of media, particularly broadcast.

buy-back allowance, an allowance based on the quantity of merchandise purchased on a preceding deal.

buyer, *noun* 1. an employee of an advertising agency who is responsible for the purchase of advertising space or time in communications media. Also *media buyer.*
2. a professional purchaser of goods.

buying agent, an agent designated as an authorized purchaser for specified goods on behalf of a client.

buying allowance, see *allowance.*

buying committee, a committee of wholesalers and retail chains that decides on new products, special offers and promotions. Cf. *advisory board, merchandising committee, plans committee.*

buying corporation, an organization that acts as a broker in finding and purchasing merchandise for a customer.

buying headquarters, the main purchasing office of a retail chain or wholesaling corporation.

buying incentive, an extra inducement for a buyer to purchase a product or service; could be in the form of a discount, gift or bonus goods.

buying loader, a premium rewarded to a retailer as a gift in exchange for the purchase of merchandise. Cf. *dealer loader.*

buying office, an office in which wholesale purchase decisions are made.

buying service, a service that buys or secures by barter television or radio time for advertisers or advertising agencies; its fee is paid by the client.

buyout, *noun* a one-time payment to television or radio talent for all rights to performance.

buy sheet, see *time sheet.*

B/W, *black and white.*

byline, *noun* (in journalism) a line below the headline or at the end of an article giving the writer's name.

C

C, *outside front cover; first cover:* used in ordering magazine advertising.

©, *copyrighted.*

C.A., *Census Agglomeration.*

cable, *noun* a wire or cluster of wires for electrical transmission. Cf. *coaxial cable.*

cablecasting, *noun* broadcasting by cable television.

cable television, 1. television paid for by subscription and transmitted by cable to a subscriber's home. Also *pay television.*
2. television employing a single antenna to pick up broadcast signals, which are amplified and distributed to local individual sets via direct cable; useful in areas where individual set reception is bad or impossible. Also *CATV.*

calendered paper, paper with a smooth, glossy finish created by treating it with steam and passing it between rollers (**calenders** or **calender rollers**) of steel and compressed cotton. Paper that has a high degree of gloss from repeated calenderings is said to be *supercalendered.*

call, *noun* 1. an offer of work made to a performer.
2. the time set for a rehearsal.

call-back, *noun* 1. (in research) a call made by an interviewer to a respondent subsequent to a previous one, as to reach a previously unavailable respondent, or as one of a series of interviews.
2. a repeated review or audition of previously screened prospects for employment (e.g., commercial talent), or a request to an individual to report to such a review or audition.

call book, a book maintained by a salesman with the locations, purchases, buying habits, etc., of regular customers, and other information useful in making sales calls.

calligraphy, *noun* 1. the art of lettering or writing by hand.
2. hand lettering or handwriting regarded as a specimen of this art.

call letters, a combination of letters assigned, in the United States by the Federal Communications Commission, to a television or radio station. In the United States, including Alaska and Hawaii, W is generally the first letter for stations east of the Mississippi and K for those west; there are exceptions, since some stations were licensed before this arrangement was devised. Canadian call letters begin with C, and Mexican call letters with X.

callout, *noun* a word or words used to more clearly identify elements depicted in an illustration; most often connected to the specific element in question by a straight line or arrow.

call report, a record of a meeting between an advertiser and an agency prepared by an agency representative. Also *conference report, contact report.*

cameo shot, (in motion pictures or television) a shot made against a neutral background, with only actors and props lighted.

camera angle, the position of a camera with regard to a subject, standing eye level being taken as a normal position: *a low camera angle.* Also *viewpoint.*

camera card, a large card carrying titles to be picked up by a television camera.

camera chain, a television camera with its related control and power equipment. Also *chain.* Cf. *film chain.*

camera cue, (in television) a red warning light or buzzer indicating that a camera is shooting a scene for transmission. Also *cue light, tally light, warning light.*

camera left, left as seen from a cameraman's position.

camera light, a camera-mounted spotlight for television close-ups.

camera lucida, an optical device for projecting an image, to a desired size or scale, on a sheet of paper so that it may be copied. Also *lucy.*

cameraman, *noun* (in motion pictures and television) a person responsible for the composition and proper exposure of a scene to be filmed or televised.

camera mixing, (in television) selection of successive shots for transmission from cameras continuously operating in various positions. Also *camera switching.*

camera-ready, *adjective* (in printing) suitable for photographic reproduction on film, a printing plate, or the like: *camera-ready copy.*

camera rehearsal, (in television) a full dress rehearsal filmed for final review before an actual performance.

camera right, right as seen from a cameraman's position.

camera shot, see *shot.*

camera switching, see *camera mixing.*

camera tube, an electronic tube for converting visual images into electrical signals, used in a television camera.

campaign, *noun* 1. a program of coordinated advertisements and promotional activities, intended to accomplish a specific sales objective.

2. a series of advertisements with a common selling idea.

Campbell's Soup position, the first right-hand page following the main editorial section of a magazine; so called because the Campbell Soup Company has often specified this position for its advertisements.

Canadian Broadcasting Corporation, a nationally owned television and radio network in Canada. Abbreviated *CBC.*

Canadian Circulations Audit Board, an organization of advertisers, advertising agencies, and publishers for the auditing of circulation statements of controlled-circulation periodicals. Abbreviated *C.C.A.B.*

Canadian Radio and Television Commission, a government-appointed commission that regulates all aspects of television and radio broadcasting in Canada. Abbreviated *C.R.T.C.*

Canadian TV Network, an independently owned Canadian television network. Abbreviated *CTV.*

cancellation date, the final date for cancelling an advertisement planned for a publication, broadcast, or outdoor advertisement. Cf. *closing date.*

cannibalize, *verb* to draw sales away from another product of the same manufacturer in a manner diminishing the maker's profit; said of new products, flanker items or line extensions.
cannibalism, *n.*

cans, *plural noun, informal* headphones worn by television or radio personnel.

canvass, *noun* a round of visits to regular customers in a sales territory for some specific purpose. Cf. *advance canvass.*

cap., *noun* (in printing) capital letter.

caption, *noun* a legend describing an illustration or a number of illustrations grouped together. Also *title.*

carbro, *noun* a continuous-tone photographic color print, usually made from three negatives; yellow, magenta and cyan.

car card, an advertising sheet for display inside or outside a vehicle of public transportation. Car cards for inside use are 11 inches high, with 28, 42, and 56 inches the standard lengths.

cardboard engineer, a specialist in the design of cardboard objects such as packages and display objects.

cardpunching, *noun* the conversion of data into stored information on punchcards.

card rate, the standard rate charged for a specified quantity of space or time by a communication medium without regard to any discounts; the charges as listed on a rate card.

carry-in charge, a charge to a retailer by a wholesaler for carrying delivered merchandise from a truck to part of a shop. Cf. *curb delivery.*

carryout, *noun* a person who carries merchandise from a store to a customer's vehicle. Also *courtesy boy.*

C.A.R.S., *community antenna relay station.*

carton, *noun* a light cardboard box, especially manufactured for a single retail item.

cartoon animation, see *animation.*

cartouche, *noun* a decorative border for a legend, designed in a generally oval form.

cartridge, *noun* a permanent plastic case housing a length of standard width audio-magnetic recording tape held in an "infinite loop" configuration on a single take-up spool.

case, *noun* 1. (in printing) a compartmented tray for holding a font of type for hand setting, the types of each character being in separate compartments.
2. a container of a stated number of product units.
3. see *display case.*

case allowance, an allowance by a manufacturer to a retailer which is proportional to the number of cases purchased, either continuously or in increments.

case-count method, a form of acceptance of a wholesale delivery by a retailer on the evidence of the number of cases listed in an invoice rather than after an actual count of cases delivered.

casein, *noun* 1. a protein derived from milk, used in paint and glue.
2. a paint vehicle containing this protein.
3. paint made with this vehicle.

case lot, 1. a lot of merchandise priced by the case rather than by the individual item.
2. a number of cases sold as a lot for a flat price.

case pack, the number of units of merchandise in a case.

cash-and-carry, *adjective* 1. (of a retailer) selling for cash only, with no delivery service.
2. (of a wholesaler) selling to legitimate buyers who provide their own transportation.

cash discount, a discount on purchases of space or time in communications media, made by the media to buyers as a reward for prompt payment.

cash on delivery, *C.O.D.*

cash refund offer, an offer by a manufacturer for a refund of money to a customer who mails in a label or the like as proof of a purchase.

cash register, a device used to record the sales transactions, item by item and in total, of a retail store, and to store money checks, coupons, and change produced by such transactions.

cassette, *noun* a permanent plastic case housing a length of audio magnetic recording tape of one quarter inch width held between two take-up spools.

cast, *verb* 1. to calculate the printed space required by a certain quantity of manuscript copy in a specified size. Also *fit*.
2. to calculate the amount of manuscript copy required to fill a certain area when set in a specified type size.
3. to cast manuscript or printed copy. Also *cast off*.
noun 4. the performers in a show or commercial.

cast commercial, a television or radio commercial acted out by members of a program to which it belongs. Cf. *star commercial*.

casting director, a person responsible for selecting actors for a performance.

casual rate, (in Canada) a one-time advertising rate.

category, *noun* a class of products or services which satisfy the same consumer need or needs, and are therefore competitors.

category development, see *market development*.

category development index, see *market development index*. Abbreviated *C.D.I.*

CATV, *community antenna television*.

CBC, *Canadian Broadcasting Corporation*.

C.B.O., *confirmation of broadcast order*.

CBS, *Columbia Broadcasting System*.

C.C.A., *Controlled Circulation Audit*.

C.C.A.B., *Canadian Circulations Audit Board*.

C county, any county other than an A or B county that has either more than 35,000 inhabitants or that is in a metropolitan area with more than 35,000 inhabitants; the designation is that of the A. C. Nielsen Co. Cf. *A county, B county, D county*.

C.C.T.V., *closed-circuit television*.

C.D., *creative director*.

CDI, *category development index*.

C.D.T., *Central Daylight Time;* see *time zone*.

cease and desist order, an order to discontinue an unlawful practice, as one issued by the Federal Trade Commission regarding deceptive advertising.

cel, a transparent plastic sheet on which a figure in an animation is drawn or painted.

cell, *noun* 1. (in statistics) a small homogeneous group within a larger sample. Also *sample cell*.
2. a single image in a film or unit on a story board. See *frame*.

cellophane, *noun* a transparent, nonfibrous cellulose film, used extensively in packaging.

celluloid proof, (in printing) an impression of a color plate on a transparent sheet. Superimposed on other such sheets, one for each plate, it provides a means of checking the register or fit.

census, *noun* see *U.S. Census Bureau*.

Census Agglomeration, (in Canada) a geographical area with an urban center of at least 1,000 population, an adjacent built-up area with at least 1,000 population, and a density of at least 1,000 persons per square mile. Abbreviated *C.A.*

Census Metropolitan Area, (in Canada) the principal labor market area within a built-up area of 100,000 or more persons. Abbreviated *C.M.A.*

center, *verb* to place an object, design element, etc. so that it rests symmetrically on a center line or central point.

center spread, the two facing pages at the center of a periodical, desirable because the pages are continuous, with little or no interruption at the gutter.

central buying, purchase of wholesale goods for individual store outlets from a central point, thus giving maximum opportunity for discounts for quantity purchases and for simplification of ordering.

centralized prepackaging, packaging of sales items before delivery to stores.

cents-off, *noun* see *price pack.*

certification mark, a mark applied to goods that certifies them as being of a certain quality or origin.

chain, *noun* 1. a group of retail outlets under a common ownership. Also *store.*
2. see *voluntary chain.*
3. a television or radio network.
4. see *camera chain.*

chain break, 1. a network affiliated station's interruption of network broadcasting for local station identification. Also *station break.*
2. a commercial delivered during this time.

chain store, 1. a retail store belonging to a chain.
2. a chain of these.

channel, *noun* a broadcast frequency assigned to a television or radio station.

channel strip, an extruded molding covering the front edge of a retail display shelf, used to exhibit price data or hold point of purchase advertising.

channel width, the range of wavelengths assigned to a television or radio channel.

charcoal, *noun* 1. a black material obtained by heating wood at a burning temperature in the absence of oxygen.
2. a stick of such material, often made from willow, used for drawing.
3. a drawing made with such a stick.

chase, *noun* (in printing) a metal frame in which foundry type, cuts, etc. are locked up either for direct printing or for the making of plates or matrices.

cheat, *verb* (of an actor) to give an illusion of occupying a certain position or making a certain movement, desirable in its relationship to the positions or movements of other actors, objects, scenery, etc.

checker, *noun* a person who enumerates, totals, and collects money for customer purchases in a supermarket.

checkerboard, *noun* a unit of magazine advertising which consists of quarter pages or spread half pages placed in diagonal opposition.

checking copy, a copy of a periodical, sent to an advertiser as proof that an advertisement was run as ordered.

checkout counter, a counter in a supermarket where purchases are checked and money collected for them. Also **checkout, checkstand.**

Cheshire, *noun, trademark* a machine for affixing printed address labels to mail.

chinese, *verb* (of a motion picture or television camera) to pan while moving away.

Chinese white, 1. a bluish-white paint used for the retouching of artwork and photographs.
2. a bluish-white pigment used as an additive to colored inks.

chipboard, *noun* a coarse grade of cardboard made from paper waste, sometimes covered with a paper of a higher grade.

chisel point, a point, as on a drawing pencil, terminating in a straight edge with sides sharply inclined rather than conical.

chi square design, see *Latin square design*.

choreographer, *noun* a person who plans the movements and steps of ballet or other dances.

chroma, *noun* see *hue*.

chrome, *verb* 1. to coat a printing plate with chromium to make it last longer during press runs.
noun, informal 2. color film. Cf. *Kodachrome*.

circle in, see *iris in*.

circle out, see *iris out*.

circular, *noun* a printed advertising sheet mailed, inserted in packages, or distributed by hand.

circulation, *noun* the total number of distributed copies of a periodical as counted at some specific moment or as averaged out over an extended period.

city-grade service, (in television) transmission of the highest quality, usually found in the geographical area around the transmitter. Cf. *contour*.

city zone, an urban area consisting of the central city of a local market along with communities sharing the general character of the city.

claim, *noun* 1. an assertion regarding a product's or service's performance in providing benefits to purchasers used in an advertisement.
verb 2. to make such an assertion.

clambake, *noun* a badly produced television or radio program.

class, *noun* a broad social group regarded as distinct from others because of its level of income, education, occupation, place of residence, life style, and status.

classification data, data by which a territory, group or medium can be characterized.

classified advertising, newspaper and magazine advertising subdivided according to the types of things offered or sought.

class magazine, 1. a magazine intended for a readership with a special range of common interests.
2. loosely, a magazine intended for a high-income readership.

class of time, the value of a certain period of television or radio station time as reflected in its rate for that time. Prime time is in Class A, the next most desirable time is Class B, and so on.

Clayton Act, a 1914 law which amplified the terms of the Sherman Act by prohibiting practices that may substantially lessen competition.

c/lc, see *upper and lower*.

clean, *verb* 1. to correct and update a mailing list.
adjective 2. (of a printer's proof) having no errors.

clean rough, a layout in which major elements of a printed page, poster, advertisement, etc. are sketched in considerable detail.

clear, *verb* 1. to obtain official permission for use of a picture, quotation, etc. in an advertisement.
2. (of an advertiser) to reserve broadcasting time.
3. (of a network) to check on the availability of a period of broadcasting time with affiliates.

clearance, *noun* 1. the act of clearing something, as the use of copyright matter in advertising or the availability of broad-

cast time.
2. the notification that something is cleared.

clear-channel station, an AM radio station allowed 50,000 kilowatts, the maximum power allowed, and priority in the use of a frequency band. At sunset, other stations on this frequency sign off, since broadcasting range is extended after dark and stations on the same frequency tend to interfere with one another. Also *powerhouse.*

client, *noun* one who employs the services of an advertising agency; an account.

clinical psychology, the branch of psychology concerned with the diagnosis and treatment of mental disorders; some of its techniques have been adapted for advertising purposes.

Clio, see *American Television and Radio Commercials Festival.*

clip, *noun* 1. a short length of film cut from a complete motion picture or television film.
2. loosely, a newspaper clipping.

clipping, *noun* an item of interest removed from a publication by a reader or clipping service.

clipping bureau, an organization that examines newspapers and magazines, and clips from them articles, references and allusions of interest to its clients, to be sent to them.

clip sheet, a sheet of material for reproduction in newspapers, distributed by a public relations office on behalf of a client.

clock-hour delay, (in television or radio) a delay in the broadcasting of a program originating in another time zone in order that the program may be aired at the same clock time in both zones. Also *live-time delay.*

close, *noun* 1. a mention of the sponsor or sponsors at the conclusion of a television or radio show.
2. the last shot or sequence of a program or commercial.

closed-circuit, *adjective* noting or pertaining to a television or radio system for distribution of video and/or audio signals to specific receivers, rather than for broadcasting; often on a one-time basis.

closed-end diary, (in research) a respondent diary of reported behavior (e.g., media or product usage), in which entries are limited to the categories given in a printed form. Cf. *open-end diary.*

close-up, *noun* (in motion pictures or television) a shot in which a single object, person, or face, dominates the screen. Abbreviated *C.U.*

closing date, 1. the final date for contracting for an advertisement. Cf. *cancellation date.*
2. the final date for supplying printing material for advertisements.

closure, *noun* a customer order placed as a result of direct mail advertising.

Cloze procedure, a method for assessing the readability and comprehensibility of a text or script developed by Prof. Wilson Tucker, Univ. of Illinois; tests respondents' ability to correctly guess every *nth* word, which has been deleted for the purpose of the test. Cf. *Flesch formula, Gunning formula, Dale-Chall formula.*

clubbing offer, an offer of subscriptions to two or more magazines jointly at a reduced combined rate.

cluster sample, (in statistics) a sample of respondents drawn randomly from groups of respondents, selected previously in a non-random manner.

clutter, *noun* the number of advertisements claiming the attention of the audience of a television or radio program, periodical, etc. Cf. *commercial time.*

C.M.A., 1. *Census Metropolitan Area.* 2. *cooperative merchandising agreement.*

CNYT, *Current New York Time.* Cf. *time zone.*

coarse screen, (in printing) a halftone screen with 100 or fewer dots per linear inch.

coated blank, cardboard coated on one or both sides.

coated cover, a coated paper stock suitable for magazine and brochure covers.

coated offset, coated paper suitable for offset printing.

coated paper, any smoothly finished paper with a mineral-based, usually white coating used for aesthetic effect and for the reception of fine halftone printing.

coaxial cable, an electrical transmission cable capable of carrying complex signal information, such as multiple telephone conversations or television transmissions.

C.O.D., *collect on delivery.*

code dating, the practice of coding packages of retail products, so as to indicate the packing date, or termination of fresh sales life, or the name of its supplier, using symbols meaningless to the customer.

code number, 1. any number meaningful in a special context, as to identify a commercial or to synchronize two lengths of film so that one follows the other without interrupting the action.
2. a number in store redeemable coupons used to identify the carrier publication, after redemption.

coding, *noun,* (in research) a numerical scheme for assigning nominal labels to responses.

coefficient of correlation, (in statistics) a measure of the strength of linear relationship between two variables; the degree to which two variables covary independent of the scalar considerations upon which each is measured. Also *correlation coefficient.* Cf. *correlation.*

coefficient of variation, (in statistics) a measure of the variability inherent in a particular variable relative to the mean or level of that variable. Used in comparing the variation in two or more series of data when the means differ significantly or when the series are not expressed in the same units. Computed by dividing the standard deviation of a series by its mean.

coffin case, a food store freezer cabinet that displays merchandise in a horizontal position.

cognitive dissonance, (in psychology) a theory of human cognition stated by Leon Festinger; holds that persons attempt to reduce conflict between their actions and opinions by changing their actions, or if actions cannot be changed, by changing their opinions. Cf. *distortion.*

coincidental, *adjective* (in research) noting or pertaining to interviewing done during an event, such as telephone interviews to determine which television or radio shows a random sample of persons are tuned to when the calls are made.

coined word, a word, especially a trade name, not in the regular vocabulary, that is created for a special purpose.

collage, *noun* a still montage image, usually prepared in a manner that gives an impression of depth.

collate, *verb* to assemble the pages or signatures of a book or the like in the proper final order.

collateral, *noun* advertising material other than that presented through communications media.

collective mark, a trade or service mark used by a membership organization, such as a union or cooperative.

collect on delivery, a delivery to a recipient who is expected to pay the purchase price of the item, and possibly postage or a handling fee as well. Abbreviated *C.O.D.*

collotype, *noun* 1. any continuous tone printing process, especially for fine picture reproduction, using gelatin as a printing surface.
2. a picture printed by such a process.

colophon, *noun* 1. a description, run at the back of a book, of the contribution of various persons to the book, the design of the book, the date when printing was completed, or similar matters.
2. a symbol used by a publisher and run on a title page; a publisher's trademark. Also *logo, logotype.*

color filter, 1. (in photography) a tinted transparent camera lens covering used: to absorb certain colors in order to allow better rendering of others; or to eliminate undesirable colors in a subject; or to produce color separation negatives.
2. (in color television) an electronic camera tube sensitive to one of three ranges of hues; the camera contains three tubes, which together produce the full color image.

color form, (in color printing) a printing plate or the like to be used for printing one of any number of multiple flat colors desired on a printed job.

color guide, a sketch prepared by an artist as a guide in preparing color plates from black and white copy. Cf. *color overlay.*

color overlay, a transparent overlay superimposed on black and white camera copy as a key for the addition of colors in printing.

color plate, *noun* 1. an illustration printed in color.
2. a plate used to print one of a desired number of colors for such an illustration.

color print, a positive full color reproduction, on photographic paper or in printed form.

color proof, a proof made from color plates, printed separately or in combination.

color separations, a set of black and white color separation negatives of full color copy made through the use of color filters for transformation into color printing plates; these commonly represent the yellow, red and blue tones, and are often combined with a black plate to enrich the shadow values.

color swatch, a sample of a desired color, used in matching ink, paint, etc.

color toning, the coloring of a black and white photograph with dyes and bleaches.

color transparency, a transparent full color photographic positive.

Columbia Broadcasting System, a television and radio network founded in 1927. Abbreviated *CBS.*

column, *noun* 1. an area of print running down a page of a periodical, composed of lines of equal width.
2. the typical or standard width of such an area of print, used as a measure of size for such a periodical.
3. a series of regular periodical articles by a journalist.

column inch, (in periodical publishing) a unit of space one standard column wide and one inch deep; in newspaper publishing, this is 14 agate lines deep.

combination buy, a media buy made at a combination rate.

combination commercial, a television commercial combining various techniques, as live acting, a film, or the display of still photographs or drawings. Cf. *integrated commercial.*

combination cut, see *combination plate.*

combination feature, a combination of retail items specially promoted for sale together.

combination plate, a printing plate that combines halftone and line or solid elements, as a photograph surrounded by a rule or combined with type. Also **combination cut,** when engraved.

combination rate, a rate, often discounted, for the purchase of advertising space or time in two or more periodicals, stations, etc., under a common ownership.

comic strip, a series of drawings, using narrative and dialogue integrated into the drawings, often in balloons, that relate an incident or story; a book of such drawings, usually relating a longer story, is a *comic book.* Also **comics.**

commercial, *noun* an advertisement on television or radio. See *spot announcement, participating announcement.*

commercial audience, the television or radio audience for a specific commercial, regarded as consisting of those persons actually in the room with a set tuned in to the program.

commercial break, (in television or radio) an interruption in a performance for a commercial.

commercial code number, a series of four letters followed by four numbers used to identify a television commercial film print's sponsor and content; assigned by the originating advertising agency in accordance with a standard industry system.

commercial delivery, the exposure of a television or radio commercial measured by the size of the commercial audience.

commercial exposure potential, the ratio of the number of sets actually tuned to a television or radio station at the time when a commercial is delivered, to the total number of sets able to receive the commercial.

commercial impression, (in television or radio audience research) a unit for measuring gross message weight, representing an exposure to a television or radio commercial. Cf. *exposure, gross rating point.*

commercial integration charge, a charge made by a television or radio station or network for the inclusion of a commercial into its broadcasting. Cf. *networking.*

commercial minute, one minute of actual television or radio commercial time.

commercial occasion, see *occasion.*

commercial pool, the selection of television or radio commercials that an advertiser has available for airing at any one time. Also *pool.*

commercial program, a television or radio program paid for by sponsors.

commercial protection, a time interval preceding and following an advertiser's commercial that a broadcaster customarily or contractually keeps free of commercials for competitive products or services. Cf. *competitive separation.*

commercial straight, a nonintegrated television or radio commercial, delivered during a break in a program or during a station break.

commercial time, a standard amount of time and number of interruptions which television and radio broadcasters who are members of NAB are permitted to devote to non-program material (credits, commercials, billboards). On a network affiliated television station, for example, each hour of network feed programming is limited to the following non-program time:

	Prime time	Non-prime time
Network commercials	6 minutes	12 minutes
Spot commercials	1 min. 10 sec.	2 min. 20 sec.
Other non-program	2 min. 20 sec.	1 min. 40 sec.
Total	9 min. 30 sec.	16 min.

commercial unit, a description of the length of a commercial occasion and the manner in which it will be used when multiple commercials are to appear within an occasion. Cf. *split unit, integrated unit,* or *piggyback unit.*

commissary store, see *industrial store.*

commission, *noun* 1. see *agency commission.*
2. compensation to a salesperson, agent, etc. as a percent of their sales.

commissionable, *adjective* (of an advertising purchase) yielding a commission to a recognized purchaser, usually an advertising agency.

commissioned representative, an agent who sells goods on a commission basis but who is not responsible for storage, delivery, or billing.

commission merchant-receiver, a merchant who stores and sells goods left with him on consignment.

commodity, *noun* 1. a raw material, especially a food product, bought and sold in bulk.
2. a product category in which it is difficult to differentiate a brand from its competition.

Communications Act of 1934, an act of Congress, as amended, for the regulation of television and radio broadcasting and other means of communication.

Communications Satellite Corporation, an organization formed to receive the first Federal license for use of communications satellites for profitable commercial leasing operations. Abbreviated *Comsat.* Cf. *Intelsat.*

communications theory, (in psychology) a body of experimental knowledge regarding the typical manner of message and respondent interactions.

community antenna relay station, a relay station in a community antenna television system. Abbreviated *C.A.R.S.*

community antenna television, see *cable television.*

community station, a television station of 1,000 watts or less serving its own community alone.

comp, *noun* 1. a complimentary subscription to a periodical.
2. see *comprehensive layout.*

company store, see *industrial store.*

comparative proved name registration, a term used by the research firm of Gallup and Robinson to designate the accurate recall of an advertisement by a number of respondents, taken as a proportion of a total number of respondents who have each seen the advertisement only once.

compatible, *adjective* adaptable to another system, as a color television signal to black and white reception or a quadraphonic record to playing on a stereophonic record player.

competitor, *noun* 1. a rival in business and advertising, as for trade or for public attention.
competition, *noun* 2. such rivals, taken as a whole.

competitive-parity method, a method for establishing a marketing budget based on matching anticipated competitive expenditures or spending rates.

competitive preference, preference for one brand of a certain product over other brands of the same product, shown by a proportion of a group of persons.

competitive separation, a quantity of media space or time separating a given advertisement, at the request of the advertiser, from directly competitive advertising. Cf. *commercial protection.*

complimentary, *adjective* granted without the customary charge, usually as a sample.

comp list, *noun* a periodical's list of its complimentary subscribers.

compose, *verb* 1. (in printing) to assemble type in a sequence.
2. to create a musical piece.

composing room, a room at a newspaper, composition house or a printing plant where type is set.

composing stick, (in printing) a device for holding hand set individual type characters in sequence before transfer to a galley for lock-up and proofing.

composite, *noun* 1. a motion picture or television film or videotape bearing both images and sound.
2. an actor or model's brochure, depicting appearance and other vital data.

composite shot, 1. (in motion pictures or television) a shot presenting two or more separate scenes simultaneously on different parts of the screen. Also *split screen.* Cf. *half lap.*
2. a camera shot in which one image is superimposed on another, as to create a special visual effect. Also *double exposure, double print.*

composition, *noun* 1. (in printing) the setting of type according to a customer's requirements.
2. (in art) the arrangement of the elements of a picture or design.
3. (in display advertising) the arrangement of the various elements of an advertisement.

composition house, a company specializing in typesetting and the preparation of repro proofs.

composition-set type, type set by a composition house. Cf. *publication-set type.*

compositor, *noun* see *typesetter.*

comprehensive layout, an advertising layout for presentation to a client, made to give the effect of a finished advertisement or display. Also **comprehensive, comp.**

Comsat, *noun* Communications Satellite Corporation.

concentration ratio, the share of market enjoyed by the four leading firms in an industry, collectively, as published by the Federal government; serves as an indicator of the degree of competition in a market.

concept, *noun* a briefly stated idea of a benefit that a product or service could provide to consumers. Cf. *strategy.*

concept test, a research project designed to assess consumer reaction to a product or service concept, or concepts, in quantitative terms.

concurrent method technique, a research technique that investigates events and activities as they occur.

condensed, *adjective* (of a typeface) narrower than is normal for a given type face or height. Cf. *extended.*

condition, *verb* to affect the attitudes and behavior of a person through psychological influences. In advertising research, the research situation itself may condition a subject's responses, thus making data gathered from him not reflective of his true attitudes.

conference report, see *call report.*

confidence interval, a range of values within which a true population value is expected to fall with a specified level of probability or assurance. This interval is a function of the variability of the sample plus a constant reflecting the desired degree of assurance.

confidence level, (in statistics) the level or degree of assurance one uses in considering results obtained from statistical tests; such assurance is expressed in probabilistic notation (e.g., one has 95% confidence in his findings).

confirmation, *noun* a statement by a television or radio station or network that a time period is available for purchase. **confirm,** *v.*

connotative mapping, a research technique used to establish a diagram or map of consumers' perceptions of a product category and individual brands location within the map. Also *perceptual mapping.*

consecutive-weeks discount, a discount to an advertiser who buys television or radio advertising time for a continuous period, usually between 26 and 52 weeks. Abbreviated *C.W.D.*

consignment, *noun* merchandise possessed by a party who is to sell it, but owned by another.

consignment selling, a system of retail selling under which a supplier is paid only as his goods are sold, the retailer having the right to return undamaged goods unsold after a certain date.

console, *noun* a control panel, as one used by recording or broadcasting engineers for blending and adjusting the volumes of signals from several microphones or video cameras.

consumer, *noun* a person who uses or is responsible for consuming a product or service; less accurately, a person who purchases such goods. Cf. *purchaser.*

consumer advertising, advertising directed at the public as a whole rather than to a profession, industry, etc.

consumer cooperative, a nonprofit consumer group, organized for the purchase and distribution of goods, whose members enjoy lower prices as a result of wholesale purchasing.

consumer goods, goods that satisfy individual human needs or desires, such as food and clothing, as contrasted with goods sold for commercial or industrial use. Cf. *industrial goods.*

consumerism, *noun* the public movement or trend that favors protection of the consumer from improper marketing practices through examination of product performance, advertising and sales practices, etc.

consumer jury, see *consumer panel.*

consumer magazine, a magazine intended for the general public rather than for a trade or profession. Cf. *professional magazine, trade magazine.*

consumer panel, a group of consumers who are retained to provide information of interest to an advertiser, advertising agency, or advertising research organization, as reactions to advertising or patterns of purchase and consumption. Also *consumer jury.*

consumer product, a product manufactured for sale to the public rather than for commercial or industrial use; a product classified among consumer goods.

consumer profile, the demographic, geographic, and psychographic characteristics of the users of a product, especially as they differ from the total population.

consumer research, research designed to describe the behavior and motives of people as purchasers and consumers.

consumer research director, see *research director.*

consumer survey, a survey of public attitudes, buying habits, etc., especially one done among the actual or potential customers of a consumer product.

consumption, *noun* the use of a product by a consumer, especially a use that so changes a product's form that its suitability for further use by the original consumer is reduced or eliminated.

contact executive, see *account executive.*

contact man, 1. an employee of a wholesaler who makes periodic calls on retailers as a sales and service representative and who advises the retailers on management and merchandising; a field man.
2. see *account executive.*

contact print, (in photography) a print made by superimposing a negative on print paper in the darkroom; generally small because they are the same size as the negatives, contact prints are used mainly for the selection of one or more photographs from a large number.

contact report, see *call report.*

container, *noun* 1. a package for shipping merchandise, especially one made of corrugated cardboard.
2. the vessel in which an item of product is held, as a box, jar, or bottle.

container board, *noun* any fiberboard or cardboard used for making shipping containers.

content analysis, (in research) separation of qualitative or subjective responses to interview questions into manageable categories.

contest, *noun* a scheme in which a prize is awarded to an entrant judged to have qualified by virtue of superior skill; entrants may be required to furnish a consideration, without violating lottery laws in many states.

contiguity, *noun* 1. proximity without intervening elements, as that of radio programs following one directly after the other.
2. (in television or radio) a condition regarded as equivalent for billing purposes, created by an advertiser's purchase of a minimum amount of time either in one day *(vertical contiguity)* or in one week *(horizontal contiguity).*

contiguity rate, (in television or radio) a reduced rate offered an advertiser who sponsors separate programs in adjacent time periods or whose sponsorship creates situations of vertical or horizontal contiguity. Cf. *contiguity.*

continuing discount, (in television or radio) a previously earned discount continued under a new contract.

continuity, *noun* 1. an acting script including all dialogue and cues.
2. (in advertising) the presence of a single theme or idea throughout a campaign.
3. the maintenance of uninterrupted media schedules.

continuity acceptance department, a department of a broadcast network, television or radio station that reviews scripts and advertising to insure its freedom from morally objectionable, illegal, or unsubstantiated claim material. Also **continuity clearance department.**

continuity girl, see *script girl.*

continuous roll insert, see *hi-fi insert.*

continuous tone, *adjective* noting or pertaining to photographs or the like that have continuous shading rather than shading rendered with halftone dots, hatching, etc.

contour, *noun* 1. (in television) either of two concentric rings on a map defining

37

zones of reception that are acceptable but inferior to that provided by city grade service; the contours are labeled A and B, B defining the outermost acceptable limit.
2. (in printing) type set around an illustration or photograph with irregularly shaped outline edges.

contour map, see *field intensity map*.

contra, *noun* (in Canada) a barter of media space or time for something else of value, as one between two communications media or between a retailer and a local medium.

contract, *noun* 1. an agreement as to terms of purchase, as that made between an advertiser or his agency and an advertising medium. Cf. *advertising contract*.
2. an agreement between an advertiser and an advertising agency or other advertising supplier which specifies terms of service and compensation.

contract feature, a sales item scheduled for a special merchandising effort for which the distributor or retailer is compensated by the manufacturer of the item.

contract year, a contractual relationship of one year, as measured by a specific communications medium with respect to an advertiser, from the placing of the first of a series of advertisements; used to establish rates and payment dates in cases where the contract is for a year or more.

contrast, *noun* the degree of difference between lightest and darkest tonal values, as in a photograph or television image.

contrasty, *adjective* (of a photograph or the like) with a high contrast between black and white; lacking the normal range of middle values.

control base, (in statistics) 1. a characteristic common to a whole sample that can serve as a basis for analysis.
2. a group or area which is not subjected to a test treatment, but is measured in the same manner as the test group or area; differences between test and control samples are regarded as the product of the test treatment. Also **control group, control**.

controlled association, see *association*.

controlled brand, a brand of merchandise distributed exclusively by one wholesaler, retailer, or group of stores. Cf. *franchised label, private label*.

controlled circulation, a form of periodical distribution which delivers most or all copies to selected persons or households at no charge. Also *qualified circulation*.

Controlled Circulation Audit, an organization that audits the circulation statements of controlled circulation publications. Abbreviated *C.C.A.*

controlled recognition, *adjective* (in research) noting or pertaining to any technique used to determine the reliability of an interview respondent in his claims to recognize an advertisement from previous exposure to it.

control room, a room in a television or radio studio from which sound and images are controlled for transmission.

control track, a secondary film sound track placed alongside the main one, used to control the timing or the volume of the sound.

convenience food, a packaged food containing all the necessary ingredients for preparation.

convenience goods, consumer goods purchased frequently in small quantities with a minimum of deliberation, e.g. cigarettes or candy.

convenience store, a store close to homes or workplaces, offering a narrow range of goods and depending on ready accessibility or extended hours for trade.

conventional wholesaling, wholesaling in which the wholesaler's markup is not revealed to the retailer. Cf. *cost-plus wholesaling*.

converter service, (in Canada) a cable television service using equipment to receive channels unavailable to a basic service.

cookie, noun see *cucalorus.*

copack, *verb* to obtain packaged goods for resale to wholesalers and retailers under one's own brand; done by manufacturers to reduce or eliminate investments in production facilities.

copacker, *noun* a supplier of copacked goods.

cooperative advertising, advertising run by a local advertiser in cooperation with a national advertiser, the latter usually supplying the copy, plates, or reproduction materials; the two share both the cost and the mention of their names.

cooperative affiliate, a retailer belonging to a cooperative wholesale organization.

cooperative association, a group of independent retailers who combine under a common name for purchasing and merchandising purposes. Cf. *voluntary chain.*

cooperative merchandising agreement, a contract between a wholesaler and a retailer that assigns merchandising costs and mutual obligations. Abbreviated *C.M.A.*

cooperative program, a network television or radio program planned for sponsorship by local advertisers.

cooperative store, a store owned by a consumer cooperative. Also **co-op store, co-op.**

cooperative wholesaler, see *retailer-owned wholesaler.* Also **co-op wholesaler.**

coordinated advertising, advertising and promotion through various media centered on a single theme or visual motif so that each type of advertisement supports the impact of the others.

copperplate, *adjective* 1. pertaining to a print made from an engraved copper plate.
2. pertaining to a delicate and elaborate script lettering style or typeface recalling the lettering style used in engraved formal announcements.

copper halftone, a copper engraving that has an overall halftone printing surface. Cf. *combination plate.*

copy, *noun* 1. textual matter to be set in type.
2. the written portions of an advertisement.
3. textual and graphic material for reproduction on a printing plate. Cf. *camera copy.*
4. loosely, advertisements.
5. a single, assembled unit of a periodical or document, or a single facsimile, printed piece, or photographic print.

copy approach, the theme or major point of emphasis of a piece of advertising copy.

copy chief, a supervisor of the work of writers. A somewhat archaic term in advertising agencies, dating from the period when copy and art were commonly separate departments.

copyholder, *noun* 1. a person who reads copy aloud to a proofreader.
2. a frame or board for holding copy from which type is being set.

copy negative, a photographic negative made by photographing other photographic material.

copy platform, a description and rationale for an advertising campaign, usually based on an established creative strategy; describes selling ideas, their importance, and may include executional considerations.

copy print, a photographic copy of artwork or an original photograph.

copyright, *verb* 1. to register a writing, work of art, design, etc. with the Library of Congress upon publication in order to establish one's exclusive right to reproduce the material in question.
noun 2. registration of such a work in this

39

manner.
adjective 3. registered in this manner.

copy slant, see *copy approach.*

copy test, (in research) a test of the effectiveness of an advertisement with purchasers, consumers, or an audience obtained for the test.

copywriter, *noun* a person employed to write advertising or editorial copy.

corner bullet, a small dot at each corner of an advertisement used to define the column width and linage depth of the advertisement for the printer. Also *corner dot.*

corner card, an initial sentence or phrase on the outside of a mailing piece intended to intrigue the recipient and persuade him to open the piece.

corporate campaign, an advertising campaign intended to benefit the image of a business corporation rather than to sell a specific product or service.

corporate chain, a chain of stores under a common ownership; in general, each store receives stock and advertising from company headquarters, which also makes all major policy decisions.

Corporation for Public Broadcasting, a government funded corporation founded in 1969 to aid in the presentation of non-commercial television.

corrected print, a photographic color print in which all hues and color values have been adjusted to create the proper balance.

correct increment method, a technique for assigning media weight to a test market, which attempts to apply the same ratio of test versus non-test weight levels as called for in the national theoretical versus actual plans. See *as-it-falls method, little America method.*

corrective advertising, advertising designed to correct an erroneous public impression created by earlier false advertising claims; required on occasion by the Federal Trade Commission.

correlation, *noun* (in statistics) the observed variation of one variable in accord with that of one or more other variables. In *simple correlation* only two variables are involved; in *multiple correlation,* one variable is compared with two or more others. In *positive correlation,* all variables vary in the same direction, i.e., toward increase or decrease; in *negative correlation,* one variable varies in the opposite direction from the others; in *zero correlation,* all variation is independent. Correlation may or may not be due to a cause-effect relationship among the variables. Cf. *coefficient of correlation.*

correlation coefficient, see *coefficient of correlation.*

corrugated board, a container board composed of an inner corrugated thickness of paper glued to smooth outer faces; used to provide strength and shock absorption. Cf. *flute.*

co-sponsorship, *noun* sponsorship of a television or radio program by more than one advertiser.

cost efficiency, the effectiveness of an advertising medium measured with reference to its actual or potential audience and its cost for advertising placement; usually expressed in cost per thousand persons, homes, or other units reached or able to be reached.

cost per commercial minute, the average price for a minute of commercial time in a program, or a media element, or media schedule.

cost per order, a measure of the effectiveness of mail-order advertising in terms of the sales value of the mail orders received divided by the cost of the advertising for the items ordered.

cost per page per thousand circulation, the cost per thousand copies of an issue for placement of a full-page black and white advertisement in a publication.

cost per gross rating point, a measure of broadcast media efficiency of particular use to media planners; represents the price of a single gross rating point for a medium. Also *cost per rating point.* Abbreviated *CPGRP.*

cost per return, a measure of the effectiveness of a communications medium in promoting a sales offer, contest, coupon promotion, etc. that invites a direct response from the public; computed by dividing the advertising cost involved by the number of returns.

cost per thousand, the advertising cost required to reach one thousand persons, homes, or other audience units. With periodicals, the advertising rate or actual advertisement cost is divided by the circulation, interpreted as the estimated number of readers or ad-noters. With television and radio, the rate charged for commercial placement is divided by the average number of persons or homes tuned in. Abbreviated *C.P.M.*

cost-plus wholesaling, wholesaling in which the wholesaler's markup appears as a separate item on his bill to the retailer. Cf. *conventional wholesaling.*

cost ratio, a term used by the research firm of Daniel Starch and Associates for an estimate of relative advertising readership efficiency. Readership is divided by the number of dollars spent on an advertisement and the resulting figure is stated as a percentage of the average number of readers per dollar spent for all advertisements in the same issue.

count and recount allowance, an allowance to a retailer or wholesaler paid for each unit of a manufacturer's specified merchandise sold to customers in a stated period of time. Also **count/recount allowance.**

count down, a film strip bearing progressively diminishing numbers preceding videotaped or filmed shows or commercials; used as a cue to the operator of playback or projection equipment.

counterprogramming, *noun* presentation of a television or radio program that is deliberately designed to appeal to the audience of a specific competing program on another station during the same time period.

country and western format, see *format.*

country edition, an edition of a newspaper distributed nationally and dated the day of its distribution; predate.

coupon, *noun* a certificate issued by a seller entitling a bearer to claim a stated discount on the purchase price of a designated item.

Coupon Clearing House, see *A.C. Nielsen Co.*

courtesy announcement, (in television or radio) an announcement of a forthcoming series or broadcast made by a station or network at its own expense in order to stimulate listener interest.

courtesy boy, see *carryout.*

cover, *noun* 1. the outer faces of a magazine.
2. advertising spaces sold on magazine covers, e.g., first cover or outside front cover, inside front cover, third cover or inside back cover, fourth cover or outside back cover.

coverage, *noun* the geographical area within which a communications medium reaches. Also **coverage area,** *signal area.*
2. the percentage of a universe under study which is represented in a sample panel.

coverage analyst, a television or radio network employee who prepares regional coverage maps and proposes new network affiliates to extend coverage.

41

coverage map, a map of the area within which the signal of a television or radio station is adequately received.

cover position, see *cover*.

cover shot, 1. (in motion pictures or television) a wide-angle shot taken for contrast with, and to, a close-up. Cf. *establishing shot*.
2. any shot taken in case it might be required in final editing.

cover stock, a heavy, strong paper used for the covers of booklets and the like, manufactured in a variety of basic weights, with a basic sheet size of 20 by 26 inches.

cowcatcher, *noun* a commercial occurring at the beginning of and forming a part of a television or radio program, and advertising a product of the sponsor that is not mentioned again in the program.

C.P.B., *Corporation for Public Broadcasting*.

C.P.M, 1. *cost per thousand*.
2. *critical path method*.

CPGRP, *cost per gross rating point*.

C print, *noun* an inexpensive type of color reproduction used where high fidelity to the original is not required. Also *type C print*. Cf. *dye transfer print*.

c.p.s., *cycles per second*.

crab, *verb* see *truck*.

crane shot, (in motion pictures or television) a shot made from above the subject or scene, using a camera mounted on the boom of a crane.

crash finish, a paper finish that simulates the texture and weave of crash or other rough open cloth.

crawl, an effect produced by a crawl roll.

crawl roll, (in motion pictures or television) a drumlike mechanism on which the titles and credits of a film are mounted so that their position can be continuously altered in printing on successive frames in order to create a creeping title. Also *title roll*. Cf. *creeping title*.

crayon, *noun* 1. a stick of pigmented waxlike material used for drawing.
2. a drawing made with one or more of such sticks.

created news, news of an event deliberately planned for its potential news value.

creative, *noun* 1. (informal) see *advertisement*.
adjective 2. noting or pertaining to the process of conceiving, developing, and executing advertising ideas.

creative boutique, an advertising organization differing from a full service agency in that its work is primarily confined to creative services, on a job-by-job or continuing basis with its clients. Also *boutique*.

creative director, an advertising agency employee responsible for managing the operations and personnel of a creative group or department. Cf. *executive creative director, associate creative director*.

creative strategy, a statement of the communications goal and basic message (not specific content) to be used in an advertisement, or series of advertisements; usually consists of a stated intent (e.g., to persuade), target prospect description, the benefit or benefits to be promised, and the facts to be used to support the believability of the benefits pomised.

credit, *noun* 1. a deduction by a medium from the amount charged an advertiser; for example, to compensate for a pre-emption in lieu of a makegood.
2. a line in a credit title, crediting a participant in a motion picture or television production with the work contributed by the participant. Also **credit line,** *line*.

3. a brief television or radio announcement used in place of a credit line.
4. a brief mention of a sponsor in a television or radio program.

credit and delivery store, a store allowing charge accounts and offering a delivery service. Cf. *cash-and-carry.*

credit title, a sign at the beginning or end of a motion picture or television film that lists the contributions of the production's various participants.

creeping title, (in motion pictures or television) a title whose legends appear to pass into the screened image from the bottom and out through the top. Cf. *crawl roll.*

critical path method, a planning technique used to control extensive projects consisting of many independent but interlocking operations; determines which linear sequence of steps (i.e., the **critical path**) will determine the minimum time in which the project can be completed.

Cromalin, *noun, trademark* a dry positive working proofing system which produces a simulated press proof (usually 4/colors).

Cromalin proof, *noun, trademark* an extremely thin polymer layered prepress proof made by the Cromalin system.

Cronapress engraving, *noun* duplicate letterpress original engraving made from mechanically contacted cronapress negatives.

Cronapress negative, *noun, trademark* a contact negative used in letterpress engraving to make duplicate originals or conversion to offset lithography.

crop, *verb* 1. to cut off an undesired part of a photograph or the like.
2. to mark a photograph or the like to indicate a portion or portions to be deleted in final processing.

crop mark, a mark, often a line, indicating the way in which a photograph is to be cropped.

cross analysis, (in research) the use of one set of data established by a survey to illuminate another set of data from the same survey. Also *cross-sectional analysis, cross-tabulation analysis.*

cross classification, (in research) further classification of data after an initial classification has taken place, in such a way that a member of any group in the first classification may be a member of any group in subsequent ones.

cross dissolve, see *dissolve.*

cross-fade, *verb* (in television or radio) to cause two kinds of sound to change volume so that as one fades out the other fades in.

cross-hatch, *verb* to hatch an area of a drawing with crisscrossed lines.
crosshatching, *n.*

crosslight, *verb* to light a photographic subject, motion picture or television scene, etc., from one side.
crosslighting, *n.*

cross merchandising, displaying of related retail items in alternate order, as on opposite sides of a supermarket aisle; done so that a customer in search of one item may buy another on impulse.

cross plug, (in television or radio) a commercial for an alternately scheduled sponsor that is not the main sponsor for the broadcast in question; arranged on a barter basis, cross plugs give continuity of advertising for each of the sponsors.

cross-sectional design, a survey design intended to compare or contrast experimentally defined groups on one or several variables of interest.

C.R.T.C., *Canadian Radio and Television Commission.*

C.S.T., *Central Standard Time;* see *time zone.*

43

C.T.V., *Canadian TV Network.*

C.U., *close-up.*

cucalorus, *noun* (in television or motion pictures) a spotlight screen or filter used to project a specific shape of shadow or outline form on a backdrop. Also *cuckoolorus, cukaloris, cookie, cuke.*

cue, *noun* 1. a perforation or beep in a motion picture film serving to indicate the time before the beginning or end of the action or film.
2. (in the performing arts) a signal to a performer or other party active in a production to begin or end a certain action.
verb 3. to provide such a signal.

cue card, a large card depicting the lines to be spoken by a performer. Also *idiot card.*

cue light, see *warning light.*

cue sheet, an outline of a dramatic performance or the like that gives all cues in consecutive order and often provides notes on hand props to be used.

cukaloris, see *cucalorus.*

cuke, see *cucalorus.*

cumulative audience, a television or radio audience, computed either in individuals or homes, that views or listens to some portion of a series of programs or commercials. Also *cume, reach, unduplicated audience.*

cumulative price discount, see *patronage discount.*

cumulative time, (in television or radio) time elapsed since the beginning of a program.

curb delivery, delivery by truck either to a sidewalk in front of or a platform alongside a shop.

Current New York Time, the present time in New York City, used as a basis for broadcast scheduling in other U.S. time zones. Abbreviated *CNYT.* Cf. *time zone.*

cursive type, see *script.*

curved plate, a printing plate used on a rotary press.

curve of distribution, see *frequency curve.*

cushion, *noun* (in television or radio) any type of material, as dialogue or music, that can be lengthened or shortened in duration to change the running time of a program.

cut, *noun* 1. a printing plate used in letterpress printing to reproduce an image.
2. (in motion pictures or television) the abrupt termination of a shot or scene.
verb 3. to terminate a shot or scene abruptly.
4. to edit in a manner that diminishes the length of a manuscript, film, etc.
5. to record information, as a phonograph record, stencil, etc.
6. (in motion pictures and television) to end recording of a scene by order of the director.

cut-in, (of a commercial) to replace a network commercial with another, locally, in order either to test the new commercial or to provide better local support for the product it advertises.

cutback, *noun* see *flashback.*

cut case, 1. a quantity of merchandise equivalent to a case lot, sold to a retailer.
2. a case of goods that has been divided by a cutting device.

cut line, a caption describing a printed illustration or a portion thereof.

cutoff rule, a printed line separating two newspaper advertisements.

cutout, a visual device affixed to the surface of an outdoor bulletin to give a three dimensional effect.

cut-rate subscription, a periodical subscription offered at a special low rate to stimulate circulation.

C & W station, see *format.*

C.W.D., *consecutive-weeks discount.*

cyc, *noun* see *cyclorama.*

cycle, *noun* (in television or radio) a period, usually a quarter of 13 weeks, used as a unit of time in negotiations for purchase of commercial occasions, or for the payment of commercial performers.

cycle discount, a discount for the purchase of television or radio time to run during an entire cycle, at a rate increasing according to the number of cycles purchased.

cycles per second, see *frequency.* Abbreviated *c.p.s.*

cyclic animation, see *animation.*

cyclorama, *noun* (in theater, motion pictures, or television) a curved backdrop used to give the effect of sky or distance. Also *cyc.*

D

DAGMAR, *noun* the title of a book by Russell Colley, published by the Association of National Advertisers; the book recommends evaluation of advertising effectiveness by its attainment of communications goals (e.g., advertising awareness) rather than only concurrent sales results. The book's title is an acronym for "Defining Advertising Goals for Measured Advertising Results."

dailies, *plural noun* see *rushes.*

daily newspaper, a newspaper sold daily Monday through Friday or Saturday. In the United States in 1974 there were 1768 of these, with a total circulation of 61,877,197. Also **daily.**

daily rate, the advertising space rate charged by a daily newspaper for all editions published Monday through Friday or Saturday.

daily report, a field report on sales and expenses made daily by a salesman.

Dale-Chall formula, a technique for assessing the ease with which a text may be read; calls for measuring sentence length and degree of use of uncommon words. Cf. *Flesch formula, Gunning formula, Cloze procedure.*

dante, *noun* a flamelike pattern created with a cucalorus.

D.A.R., *day-after recall.*

dark week, see *black week.*

data bank, a collection of information regarding an organization's experience, not necessarily centralized or computerized.

dating, *noun* the line on an order form indicating when payment is due.

day-after recall, audience recall measured the day after an advertisement is exposed. Abbreviated *D.A.R.*

day-after survey, an advertising research survey made 15 to 24 hours after a test treatment, e.g., the broadcast of a test commercial.

Day-Glo, *noun, trademark* a luminously brilliant matte paint, available in a variety of colors, used mainly for display cards and outdoor advertisements.

day letter, a daily bulletin sent to retailers by a chain or wholesaler.

daypart, *noun* any of the time segments into which the broadcasting day of a television or radio station is divided. Typical dayparts for television are: *daytime* (sign-on - 5:00 P.M.), *early fringe* (5:00 - 7:30 P.M.), *access* (7:30 - 8:00 P.M.), *prime* (8:00 - 11:00 or, on Sundays, 7:00 - 11:00 P.M.), and *late fringe* (11:00 P.M. - sign-off). Typical dayparts for radio are *morning drive* (sign-on - 10:00 A.M.), *housewife* (10:00 A.M. - 3:00 P.M.), *afternoon drive* (3:00 - 7:00 P.M.), *night* or *teen* (7:00 P.M. - sign-off). Also *daytime.*

daytime, *noun* see *daypart.*

daytime drama, see *soap opera.*

daytime station, an AM radio station restricted to broadcasting between sunrise and sunset so that its signal, which nocturnal conditions would greatly strengthen, will not interfere with that of a clear channel station. Also *daytimer.*

D.B., *delayed broadcast.*

db, *decibel.*

D county, any county that is not an A, B, or C county. The designation is that of the A. C. Nielsen Co. Cf. *A county, B county, C county.*

dead matte, (of a photographic print or photostat) having a dull finish so as to be easily marked with pencil or pen. Cf. *glossy.*

dead matter, (in printing) composed type which is no longer needed.

dead metal, (in printing) metal left in non-printing areas of an original engraving or metal inserted in type forms, type high, so that pressure used in molding duplicate or printing plates does not break down type or vignetted edges of halftone illustrations. Dead metal is then routed out of the printing plate.

deal, *noun* a temporary offer to sell goods under terms which vary from the customary terms in a manner which favors the buyer. Cf. *allowance.*

DEALER LISTING

dealer, *noun* see *retailer.*

dealer imprint, the name and address of a local retailer, added to a manufacturer-prepared advertisement or advertising piece. Also *hooker.*

dealer listing, a listing of local dealers added to an advertisement used over a large geographical area. Such a listing can be changed by state, metropolis, or region when an advertisement is run nationally, depending on the publication's capability of production of such local editions.

dealer loader, a premium given to retailers as an incentive to purchase a stated quantity of merchandise. Also *loader.* Cf. *buying loader, display loader.*

dealer super, see *local tag.*

dealer tie-in, a listing of local dealers in an advertisement paid for entirely by a manufacturer.

deal pack, 1. merchandise whose units have been packaged in a manner providing a special sales incentive, e.g., cents-off pack, bonus pack or premium pack.
2. merchandise which is sold on a deal basis.

decal, *noun* an adhesive design in paint, ink, or the like, backed with a protective layer of water-soluble paper which is removed when the design is applied to a surface to be decorated. Also **decalcomania,** *transfer.*

decentralize, *verb* (in chain retailing) to give a measure of autonomy to divisional or store managers within the general regulations of a parent company.

decibel, a measure of the intensity of sound. Abbreviated *db.*

decile, *noun* (in statistics) any of ten equal parts into which the whole population of a sample is divided, the parts being arranged in some meaningful order; every tenth centile in ascending or descending order.

47

decision tree, the range of alternative courses of action, and the alternative consequences which may result from each, about which a decision or choice of alternative actions must be made.

deck, see *tape deck.*

decker well, a food store freezer cabinet that displays merchandise in a vertical position; usually prefixed by the number of available tiers or shelves (e.g., three-decker well).

deckle, *noun* the untrimmed edge of a sheet of paper, sometimes retained for its decorative effect. Also *deckle edge.*

decline, *noun* see *product life cycle.*

decode, *verb* to give a personal interpretation to the elements of an advertisement with a greater or lesser amount of interest, comprehension, and belief, according to the advertisement's success. The concept is derived from communications research. Cf. *encode.*

deep etching, additional etching of engravings to create proper molding depth or to sharpen the highlights of halftones. Also to add depth in type areas on combination line and halftone engravings.

defensive spending, expenditures for marketing activities intended to protect an established business from competitive inroads.

deferred discount, see *patronage discount.*

definition, *noun* (in television or radio) the clarity of a signal.

defocusing, *noun* see *out-of-focus dissolve.*

delayed broadcast, a television or radio program recorded during the original broadcast for further broadcast at a later time. Abbreviated *D.B.*

delete, *verb* to remove part of a manuscript, or copy that has been set in type.

deluxe urban bulletin, a painted outdoor advertising bulletin 13'4" high by 46'10" wide.

demand, *noun* (in economics) the amount of desire on the part of the buying public for a type of product or service, or for such a product or service from one company.

demographic, *adjective* noting or pertaining to the study of population group data in terms of external characteristics, e.g., age, income, types of occupation, educational levels, race, and national origin, the number of persons in each category being established. Cf. *psychographic.*

demographic edition, an edition of a periodical intended for a specific demographic group; advertisers interested especially in such a group are offered space at premium rates.

demonstration, *noun* an active display showing a product or service in use or being consumed. Also **demo.**

demo reel, a sample reel of commercials or the like, used by production studios, directors, etc. as a means of exhibiting their work. Also *sample reel.*

departmental display, a unified retail display of all related items from one manufacturer.

department store, a large retail outlet offering a wide variety of durable goods organized by departments, each of which may be as large as an independent specialty shop; usually operated on a credit and delivery basis.

dependent variable, (in statistics) a variable to be predicted whose value is a function of other variables or constants in an experimental design. Cf. *independent variable.*

depth, *noun* 1. the distance on a printing plate between the printing surface and the

level to which the nonprinting portions of the plate have been etched.
2. the top-to-bottom length of a column in a periodical, measured in inches or, in newspapers, in agate lines.

depth interview, an interview in which a respondent is questioned for the purpose of obtaining full information about his knowledge, attitudes, etc.

depth of exposure, the extent to which the size or duration of an advertisement or the frequency of its repetition heightens the conciousness of it on the part of a newspaper reader, television viewer, etc.

depth of field, (in photography) the depth between nearer and farther points of a scene that are in acceptably sharp focus.

depth of focus, (in photography) the distance a camera may be moved toward or away from a subject, while the subject remains in acceptably sharp focus.

descender, *noun* (in typography) a stroke of a lower case letter descending below the base line; g, j, p, q, and y have descenders. Cf. *ascender.*

descending letter, (in typography) any lower case letter with a descender.

design, *noun* 1. a visual plan depicting the appearance of a symbol, trademark, object, or setting intended to communicate desired qualities.
2. the visual execution of such a plan.
3. the art of preparing such depictions.
4. see *experimental design.*
verb 5. to prepare visual or research plans.

designated market area, a term used by the A.C. Nielsen Co. to define a group of usually adjacent counties in which the major share of audience is obtained by television stations located within these counties; each U.S. county is part of only one such area. Abbreviated *D.M.A.* Cf. *area of dominant influence.*

designer, *noun* a person who creates or executes designs.

detailer, *noun* a salesman whose work is primarily the promotion of goodwill among professionals, especially doctors, etc., who may influence the purchase of their employee's or client's products or services.

detail man, a manufacturer's or broker's representative who calls on retailers to check sales and the condition of stock and to render sales aid. Cf. *retail man, field man.*

develop, *verb* 1. to bring forth photographic images on exposed film or paper by the use of a suitable chemical solution (**developer**). Cf. *fix.*
2. to encourage the growth of sales of a product or product class. Cf. *brand development, market development.*

dex, *noun, trademark* a Graphic Sciences, Inc. system for transmitting document facsimiles from and to properly equipped telephone terminals.

D.G.A., *Directors Guild of America.*

dial shopper, (in Canada) a person who dials stations on a television or radio set at random with no fixed intention of tuning in to a specific program.

diary method, a method of consumer research in which respondents keep a log of periodicals read, television or radio programs heard, products purchased, etc.

die cut, 1. a sheet of paper cut with a die to the shape desired.
2. the cut so made.
die-cut, *adj.*

die stamping, the embossing of paper by means of dies to create a raised or recessed design or image on the sheet.

differential, *noun* see *rate differential.*

differentiation, *noun* see *brand differentiation.*

diffuser, *noun* 1. (in photography, motion pictures and television) a translucent screen or the like used to soften shadows and highlights created by bright lights.
2. a device used to blur the focus of a camera image.

digest, a periodical providing a summary of a variety of subjects, including condensations of longer works which may have appeared in other publications.

digest-sized page, a unit of magazine advertising space measuring 5 inches by 7 inches, included in a magazine of larger page size; so called from the page size of the *Reader's Digest.*

dig out, (in printing) to remove a portion of a plate by hand; route out.

dinky inkie, see *baby spotlight.*

diorama, *noun* 1. (in motion pictures or television) a mockup of a scene shot in such a way as to give the illusion of being an actual scene.
2. an advertising display, usually three dimensional, specially lighted and often animated.

direct buyer, a person who is permitted to buy directly from a manufacturer, usually a retailer with a number of stores and his own warehouse.

direct halftone, a halftone made as an object is photographed rather than from a photographic negative or print. Cf. *direct halftone process.*

direct halftone process, (in color engraving) production by photography of halftone separation negatives for each color, using appropriate color filters and halftone screens simultaneously. Also *direct process.*

directional microphone, a microphone sensitive to sounds within a limited arc; useful for screening out potentially distracting background noise.

directive interview, an interview in which the respondent's answers are restricted to those offered for choice in a questionnaire. Cf. *nondirective interview.*

direct mail advertising, use of the postal system as a medium to deliver advertisements to prospects. Also **direct mail.**

Direct Mail Advertising Association, an organization of national and local users of direct mail advertising, formed to further member interests and to promote this advertising medium. Abbreviated *D.M.A.A.*

director, *noun* a person responsible for supervising all audience-visible aspects of a play, motion picture, television show, etc. Cf. *producer.*

director of research, see *research director.*

direct order, an order to a manufacturer from a direct buyer.

Directors Guild of America, a professional organization of film and television directors. Abbreviated *D.G.A.*

directory advertising, 1. advertising in a directory.
2. loosely, advertising consulted by a market as a guide for its purchases, as that of a department store or supermarket.

direct positive, a photographic positive made by a process requiring no negative.

direct process, see *direct halftone process.*

direct recording, 1. see *lip synchronization.*
2. to make a phonographic recording direct from a live performance, rather than a magnetic tape.

direct response advertising, advertising which attempts to obtain orders for purchase to be made directly to the manufacturer or servicer, rather than through agents, stores, or other dealers. Also **direct response, direct response marketing.** Cf. *mail order advertising.*

direct sale, a sale made by a manufacturer to a direct buyer.

direct store delivery, a delivery of merchandise from a manufacturer directly to a retailer. Also *drop shipment, store door delivery.*

disc, *noun* a phonograph record. Also **disk.**

disc jockey, a radio entertainer whose program consists mainly of popular records, interspersed with commentary, live and recorded commercials, and other announcements. Also *jock,* **disk jockey.** Abbreviated *D.J.*

discount, *noun* any reduction from a stated price or rate of payment, made for various reasons. An advertiser may receive a discount, for instance, for purchasing a certain large quantity of space or time in a communications medium; an advertising agency receives much of its revenue in the form of discounts from media on billings to advertisers; a retailer buys from a wholesaler at a discount from the established retail price.

discount house, a retail outlet offering a variety of durable or non-food packaged goods at a relatively low markup, usually featuring a minimum level of credit, delivery, and guarantee services. Also **discounter,** *discount store.* Cf. *mass merchandiser.*

discount store, see *discount house.*

discrepancy, *noun* 1. an incongruity between two related things, as media space or time ordered and that billed to the advertiser.
2. an inadequacy of competitive separation or commercial protection provided by a medium.

discriminant function analysis, a multivariate statistical technique which seeks to maximize group differences relative to the error or variability found within such groups; groups are defined through the experimental design and each is evaluated on a number of dimensions by separate, independent groups assigned randomly to each such concept. Some combination or combinations of these dimensions forms in a manner which tends to maximally differentiate these groups.

dispersion, *noun* (in statistics) the degree or pattern of distribution of measurements of frequency or other observed factors.

dispersion pattern, 1. (in television or radio) audience flow at the end of a program.
2. the placing of advertising messages, in terms of coverage and frequency, to attain an objective.

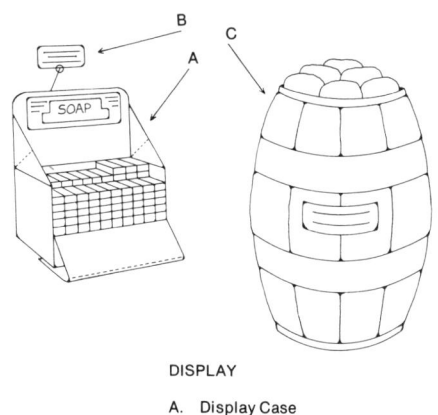

DISPLAY

A. Display Case
B. Display Card
C. Display Bin

display, *noun* a physically contiguous arrangement of goods or advertising, possibly with decorative material, intended to call attention to and prompt the sale of a product or service.

display advertising, 1. advertising in print that usually uses illustration(s) as well as type.
2. advertising mounted in a display.

display allowance, a merchandising allowance granted to retailers in return for the opportunity to display merchandise, usually off-shelf.

display bin, an open bin, usually of heavy paper or cardboard, for the display of small items piled inside; usually a dump bin.

display card, a printed or hand lettered advertisement attached to a store display. Cf. *shelf talker.*

display case, 1. a cabinet with glass panels allowing the contents to be protected, to be refrigerated, etc., while remaining on display. Also *case.*
2. a container for merchandise that becomes a display setting when opened.

display classified advertising, classified advertising that uses display type, illustrations, and other special features, and that occupies more space for its verbal content than the regular advertising of a classified section.

display loader, a dealer loader premium that is built into a display, and received by the dealer when the display is taken down.

display type, large, boldface type used for headlines and subheadlines, rather than text.

dissolve, *noun* (in motion pictures or television) any beginning or termination of a shot made by putting the camera gradually out of or into focus. Also *cross dissolve.* Cf. *cut, lap dissolve, out-of-focus dissolve.*

distant signal, a broadcast media signal received outside the normal reception area of a locality and relayed to it by cable. Also *imported signal.*

distortion, *noun* 1. the false recollection of an experience; e.g. that of an advertising message, so as to make the message fit readily into a personal frame of reference. Distortion, as a rule, either "sharpens" the message in attributing a false meaning to it or "levels" it by eliminating part of its significance. Cf. *cognitive dissonance.*
2. bad reception of a video or audio signal.
3. intentional distortion of the width of a newspaper advertisement in order to accommodate individual newspaper column width requirements; an alternative to cropping or completely resizing an advertisement.

distribution, *noun* 1. the extent to which dealers carry a retail item; usually measured by either the percentage of the number of all dealers who carry the item (*store count basis*), or by the percentage of the total volume of business done by those who carry the item (*all commodity volume basis*).
2. the means by which a manufactured product reaches the customer including storage, transportation, sales, etc., and the way these are organized.

distribution allowance, a discount made by a manufacturer to a wholesaler or store chain to cover the cost of distributing a product, especially for the first time.

distributor, *noun* 1. a person or organization who supplies stock to retailers or wholesalers from a central warehouse. Also *jobber.*
2. a retail or wholesale sales merchant.

distributor's brand, a brand owned by a wholesaler or chain rather than by a manufacturer or single retailer.

district, a geographical sales territory covered by one salesperson or broker. Also *section.*

D.J., *disc jockey.*

D.M.A., *designated market area.*

D.M.A.A., *Direct Mail Advertising Association.*

documentary, *noun* a motion picture, television, or radio presentation of actual events, especially as illustrations of a theme being discussed.

dollar volume discount, a discount to a purchaser who purchases a certain number of dollars' worth of merchandise, usually increasing with the amount purchased.

dolly, *noun* 1. a small carriage for a motion picture or television camera.
verb 2. to shift the viewpoint of such a camera during a shot (**dolly shot**) by causing it to go forward (**dolly in**) or backward (**dolly out**).

Domsat, *noun* a domestic U.S. communications satellite system. Cf. *Comsat, Intelsat.*

donut, *noun* a recorded television or radio commercial distributed to local stations and having a blank central section to be filled with a local advertiser's message.

door opener, an inexpensive gift from a salesman offered as an inducement to gain a prospect's attention.

door-to-door sales, a distribution system which employs salespersons to make retail sales calls on individual consumers at their homes.

dot, *noun* one of the minute individual printing surfaces in a halftone plate that, as its diameter and those of adjoining dots vary from larger to smaller, cause the areas of the plate to print darker or lighter.

dot formation, the arrangement and relative size of the dots of a halftone film or plate.

double coating, an unusually heavy paper coating; the term is used regardless of the number of coating operations.

double-decker, *noun* an outdoor advertising display in two separate tiers.

double-duty envelope, an envelope so formed that when portions are torn away a self-addressed return envelope remains.

double exposure, 1. (in photography, motion pictures, and television) a composite image created by two exposures of one film or blended images from two television cameras. Also *double print.* Cf. *composite shot.*
2. a television film shown over two different stations in the same week.

double image, see *ghost.*

double-page spread, see *double spread.*

double post card, a post card in the form of a folded double-sized sheet, one leaf addressed to the recipient, the other addressed to the sender; privately printed and often sent bulk rate. Cf. *double postal card.*

double postal card, a post card similar in form to a double post card, but issued by the U.S. Postal Service.

double print, 1. (in printing) a combination on a printing plate of line and halftone, created by the photographic exposure of two different negatives in register in the same area, type overprinting the photographic area.
2. a sheet printed from such a plate. Cf. *surprint.*
3. (in photography) a print made from the superimposition of two negatives. Also *composite shot, double exposure.*

double pyramid, a form of newspaper layout in which a center section of editorial matter is flanked by columns of advertising. Cf. *pyramid makeup.*

double spotting, (in television or radio) running of one spot announcement directly after another.

double spread, two facing pages in a periodical. Also *double-page spread, double truck.* Cf. *center spread.*

double system, (in motion pictures or television) the recording of images and sound on separate occasions for later combination.

53

double truck, 1. an advertisement running across a pair of facing pages in a periodical.
2. see *double spread.*

down-and-under, *adverb* (in motion pictures, television, or radio) down to a volume permitting dialogue to be heard; a direction to a musician or sound-effects man.

down-scale, *adjective, adverb* at the lower end of a range in a demographic parameter, in terms of education, income, etc.

downstage, *adjective, adverb* (in the performing arts) toward the audience or camera. Cf. *upstage.*

down-the-street sell, that portion of a promotion drive period following headquarters sales office calls, when salesmen and detail men place sales and service calls on store managers and independent store owners.

dragon's blood, a fusable powder used in engraving letterpress plates, which protects all sides of the relief printing areas of the engraving during the etching process.

dress, *noun* 1. (in theater, motion pictures, or television) properties and the like intended to add realism or interest to a scene but not required specifically by the action. Cf. *dress rehearsal.*
verb 2. to ready a scene for a performance.

dress rehearsal, *noun* a final and complete rehearsal of a theatrical performance or the like in full costume. Also *dress.*

drive-in, *adjective* noting or pertaining to a customer sales or service facility equipped to accommodate customers in their cars.

drive period, a limited period of time scheduled by a manufacturer or wholesaler sales organization for representing deal and promotional terms to retail sales prospects, and consumers. Also *promotion drive period, promotion period.*

drive time, see *daypart.*

drop-in, *noun* (in television or radio) a local commercial inserted into a nationally sponsored network program. Cf. *cut-in.*

drop-out halftone, a halftone in which dots are dropped out in the highlight areas of the plate to give the whitest effect possible for good contrast.

drop shipment, a direct shipment of merchandise to a retailer from a manufacturer, billed to him through a wholesaler or chain headquarters. Cf. *direct store delivery.*

drop shipper, an agency that sells a product delivered directly to a customer by a manufacturer.

drug store, a store which sells pharmaceutical products as an important portion of its total sales; increasingly, drug stores have evolved into, or been incorporated in, mass merchandiser outlets which treat pharmaceutical products as one of many departments.

dry, *adjective* noting or pertaining to products that are not perishable.

dry-brush, *adjective* noting or pertaining to painting on textured paper with a brush slightly moistened with water color or ink, so as to allow the texture of the paper to appear.

dry mount, *verb* to process two pieces of paper, cardboard, or the like, under heat and pressure, with a paraffin-treated sheet between, so as to make them adhere together as a unit.

dry offset printing, a form of offset printing in which the areas to be inked are raised by etching around them, in contrast to the ordinary planographic form of offset printing. See *letterset.*

dry run, (in motion pictures and television) a rehearsal in which various aspects of a production are perfected. Cf. *walkthrough.*

dual channel market, a market area in

which two local or nonlocal television stations are readily received.

dub, *verb* 1. to blend sound into the previously recorded sound track of a film, or audio or video tape. Also **dub in.**
noun 2. a tape recorded or filmed duplicate; especially a tape copy intended for release to media.

due bill, 1. a statement of television or radio barter time acquired.
2. an agreement for the barter of services from an advertiser, as a hotel, in exchange for space or time in a communications medium.

dull, *adjective* 1. (of paper) without gloss; matte finish.
verb 2. to remove unwanted reflections from an object being photographed.

dull-coated, *adjective* (of paper) having a nonglossy coating.

dummy, *noun* (in printing) a simulation of a finished printed piece prepared prior to the printing of multiple copies, and indicating the finished characteristics of any of a number of design and production factors (e.g., size, content, weight, etc.).

dump bin, a display bin in which merchandise items are dumped rather than stacked.

dump table, a display table on which merchandise items are dumped rather than stacked.

duotone, *noun* a two-color printing process for enriching the effect of black and white halftone illustration printing by adding an additional color from a second halftone plate, in register, using a different screen angle. Also **duograph.**

dupe, *noun, informal* a duplicate, as of a photographic negative, film, recording tape, or printing plate.

duplex technique, a telephone audience-interviewing technique in which the activities of a potential audience at the time of the interview and over the previous fifteen minutes are examined.

duplicated audience, audience produced by media duplication.

duplicate plate, any printing plate made from an original, as for multiple distribution to newspapers or magazines.

duplicating paper, any paper intended for use with a duplicator.

duplication, *noun* the amount of exposure of the known audience of a medium to another medium of the same type carrying the same advertising, or to more than one appearance of the same advertising in the same medium, e.g., successive issues of the same magazine.

duplicator, *noun* a machine for printing multiple paper copies of typing, drawings, etc. from a master or stencil.

durable good, an imperishable product which need not be consumed in bulk in order to obtain its primary benefits. Also **durable.**

dust jacket, a paper wrapper for a book. Also *jacket, wrapper.*

dutch door, a magazine space unit, produced under special circumstances; consists of two-part, full-page gatefolds folding to a common center, or stacked or single half-page gatefolds.

dutchman, *noun* 1. any of various devices for concealing bad workmanship or discontinuities in the surface of something.
2. (in theater, motion pictures, or television) a strip of cloth used to cover the gap between two stage flats.

dye transfer print, an opaque color photographic print made from a transparency; while expensive, it is of high quality and permits a large amount of retouching.

E

E.A., *editorial alteration.*

ear, *noun* either of the extreme upper corners of the front page of a newspaper, flanking the title; sold as advertising space by some papers.

earlug, *noun* (in Canada) an ear of a newspaper.

early fringe, see *daypart.*

earned rate, the actual rate for advertising space or time charged to an advertiser, taking into account all discounts for volume and frequency. Cf. *card rate.*

earth station, a television or radio relay station equipped to receive transmissions from earth orbital satellites.

E.C.A., *extended central area.*

echo chamber, a resonant acoustic chamber used to give sounds an echolike effect in television, motion picture, or radio performances. Cf. *reverberator.*

E.C.U., *extra close-up.*

E.D., (to appear) every day; used as an instruction in scheduling newspaper advertising.

edit, *verb* 1. to alter the content of a manuscript, film, etc.
2. to splice or record a replacement commercial into a television film or videotape in place of a commercial originally recorded.

edition, *noun* 1. one of a series of sequential or geographic, etc., revisions of a single issue of a periodical.
2. one of a series of revisions in form or content of a book volume or set.

editorial, *noun* 1. a statement of a point of view regarding public issues expressed by the management of a periodical or broadcaster.
2. see *editorial matter.*
adjective 3. noting or pertaining to editorial matter.

editorial alteration, (in proofreading) any alteration made by a publisher other than one made at an author's request or one to correct a printer's error. Abbreviated *E.A.* Cf. *author's alteration, printer's error.*

editorial authority, 1. a credibility advantage established by a media vehicle's public reputation for accuracy and objectivity in its editorial content.
2. a goal of advertising, sought either by placement of advertisements in media vehicles judged to be of high authority to purchase prospects, or by designing advertisements to imitate the appearance of editorial matter in the media in which they appear.

editorial classification, the system of major sections or departments used to organize a periodical, especially a newspaper.

editorial content, see *editorial matter.*

editorial environment, the standard editorial content, tone, and philosophy of a medium; seen as potentially supportive or destructive of the effectiveness of advertising using the medium.

editorial matter, (in periodical publishing) reading matter prepared by the staff of a publication or accepted from contributors, as opposed to advertising, which is run for a fee. Also *editorial, editorial content.*

E.D.P., *electronic data processing.*

E.D.T., *Eastern Daylight Time;* see *time zone.*

educational television, noncommercial television devoted to educational material. Abbreviated *E.T.V.*

E.F., *English finish.*

effect, *noun* (in motion pictures, radio, and television) a technique or device for producing a visual or auditory illusion, as sound effects, special effects, optical effects, etc.

effective, *adjective* noting or pertaining to advertising which accomplishes its objectives, as demonstrated in a market or as inferred from its performance in pre-test measures.
effectiveness, *n.* Also *impact.*

effective circulation, (in outdoor advertising) an estimate of the number of passers-by who might reasonably be considered capable of seeing an advertisement. Calculated as half of pedestrian, truck, and automotive traffic, and a quarter of public transit riders, by the Traffic Audit Bureau.

effective distribution, all commodity distribution after deduction of out-of-stock distribution from total distribution. Also *net effective distribution.*

effective sample base, a sample size used by Arbitron for assessment of the statistical variance of audience data, representing the size of simple random samples required to produce the same degree of accuracy as those actually employed. Abbreviated *ESB.*

effects track, a sound effect recording for a television or radio performance.

efficiency, *noun* advertising audience size in comparison with the cost of placing the advertising; usually expressed as a cost-per-thousand exposed audience units (households, readers, viewers, listeners, prospects, target audience members, etc.). With newspapers, milline rates may be used.

ego ideal, (in psychology) a person's idealized self concept, which serves as a behavioral goal.

ego involvement, (in psychology) the degree to which a person acts toward the outside world in ways due to his identification of its characteristics, problems, etc. with his own.

8mm, see *motion picture film.*

8vo, see *octavo.*

Ektachrome, *noun, trademark* a positive color transparency film manufactured by the Eastman Kodak Company.

Ektacolor, *noun, trademark* a professional grade, high-speed color film manufactured by Eastman Kodak Co., used for making full color negatives and studio processed positives to order.

elasticity, *noun* the degree of demand responsiveness to price or marketing support variances for a product, service, or category.

electrical etching, the use of electrolysis to etch relief printing plates.

electrical transcription, an obsolescent synonym for transcription. Abbreviated *E.T.*

electric spectacular, an outdoor advertisement whose words and designs are formed by lights.

electronic data processing, the use of computer systems to process, store, etc. information. Abbreviated *E.D.P.*

electronic editing, use of a control board rather than manual splicing for editing magnetic tape.

electronic flash, a high-intensity, rechargeable flash lamp used in still photography.

electrotype, *noun* a duplicate letterpress printing plate made by electroplating the surface of a mold of the original plate. Also **electro.**

element, *noun* original negative film footage used in a master finished commercial; typically composed of a single shot.

elementary sampling unit, (in statistics) the subject upon which measurement of some set of variables is taken.

elements package, all negative film elements necessary to produce a master finished commercial from which film prints may be derived after processing.

elite, *noun* a typewriter type size with twelve characters per linear inch. Cf. *pica.*

Elliot machine, a device for printing mailing addresses on envelopes using flexible stenciled cards as printing masters.

Elrod, *noun, trademark* a machine for making leads and rules for use in typesetting.

em, *noun* a unit of horizontal measurement equal to the point size of the type being set. A 12-point type em is 12 points wide. Indentations are measured in ems, as are dashes. Cf. *en.*

embellished painted bulletin, see *semispectacular.*

embellishment, *noun* a shaped piece which extends a visual image beyond its customary frame, as in a storyboard cell or outdoor bulletin; in outdoor, a standard embellishment size is 5'6" at top, 2' at its sides, and 1' to 2' at its base. Also *extension.*

emboss, *verb* to raise portions of the surface of a sheet of paper, metal, etc., in order to form a design by pressing the material between concave and convex dies.

emcee, *noun* see *master of ceremonies.*

em quad, see *quad.*

emulsion, *noun* a light sensitive coating on the surface of photographic film, paper, or printing plates that develops the image on the medium used, when exposed to light.

en, *noun* a unit of horizontal measurement in printing, equal to one half the point size being set. A 16-point type en is equal to 8 points in width. An en dash, one en long, is used between numbers to indicate a range: the *0 - 10 age group.* Cf. *em.*

enamel, *noun* the calendered finish of clay and sizing on a coated paper.

enamel proof, see *repro proof.*

enclosure, *noun* anything mailed in an envelope or the like, especially in addition to the principal content. Also *insert.*

encode, *verb* (in communications theory) to substitute a symbol for an idea or emotion. Cf. *decode.*

end aisle display, a mass display of merchandise at the end of a row of retail shelving, as in a supermarket.

endpaper, a paper at either end of a book, lining the cover and forming a flyleaf. Also *bookend.*

end rate, a rate charged for advertising space or time which incorporates the maximum standard discount.

English finish, a hard, textureless, matte finish for book paper. Abbreviated *E.F.*

engraver's proof, a proof pulled from black and white, 2-color, 3-color or 4-color engravings, usually with color bars for checking ink density, submitted for approval.

engraving, *noun* 1. a printing plate prepared by etching or cutting into the surface of the plate.
2. an intaglio printing plate prepared by incising the areas that are to print with a tool, as a burin.
3. a print made from any such plate.

engrossing, *noun* decorative hand lettering.

enlargement, *noun* a reproduction, especially of a photograph, that is larger than the original.
enlarge, *v.*

en quad, see *quad.*

enrich, *verb* to add to processed foods a significant amount of nutrients which were not necessarily present in such foods prior to processing; can be done to replace dietary nutrients lost from substitution of such foods for other foods. Cf. *fortify.*

envelope stuffer, a printed advertising piece enclosed with a bill or other matter in a mailing envelope.

E.O.D., every other day; a term used in scheduling or ordering newspaper advertising.

E.O.W., every other week; a term used in ordering or scheduling newspaper advertising.

E.O.W.T.F., every other week till forbid; a term used in scheduling or ordering newspaper advertising.

equivalent live time program, a television or radio program recorded so as to be broadcast at the same clock time in more than one time zone; the broadcasts need not be on the same day.

error, *noun* (in statistics) the extent of variability not accounted for in a controlled experiment after a prediction has been made. The difference between an actual value and the prediction of that value.

ESB, *effective sample base.*

esquisse, *noun* a rough layout sketch; thumbnail.

E.S.T., *Eastern Standard Time;* see *time zone.*

establishing shot, (in television or motion pictures) an opening shot providing a comprehensive view of a scene which in subsequent action will be shot from closer positions.

estimate, *noun* 1. a notice of anticipated costs, often sent from agency to client as a request for approval of anticipated cost details.
verb 2. to produce such a notice.

estimated rating, a predicted rating for a television show or radio show to be broadcast at a certain time on a certain station.

estimator, *noun* an advertising agency employee who prepares media cost estimates, usually for media buys.

E.T., *electrical transcription.*

etch, *verb* to selectively remove metal from an intaglio or letterpress printing plate by means of corrosive chemicals or electrolysis. In the strictest sense, etching differs from engraving in that an engraved plate is incised with a tool. Cf. *intaglio.*

etched depth, the depth to which a printing plate has been etched.

etching, *noun* a printer's proof made from an etched plate.

ethical, *adjective* 1. (of advertising) conforming to industry standards of fairness and honesty.
2. noting or pertaining to advertising of ethical (as opposed to patent) medicines.

ethical medicine, a drug sold only with a doctor's prescription.

ethnic media, communications media that reach specific ethnic groups.

E.T.V., *educational television.*

evo, see *octavo.*

exclusive distribution, distribution of a product within a certain territory by a distributor with the sole license to do so. Cf. *open distribution.*

exclusive market area, a group of counties or other areas whose radio or television audiences are predominantly drawn to stations in a designated market area; used for spot broadcast audience measurement data. Each measurement service employs a proprietary, synonymous term to describe such areas. For A. C. Nielsen Co., see *Designated Market Area*; for Arbitron, see *Area of Dominant Influence*; for Pulse, see *Radio Area of Dominant Influence.* Also *exclusive coverage area.*

exclusivity, *noun* freedom from competing advertising within a given communications medium enjoyed by one advertiser; requires major space or time purchases.

execution, *noun* an advertisement prepared to a stated creative strategy.
execute, *v.*

executive creative director, an advertising agency employee responsible for managing the operations and personnel of a creative department. Cf. *creative director.*

expansion plan, a plan for expanding distribution, advertising, and sales of a product or service from a narrow geographic base to a broader or national base, usually in a series of stages.

experimental design, (in research) a plan for measuring the effect of test variables or treatments in a manner that minimizes the influence of other variables. Also *design.*

experimental error, (in research) variation in response from subjects that have been uniformly treated by the experimenter; used as a check on variations in response by similar subjects when treated in a nonuniform way.

explosion wipe, (in television or motion pictures) a sudden, ragged wipe radiating outward from the center of the image.

exposition, *noun* (in television or motion picture dramas) a discourse intended to provide an audience with an explanation of events which either have preceded the action they are to see, or which occur outside the visible action they do see (e.g., player's thoughts, nondepicted events, etc.). One who provides such exposition is known as an **expositor.**

exposure, *noun* 1. the presentation of an advertisement to an audience, measured in terms of the number of people able to perceive it.
2. (in surveys of print media) the act of opening a publication to a space containing advertising.
3. the act, or rate, of exposing photographic film to light.

express lane, a checkout lane in a supermarket intended for use by customers purchasing a small number of items. Also **express checkout.**

extended, *adjective* (of a typeface) a face that is broader than is normal for a given height. Cf. *condensed.*

extended central area, (in Canada) a BBM Bureau of Broadcast Measurement designation for an area outside a local television market but within its coverage area and influenced primarily by its broadcasting. Abbreviated *E.C.A.*

extended cover, a pamphlet or brochure cover that extends beyond the trim of the pages. Also *overhang, overlap.*

extended product, see *product.*

extender, *noun* see *shelf extender.*

extension, *noun* (in television or radio) 1. a seller's agreement to prolong the time available to a prospect for consideration of an option to purchase.
2. a seller's agreement to prolong the terms of a previously agreed-upon purchase.
3. see *embellishment.*
4. an additional period of time granted by a periodical after a closing date for receipt of printing materials.
extend, *v.*

exterior, *adjective* (in theater, motion pictures, and television) noting or pertaining to sets, shots, and the like intended to simulate, or taking place, outdoors.

external house organ, see *house organ.*

extra, *noun* 1. a player in a drama or the like who has no spoken lines, and whose performance is confined to making an appearance which will enhance the realism of the scene.
2. a special edition of a newspaper, designed to provide detail on late breaking news; increasingly rare practice.

extra close-up, (in motion pictures or television) a close-up showing only one detail of an object. Also **extreme close-up.** Abbreviated *E.C.U.*

extract, *noun* see *flashback.*

extrapolate, *verb* (in statistics) to estimate unknown data by projections from known data, as for forecasts of future trends. Cf. *interpolate.*
extrapolation, *n.*

eye camera, (in research) a camera for recording eye movements; used in advertising research to measure relative amounts of visual stimulation.

eyepatch, *noun* a distinctive visual or symbolic device used to identify a specific series of advertisements; derived from the prop used in "classic" Hathaway shirt advertisements.

F

f, see *f stop*.

face, *noun* 1. the printing surface of a piece of metal type.
2. the specific design of a whole alphabet of type, with its numerals, punctuation marks, and other accompanying characters; usually repeated with minor variations in a range of type sizes. Cf. *font*.

face up, to arrange retail merchandise on a shelf or in a display in an orderly manner. Cf. *facing*.

facilities, *plural noun* 1. the technical equipment and capabilities of a television or radio station. Also *fax, facs*.
2. the station lineup of a network and its broadcasting resources.

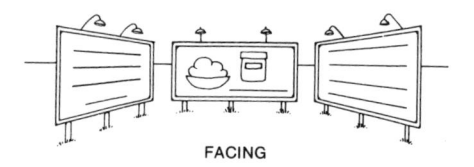

FACING

facing, *noun* 1. (in outdoor advertising) a single billboard, or a number of billboards so arranged as to permit a visually coordinated display; termed "single", "double", etc., according to the number of adjacent billboards separated by no more than twenty-five feet.
2. (in outdoor advertising) the direction in which a billboard faces: *a north facing*.
3. a single exposure of a retail item on a store shelf; the appearance of the shelf is measured in terms of the number of facings per item.

facing text matter, a descriptive position request for advertising in periodicals, which calls for placement of the advertisement opposite editorial matter. Cf. *Campbell's Soup position*.

facs, *noun* see *facilities*.

facsimile, *noun* an exact, or nearly exact, reproduction of flat visual material (writing, graphics, print, etc.).

facsimile broadcasting, the use of radio waves to transmit signals used to reproduce visual material.

factor, *noun* 1. (in mathematics) a number used for multiplication or division.
2. anything having a more or less constant influence on a certain class of events.

factor analysis, (in statistics) a variety of techniques used to study the degree of association between, and corresponding significance or meaningfulness of variables involved in, phenomena under study.

fade, *verb* (of reproduced or transmitted sound) to change in volume so as to become inaudible (*fade out*) or audible and louder (*fade in*). Cf. *cross-fade*.

fade to black, (in television or motion pictures) a gradual obliteration of an image by means of a steadily decreased camera aperture, until only black remains.

fading, *noun* (in television or radio) an intermittent or continuous reduction in the strength of a broadcast signal at a receiver.

fading area, a geographical area within normal broadcasting range in which fading of signals from a television or radio station is common.

fair trade, a principle according to which retailers agree to sell a commodity at no less than the price agreed upon between the manufacturer and the other retailers in the area; until recently suspended, such practices were often enforced by a state law (**fair-trade law**).

fake color process work, the reproduction of a black and white illustration or photograph in full color by introducing yellow, red and blue printing plates in proper tonal values to approximate true color overall.

family, *noun* a group of typefaces visually related to one another.

fanfare, *noun* a piece of music that introduces a show, announcement, etc.

fan wipe, (in motion pictures or television) a wipe in the form of a line moving radially so as to pass through an arc.

F.A.P., *field-activated promotion.*

farm publication, a periodical edited to interest farmers and their families.

Fast Evening Persons Report, an A. C. Nielsen Co. service providing overnight program audience size data from New York, Chicago, and Los Angeles audimeter homes via TWX access for clients to Nielsen's time sharing computer.

fast food, 1. noting or pertaining to a restaurant providing quick, inexpensive service, usually by orders for a selection of a few standard items placed at a counter.
2. noting or pertaining to a regional or national chain restaurant emphasizing value and service; usually franchised, these include full menu, table service operations.

fast-motion, *adjective* (in television or motion pictures) noting or pertaining to a shot or sequence in which time appears compressed, and the rate of action accelerated; accomplished by recording film or tape at a slow rate, and using regular playback rates, or (less commonly) raising the playback rate above the regular rate at which the film or tape was recorded. Cf. *slow motion.*

Fast Weekly Household Audiences Report, a weekly A. C. Nielsen Co. report on network household audiences issued in advance of more comprehensive reports. Also *fast weeklies.*

favored-nations clause, an agreement by a medium with an advertiser that no comparable purchase shall be made by another advertiser on more advantageous terms without an adjustment in the original terms of purchase.

favoring shot, (in motion pictures or television) a close-up that gives prominence to one or more actors.

fax, *plural noun* see *facilities.*

F.C.C., *Federal Communications Commission.*

F.C.C. coverage area, a television or radio coverage area within which a stated percentage of all receivers can be expected to receive the signal of a given station satisfactorily; as defined by the Federal Communications Commission.

F.D.A., *Food and Drug Administration.*

fearless dolly, (in motion pictures or television) a camera dolly mounted on a short crane boom.

feature, *noun* 1. a retail item being given special sales promotion, especially cooperative advertising of a price reduction.
2. an important characteristic of a product or service.
verb 3. to give a retail item special sales promotion.

Federal Communications Commission, A United States government agency, established in 1934, that licenses television and radio broadcasting stations, assigns transmitting frequencies, and supervises station activities. Abbreviated *F.C.C.*

Federal Trade Commission, a U.S. government administrative agency created in 1915 to assist in maintaining a free enterprise, competitive economic system. Abbreviated *F.T.C.*

fee, *noun* a payment for services made to an advertising agency by an advertiser either as an agreed-upon alternative to commission compensation, or in situations where commission is not provided by the agency's supplier.

feed, *verb* 1. to transmit (a television or radio program) from one station to another for rebroadcast.
noun 2. a program so transmitted.

feedback, *noun* 1. meaningful response from an audience to an advertiser or a communications medium regarding an advertisement or the like.
2. (in audio) a loud keening noise caused either by a microphone picking up the sound of amplified ambient or circuit noise through a speaker, or by the accidental closing of a circuit.

feed point, the origin of a television or radio program fed to other stations. Also *origination point.*

fiberboard, *noun* a heavy cardboard made of compressed wood or vegetable fibers. Also **fibreboard.**

fidelity, *noun* faithfulness of reproduction of a sound or image, as in audio, film, or television, to an original.

field, *noun* 1. (in research) the geographic area in which consumers are involved with products or services in real life; hence such terms as *field research.*
2. (in motion pictures or television) the area of a set or scene appearing in view at any given moment. Also **field of view.**
3. (in television) either of two scanning lines which alternate to form one frame of a television transmission. In the United States, there are 60 fields and 30 frames per second.

field-activated promotion, a promotion initiated by a salesman and a retailer or store manager, rather than a marketer's drive period schedule or a chain's headquarters. Abbreviated *F.A.P.*

field-intensity map, a map showing the areas of relative signal strength of a television or radio station. Also *contour map.*

field-intensity measurement, measurement of the strength of a radio signal at a certain point of reception, usually in terms of microvolts or millivolts per meter of effective antenna height.

field man, a manufacturer's or wholesaler's sales representative who visits retailers to give service. Cf. *detail man, retail man.*

field strength, the strength of a television or radio signal within its coverage area.

F.I.F.O., *first-in-first-out.*

fifo, *adjective* see *first-in-first-out.*

fifteen and two, a 15% commission on the card rate and a 2% discount for prompt payment; used to describe the typical discounts offered by print communications media to advertising agencies.

fifty-fifty plan, a plan by which the cost of cooperative advertising is shared equally by a manufacturer and a wholesaler or retailer.

filler, *noun* a short item placed at the bottom of a newspaper column to fill empty space; can be used for public relations releases.

fill-in, *noun* 1. a special order from a retailer, made to maintain stock, to correct an error in ordering, or to obtain items whose delivery could not be made at the time of the original order.

2. the name and address of an addressee, added with an appropriate salutation to a form letter.

fill light, see *balancing light.*

film chain, a complete array of equipment for presenting motion picture films, especially on television: a projector, television camera, and various equipment for control, power, etc.; a camera chain adapted to the showing of films. Also *telecine.*

film clip, filmed footage, usually short, for insertion into a live television performance or into a longer film. Also *film sequence.*

film commercial, a commercial recorded on film.

film cue, see *cue.*

film element, see *element.*

film I.D., notification that a television program is filmed rather than live (obsolescent).

film library, a place for the storage of film, especially stock footage.

film loop, a piece of motion picture film spliced into a continuous, unending sequence.

film pickup, a televised transmission of a film.

film print, a motion picture film reproduction, complete with all visual and audio components, for projection or transmission.

film sequence, 1. a filmed portion of a live telecast.
2. see *film clip.*

film speed, the rate at which a type of photographic film reacts to light; usually expressed in an ASA number.

film strip, *noun* a motion picture film composed of a number of still photographs, shown sequentially.

film studio, 1. a studio in which motion picture films are recorded.
2. a firm which specializes in arranging the production of movies or commercials.

film transfer, a television film made from videotape; used in stations without videotape equipment. Cf. *kinescope.*

filter, *noun* 1. a transparent or semi-transparent camera lens fitting used for special effect; e.g., to reduce glare, diffuse light, add hue, simulate night, etc.
2. see *color filter.*
3. an electronic device used to diminish specific audio frequencies.
4. a device for distorting sound for special effect; e.g., to simulate telephone conversations, or other peculiar acoustic conditions. Also **filter microphone.**

find-time test, a test of the time required for a customer to locate a specific package on a section of shelves bearing similar packages of a number of other brands.

fine cut, (in motion pictures or television) a finished work print, fully edited and ready, barring final approval, for reproduction and distribution. Cf. *rough cut, answer print.*

fine-grain, *adjective* 1. noting or pertaining to photographic positives that are free of any textural effects except for those provided by the subjects. Also **fine-grain printing, fine-grain printing paper.**
noun 2. a fine-grain print.

finish, *noun* the textural quality of a sheet of paper.

firm order, an advertiser's positive order for media space or time.

firm order date, a date after which an order for advertising space or time cannot be cancelled.

65

first cover, the front outside cover of a magazine; in trade magazines often available for advertising.

first-in-first-out, *adjective* 1. noting or pertaining to a system of inventory management which calls for oldest stock to be disposed of first.
2. noting or pertaining to an accounting system in which the inventory at the close of an accounting period is valued at the price prevailing at the beginning of the period. Also *fifo*. Abbreviated *F.I.F.O.* Cf. *last-in-first-out.*

first refusal, an offer of a prior claim to sponsorship made by a medium to an advertiser. Also *right of first refusal.*

first telecast, the first date on which a program, commercial, or series of commercials is to be telecast. Abbreviated *F.T.*

fiscal year, a period of roughly twelve months in length designated by an organization as its basic annual financial planning unit. Abbreviated *FY.*

fishbowl, *noun* an observation booth in a television or radio studio available for use by advertisers and advertising agency personnel.

fit, *verb* see *cast.*

fix, *verb* to arrest and complete the development of a photographic image by use of a suitable chemical solution. Cf. *develop, fixative.*

fixative, *noun* a liquid or spray applied to a painting or drawing to set the pigments in place and protect the surface. Also **fixatif.**

fixed location, 1. a space in a periodical occupied by one advertiser for two or more consecutive issues.
2. a space in a periodical specified by an advertiser.

fixed position, a specific period of station broadcasting time reserved for an advertiser and sold at a premium rate.

fixer, *noun* a chemical solution used to complete and arrest the development of photographic images on film or paper.

flag, *noun* 1. the logotype or title of a publication, printed on its front cover or front page.
2. a package design element intended to dramatize and convey special information.

flagging, *noun* the peeling of outdoor posters at corners and edges.

flagship, *noun* 1. the principal station of a television or radio network.
2. the best selling brand or item in a manufacturer's line.

flanker, *noun* a new product marketed under an existing brand name, intended for use in a different (but usually related) product category than the "parent" brand's original product or product line. Also **flanker item.**

flap, *noun* a sheet of paper attached to the back top of a piece of artwork and folded over the front for protection.

flash, *noun* (in television and radio) a very short scene, sequence, or announcement.

flashback, *noun* (in motion pictures or television) an interruption of development of the main action of a drama in the form of an episode from a previous time. Also *cutback, extract.*

flat, *adjective* 1. (of a photographic, motion picture, or television image) without contrast and a consequent feeling of depth.
noun 2. a flat piece of painted scenery, as for a theater set. Also *stage flat, set flat.*
3. (in printing) the assembled film with all elements in position for development on a printing plate.
4. a collapsed carton designed to hold one product unit when erected. Also *package flat.*

flat-bed press, a printing press (used in letterpress printing) having type locked into a flat bed that moves back and forth under a rotating cylinder which applies pressure. Paper is printed as it passes between the form and the cylinder.

flat light, see *balancing light.*

flat proof, 1. a printed proof pulled directly from type on a compositor's table rather than by means of a printing press. Also *stone proof.*
2. a printed proof pulled before make-ready and thus unlikely to be evenly inked. Used for proofreading for copy accuracy and positioning of elements in an advertisement.

flat rate, a stated price, as for advertising space or time, that is not subject to discounting of any kind.

Flesch formula, a technique for assessing the ease and interest with which a text may be read, devised by Rudolf Flesch; method calls for measuring average sentence length and average syllables per word (*Reading Ease Score*), and the percentage of personal words and sentences (*Human Interest Score*). Cf. *Dale-Chall formula, Gunning Formula, Cloze procedure.*

flex-form advertisement, a periodical advertisement with an irregular outline rather than a rectangular or regularly shaped outline.

flexichrome, *noun* a black and white photograph that has been hand colored to approximate natural colors when reproduced.

flier, a printed piece, usually consisting of a single sheet, used as an advertising handbill or mailing piece.

flight, *verb* 1. to alternate active and inactive or hiatus periods of advertising schedules.
noun 2. a period of advertising activity scheduled between periods of inactivity. Also *burst.* Cf. *hiatus.*

flight saturation, maximum concentration of spot television or radio advertising within a short period, to a point at which any further advertising would presumably have diminishing or negative effects.

flip card, a card bearing one of a sequence of messages or legends for display in a television commercial.

flip chart, a tablet sheet bearing one of a sequence of messages for use in a presentation.

float, *noun* 1. (in advertising agency finance) money received from client billings but not yet paid to the supplier of the merchandise or services billed.
verb 2. (in periodical advertising) to run an advertisement within a space which is larger than that for which its printing plate was intended.

floating time, see *run-of-schedule.*

floodlamp, *noun* a photographer or cameraman's light, which illuminates a wide area. Also **flood,** *scoop.*

floor, *noun* 1. the performance area of a stage, television or radio studio.
2. the sales display area of a store.

floor manager, *noun* (in television or radio) a director's assistant who supervises activities on a studio floor during a program; his responsibilities parallel those of a stage manager in the theater.

floor plan, a selected plan of a stage or studio, used by directors in theater, motion pictures, and television to lay out sets and plan all activities connected with a performance.

floor pyramid, a merchandise display of several levels, approximately to eye height.

floor stand, a standing mount for the display of retail merchandise.

floor stock protection, a manufacturer's agreement to protect a distributor's inventory of the manufacturer's goods against a price decline for a specified time. In the event of such declines, the manufacturer is to issue a rebate to the distributor.

flop, *verb* to reverse artwork, etc. from right to left or vice-versa on film so that a mirror image of the original form results.

fluff, *verb* (in motion pictures and television) to err in the delivery of spoken lines of a script, especially in a manner apparent to a potential audience.

flush, *adjective, adverb* (in typesetting) not indented from a specified point; type may be specified "flush left" and/or "flush right." Cf. *justify, ragged.*

flush blocking, mounting of a printing plate so that its edges are flush with those of its block.

flush cover, a cover of a booklet or the like trimmed even with its pages.

flute, *noun* 1. a corrugation in the paper core of a piece of corrugated board.
2. the entire paper core of such a board. Corrugated board is described by the number of flutes per foot it contains, standard types being the A flute (36 flutes per foot), the B (51 per foot), and the C (42 per foot), the numbers being approximate.

fly, *verb* (in theater, motion pictures, or television) to suspend scenery, lights, etc. above the visible performance area.

flyleaf, *noun* an unprinted page at the beginning or end of a book or the like, usually a portion of an endpaper not glued to an inside cover.

fly sheet, *noun* a form used by a salesman to record the authorization of a display order. Also *survey sheet.*

FM, 1. radio stations from 88 to 108 megahertz licensed to employ frequency modulation as a means of signal delivery.
2. see *frequency modulation.*

F.O.B., *free on board.*

focus, *noun* 1. the point where rays of light that have passed through a lens meet to form an image.
2. the state of definition of an image recorded by a camera.
3. the sharpest form of such a state: *in focus.*
verb 4. to bring into focus, as a lens.

focus group interview, a research technique that employs small consumer group discussions led by trained moderators to obtain insight into consumer behavior and perceptions. Also **focus group, focused group interview.**

focus in, (in motion pictures or television) to begin a scene by bringing the camera image into focus from a blur. Cf. *iris in.*

focus of sale, the basic claim or claims employed by a brand in its advertising creative strategy, together with supportive material designed to insure the believability of such claims.

focus out, (in motion pictures or television) to end a scene by deliberately putting the camera image out of focus, to a blur. Cf. *iris out.*

folio, *noun* 1. a size of paper measuring 17 by 22 inches.
2. a book with signatures formed of a single sheet of paper folded once, and thus of four pages each.
3. loosely, any book with very large pages.
4. any of the numbers that identify the successive pages of a book.

following and next to reading matter, immediately after and alongside part of the main editorial section of a periodical; used in ordering advertising. Also *Campbell Soup position.*

following shot, (in motion pictures or television) a shot of an actor who is moving away from a camera that is moving after him. Also *follow shot*.

follow style, (in typesetting) an instruction to a typesetter to set in accordance with previously established style.

follow-up, *noun* 1. a mailing to a potential customer who has expressed interest in a product or service.
2. a sales visit to such a potential customer. Also **follow-up call.**
3. actions subsequent to introduction of a new product or advertising campaign.

font, *noun* a complete alphabet of type in a specific face and size. Cf. *face*.

Food and Drug Administration, a U.S. government regulatory agency created in 1938 to regulate the content, labeling, recommended use, and advertising claims for a variety of food and drug products, as specified in the Food, Drug, and Cosmetic Act.

Food and Drug Index, see *A.C. Nielsen Co.*

food day, see *best food day*.

Food, Drug, and Cosmetic Act, a federal act of 1938 prohibiting the misbranding, falsification, or adulteration of any of certain articles of interstate commerce; enforced by the Food and Drug Administration.

Food Index, see *A.C. Nielsen Co.*

food service, sales of food purchased and used by institutions on a continuing basis.

food store, see *grocery*.

footage, *noun* photographic film in bulk, especially exposed, unedited motion picture film.

forced combination, a combination of media, particularly newspapers, whose advertising space or time must be purchased in equal quantities by an advertiser in any one of them.

forced distribution, 1. distribution of a product by retailers as a consequence of anticipated or actual customer demand created by advertising or consumer promotion.
2. in test markets, automatic placement of products in panels of cooperating stores.

foreign advertising, 1. newspaper advertising purchased by an advertiser whose business is principally outside the locality.
2. advertising by a national placed outside his own country.

form, *noun* 1. an assemblage of type, cuts, etc. for printing half a book signature or the like, locked up in a chase for printing or plate making.
2. see *format*.
3. the physical properties of a product, e.g. powder, liquid, cream, aerosol, etc.

format, *noun* 1. the size of a book or periodical page; described as folio, quarto, octavo, etc., according to the number of pages in a signature.
2. the general design of a book or periodical page, or piece of graphic art. Cf. *layout*.
3. the general organization scheme of a book, periodical, or program. Also **form.**
4. the general character of the programs aired by a radio station. Currently successful formats include popular youth music (*top 40, rock*, or *R and R format*), country and western music (*country* or *C and W format*), serious music (*classical format*), light music (*easy listening* or *background format*), discussions or audience participation (*talk format*), news reports (*all-news format*), or mixtures designed for general appeal (*middle-of-the-road format*) or special appeal (*Black, Spanish, or Bible format*).

forms-close date, the final date for getting advertising copy, cuts, etc. to a printer.

fortify, *verb* to restore nutrients to processed food which were lost or destroyed in processing. Cf. *enrich*.

69

Fototype, *noun, trademark* a brand of printed characters, available in various fonts, for assembly into camera ready display copy.

foundry, *noun* (obsolescent, in printing) a commercial firm which produces duplicate letterpress printing plates, i.e. electrotypes, plastic plates, stereotypes made from engravings or metal type.

foundry proof, a printing proof pulled from type and/or cuts assembled in a metal frame in preparation for plate making.

foundry rule, a heavy bordering piece of metal enclosing set foundry type that is to be used for plate making; on a foundry proof it prints as a heavy border.

foundry type, letterpress type of individually cast metal characters set by hand. Also *hand type.*

Four A's, see *American Association of Advertising Agencies.*

four color, *adjective* noting or pertaining to halftone printing in yellow, red, blue, and black, in combination, to give a complete range of hues and tonal values to match the artwork. Abbreviated *4/C.*

fourth cover, the outside back cover of a magazine. Also *back cover* (see *cover*). Abbreviated *BC.*

fractional page space, periodical advertising space occupying less than the whole area of a page.

fractional showing, a showing of outdoor advertising panels in a quantity of less than one-fourth that deemed adequate for full coverage.

fragmentation, *noun* use of a great variety of types of media (e.g., television, radio, magazines, newspaper, outdoor, etc.) for a single advertising campaign, with no single medium used predominantly, or heavily.
fragment, *v.*

frame, *noun* 1. any of the single images of a motion picture or television film. Cf. *field.*
2. a single audio/video unit of a television storyboard. Also *cell.*
3. (in research) a basic reference source for finding names for a population sample as a directory, set of tax records, etc.
verb 4. to adjust a projected image so a full frame appears.

franchise, *noun* 1. a contract between a supplier of products or services and an individual or organization granting the right to market the supplier's goods, usually in a prescribed territory or location; may pertain to a distributor or retailer carrying the supplier's line among other lines, or to operators of retail outlets who pay the supplier for use of his brand name, products, services, methods, or other support.
2. an agreement granting an advertiser the right to retain the sponsorship of a television or radio program with no obligation to do so.
verb 3. to grant such rights.

franchised label, a label or brand (i.e., a logotype and trademark) granted to a local distributor through a franchise for exclusive use in his territory.

franchise position, a position in a periodical reserved to an advertiser through a franchise.

fraternal magazine, a magazine for members of a fraternal order or society.

fraud order, an order from the Postmaster General to halt mail used for fraudulent or other unlawful purposes.

free association, 1. see *association.*
2. an interview technique in which respondents are encouraged to state the first word or phrase that comes to mind in an uninhibited response to a word or phrase stated by the interviewer.

free-association interview, a nondirective interview in which free association is encouraged.

free goods, 1. merchandise conferred without charge or obligation.
2. a former synonym for bonus goods; use discouraged as misleading by the Federal Trade Commission.

free hand, noting or pertaining to visual images, designs, or symbols composed by hand, without mechanical guides.

freelance, *verb* 1. (of a writer, artist, etc.) to work independently, being paid by the job.
2. to do a job while freelancing.
freelancer, *n.* a person who freelances.

free on board, with no charge for loading and delivering goods on the truck or carrier that delivers the job to a customer. Abbreviated *F.O.B.*

free publication, 1. a publication distributed without cost, especially to a selected list of readers. Also *controlled circulation publication.*
2. a periodical which does not meet the ABC requirement of 70% paid circulation during a six-month period.

free standing insert, a preprinted advertisement in single or multiple page form that is inserted loose into newspapers, particularly Sunday editions. Also **free standing stuffer.**

freeze frame, (in television or motion pictures) an effect of suspended time and action produced by repetition of a single still frame. Also *stop action.*

freezer case, a case for the retail display of frozen food.

French fold, a fold used for four-page leaflets made from sheets, printed on one side only, in which pages one and four are printed on one half of the leaflet upside-down, and pages two and three on the other half upside-up; a transverse fold is followed by a vertical one.

frequency, noun 1. the number of television or radio broadcasts or commercials aired in a given period of time.
2. the number of exposures to an advertiser's advertisements on the part of an average household or person over a given period of time.
3. the number of cyclical repetitions of a radio or sound wave in a second. Also *cycles per second.*

frequency discount, a discount to an advertiser for running a certain number of advertisements within a specified period. Also *quantity discount, time discount.*

frequency distribution, (in statistics) a graph curve joining all points to indicate the distribution of frequencies of observations over the total range of a sample. Also *curve of distribution.* Cf. *graph, normal distribution curve.*

frequency modulation, a high fidelity, line-of-sight method of radio broadcasting that employs alterations in the frequency of a carrier wave to transmit source (e.g., microphones, records, etc.) signals to receivers. U.S. television and radio stations employ this broadcasting method. Abbreviated *FM.*

frequency response, the output of an audio system or the like to source signals, as expressed in terms of either the extreme frequencies reproduced or the degree of fidelity to the source.

fringe area, the outermost perimeter capable of receiving a television or radio signal. Cf. *coverage.*

fringe time, see *daypart.* Also *transition time.*

frisket, *noun* 1. a paper for masking those areas of a photograph or piece of art work that are not to be retouched.
2. a cut-out paper mask that covers dead metal areas in engraved plates and prevents those areas from printing on an engraver's proofing press.

front end, 1. the checkout area of a supermarket.
2. the advertising area under the front windows of a bus or the like.

frontload, *verb* to schedule the use of the bulk of a budget for the first part of a planning period; serves to assure that all of a budget is used for its originally designated ends. Cf. *backload.*
front load, *n.* Also **front-end load.**

frontispiece, *noun* (in magazine publishing) the first page containing editorial material, often the table of contents and masthead.

front lighting, lighting of a photographic subject or cinematic scene from the general direction of the camera or spectator.

front of book, the section of a magazine preceding the main editorial section.

frozen food locker, a freezer with spaces rented to private persons for the storage of meat, etc.

F.S., *full shot.*

f stop, a standardized measure of the aperture of a camera's diaphragm; along with film speed and shutter speed, one of the three key variables in calculating the proper exposure of photographic film. Also *f.*

F.T., *first telecast.*

F.T.C., *Federal Trade Commission.*

full-line wholesaler, a wholesaler who professes to supply retailers with most, if not all, of their needs.

full measure, (in printing) to the standard column width, without indentation: *to set a line full measure.*

full-net program, a television or radio program carried on all the stations of a network.

full-network station, a network television or radio station carrying at least 85 percent of network prime-time programs.

full-program sponsorship, sponsorship of a television or radio program by one advertiser only.

full run, 1. insertion of an advertisement in every edition of a daily newspaper during one day.
2. see *full showing.*

full service agency, an advertising agency offering its clients a full range of staff service capabilities, including marketing planning and management, creative, media, research, accounting and often such services as merchandising and advertising-related legal counsel.

full shot, 1. (in motion pictures or television) a shot showing a person completely, from head to foot.
2. (in television) a shot of an entire scene.

full showing, 1. (in outdoor advertising) posting of the number of boards conventionally regarded as adequate in a given geographical area; Cf. *intensity, showing.*
2. (in transit advertising) a showing with a car card in every vehicle. Also *full run.*

full-time station, a television or radio station licensed to broadcast 24 hours a day.

functional discount, see *trade discount.*

furniture, *noun* (in typesetting) wooden or metal blocks and spacing material less than type-high for holding set type firmly in position in a chase.

FY, *fiscal year.*

G

gaffer, (in motion pictures and television) a person employed as an electrician on a production.

gaffoon, *noun, informal* a radio or television sound-effects man.

gag, *noun* 1. a joke.
2. (in television or radio) a comical situation.

gain, *noun* (in audio) 1. an increase of sound volume.
2. a control which varies sound level. Cf. *potentiometer.*

gallery, *noun* the camera site and film developing area of a photoengraving or printing plant.

galley, *noun* 1. a tray for holding metal type.
2. a proof or print made from type set in metal or film before makeup into pages or final positioning. Also **galley proof.**

Gallup and Robinson, a communications research service best known for syndicated general survey sweeps of television advertising recall, as well as other measures of advertising effectiveness.

galvanic skin response, a physiological reaction to psychological stimuli (e.g., fear or arousal), whose intensity is measurable by the degree of skin conductivity created by varying perspiration rates; used to determine respondent's reactions to advertising. Also *psychogalvanic skin response.* Abbreviated *G.S.R.* Cf. *arousal method.*

galvanometer, *noun* see *psychogalvanometer.*

gang, *noun* 1. an assemblage of type matter, cuts, etc. for printing together as a form.
2. a sheet printed from such an assemblage.
3. a set of multiply reproduced legends, cuts, etc., as for the printing of a number of labels at one time.

gatefold, *noun* a special two-part page in a magazine, with an outer part that folds over an inner part that is slightly narrower than the trim size of the magazine.

gathering, *noun* 1. the process of assembling book signatures for binding.
verb 2. the assembling of individual printed pieces of a collateral print job prior to inserting in envelopes.

gauge, *noun* a measure of thickness in various industries, especially for thin or narrow objects; stated as a specific measure, it generally follows a gauge number: *a 16-gauge electrotype is as thick as an original engraved plate.*

Gaussian curve, see *normal distribution curve.*

gaze motion, the movement of a viewer's or reader's eyes. Cf. *eye camera.*

gel, *noun* a translucent color filter for a spotlight. Also **gelatin.**

general editorial magazine, a consumer magazine edited for a broad, general readership.

general rate, see *national rate.*

generation, *noun* a stage in the duplication of a film or recording, the first generation being that of the original that succeeding generations reproduce.

generic, *adjective* noting or pertaining to a product or service category as a whole.

generic product, see *product.*

geographic split run, (in periodical advertising) a split run determined by geographical area of distribution.

gestalt theory, (in psychology) a theory that asserts that each thing in a group of associated things must be considered in its relation to the whole group rather than merely as an independent object, since a subject will respond to the group as a whole as well as to its components. Cf. *principle of closure.*

ghost, *noun* a secondary, weaker image on a television screen imitating the principal image and usually caused by a reflected as well as a direct transmission of the signal. Also *double image.*

ghosted view, see *phantom section.*

gimmick, *noun* any expedient for giving an air of distinction or novelty to a product, promotion, etc.

giveaway, *noun* 1. something given away for promotional purposes.
2. a television or radio show where merchandise is given away to contestants or to members of the audience.

glassine, *noun* a semi-transparent paper used for various wrapping and packaging purposes, for artwork, and in printer's proofs to check the fit of set type to space designed for it.

glossy, *adjective* 1. (of a photographic or photostatic print) bearing a smooth, reflective finish on the side on which the image appears. Cf. *dead matte.*
noun 2. a glossy photographic or photostatic print.
3. see *repro proof.*

G.N.H., see *gross night hour.*

gobbo, *noun* 1. a sound-absorbent screen used to deaden echoes while a motion picture or television program is being made.
2. a screen for cutting out unwanted light under the same conditions. Also **gobo.**

going year, a period of twelve consecutive months of advertising budgeting for a product or service. Cf. *sustaining advertising.*

golden time, (in theater, motion pictures, or television) time for which workers are compensated at special overtime rates, e.g., Sundays and holidays, generally as indicated by union contracts.

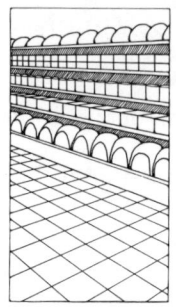

gondola, *noun* a bank of shelving, open on both sides, in a retail store.

GONDOLA

Gothic, *noun* 1. see *sans serif.*
2. see *black letter.*

go to black, let the image fade out entirely: a direction to a motion picture or television cameraman.

gouache, *noun* 1. an opaque watercolor paint.
2. a painting executed with such opaque watercolor paint.

grain, *noun* 1. the direction in which the fibers of certain materials, as wood or paper, run.
2. a spotty effect on a photographic print, caused by excessive enlargement.
3. a rough, gritty sound produced by an audio system, or poor recording or copy.
grainy, *adj.*

graph, *noun* a two or three-dimensional grid used in statistics to plot the relation of one quantifiable variable to another by ranging the incidence of one along the abscissa, the other along the ordinate according to some regular system of division. A *line graph* shows the relationship of the variables by a curve of distribution; a *bar graph* or *histogram* shows it by solid columns rising or descending from the x-axis.

graphic, noun a visual device of an informative, symbolic, or decorative nature used to embellish material and structures.

graphic designer, a person who designs graphics.

graphic structure, a three dimensional object intended primarily to serve graphic purposes.

gravity feed, any device or system that employs gravity as the force to move objects or materials to a desired place.

gravure, noun a printing process used where fine detail and subtle shading are required. The printing is done with semitransparent ink deposited in minutely varied depressions etched in the printing surface of the plate or cylinder, whose depth controls the relative density of the tone.

gray scale, 1. a scale of standard values of shading, from white to black, used in judging the appearance of colors on black-and-white television.
2. (in printing) a scale used to judge tonal values in color separation negatives for balance and uniformity of tone.

Greek, noun (in advertising artwork), a legend of meaningless shapes or garbled letters, intended to show the location and size of type to be added later or to test public response to the design alone of a package, advertisement, etc.

Green Book, the title of the New York chapter of the American Marketing Association's annual international directory of marketing research firms.

grid card, a tabulated rate card issued by a television or radio station, showing the different rates for various commerical positions.

grip, noun (in motion pictures and television) a person employed to provide manual assistance on a production; a general handyman.

gripper edge, the leading edge of a sheet of paper that passes through the press so as to receive the first charge of ink; used as a reference location in discussing print on the sheet.

grocery, noun 1. a retail store primarily designed to provide household food, beverages, and basic laundry and cleaning consumable products. Also *food store*, **grocery store.**
2. a food product sold by a grocery.

gross audience, the total audience reached by communications media as counted in surveys of several media at one time and surveys of one such medium at several times, without regard to repeated counting of individual members. Cf. *net unduplicated audience.*

gross billing, 1. an advertising cost billed to an advertiser, which includes charges for agency commission.
2. the total amount of advertisers' funds handled annually by an advertising agency.
3. (in media) a charge for one-time advertising at card rate.

gross circulation, (in outdoor advertising), the total number of persons passing an advertisement during a given period, without regard to the direction these persons may be facing. Cf. *net circulation.*

gross cost, 1. the cost for services by an agency, including the agency commission.
2. see *gross rate.*

gross impression, the sum of all exposures to an advertiser's advertising in a given media schedule.

gross less, *informal* an expression for the actual cost of an advertisement after a discount from the gross rate.

gross margin, see *margin.*

75

gross message weight, the total gross weighting points received by an advertisement or advertising effort over a stated period of time.

gross night hour, the card rate for sponsorship of one hour of television or radio station prime time; used as a basis for determining other commerical rates. Abbreviated *G.N.H.*

gross rate, the published rate for advertising space or time charged by a communications medium without regard to agency or seller's commissions. Also *card rate, gross cost.*

gross rating point, a unit of measurement of television, radio, or outdoor advertising audience size, equal to 1% of the total potential audience universe; used to measure the exposure of one or more programs or commericals, without regard to multiple exposure of the same advertising to individuals. Also, the product of media reach times exposure frequency. Abbreviated *G.R.P.*

grotesque, *noun* see *sans serif.*

ground row, (in theater, motion pictures, or television) a low scenic element placed in the foreground or middle ground of a stage or studio floor to give a naturalistic effect or to conceal lighting.

ground wave, an AM radio wave running parallel to the ground. Cf. *sky wave.*

group advertising, advertising by a group of independent retailers, often members of a voluntary chain.

group discount, a discount for advertising simultaneously in a group of television or radio stations.

growth, *noun* see *product life cycle.*

G.R.P., *gross rating point.*

G.S.R., *galvanic skin response.*

guarantee, *noun* 1. a commitment from a medium assuring an advertiser of an agreed upon rate or audience level.
2. a manufacturer's commitment to retail purchasers that a product or service will perform as specified, or be replaced, repaired at no cost, or purchase price refunded.

guaranteed sale, a sale of goods to a retailer with the proviso that the retailer may receive full credit on any of the goods not sold within a certain period if returned in their original cases.

Gunning formula, a technique for assessing the ease with which a text may be read; calls for measuring average sentence length, verb force, proportion of familiar and abstract words, and percentage of personal references and long words. Cf. *Flesch formula, Dale-Chall formula, Cloze procedure.*

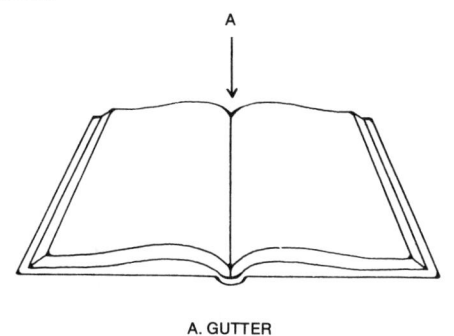

A. GUTTER

gutter, *noun* (in a book or other publication) the margins at the crease formed by a pair of facing pages at their bound or folded juncture.

gutter bleed, to run an illustration in a book, or a magazine advertisement, etc., so that it passes uninterrupted through the gutter into the binding edge of the sheet.

gutter position, an advertising position beside the gutter on a page of a periodical.

H

H.A.B.A., *health and beauty aids.* Also H & BA.

hairline, *noun* (in printing) a fine rule.

halation, *noun* a blurred glowing effect caused by diffused light.

half apple, (in television) a stand for performers or props lower than an apple box.

half binding, a book binding in which the spine and a portion of the boards are covered in one material, the remainder of the boards being covered in another.

half-lap, *noun* (in motion pictures or television) a shot in which two images appear simultaneously on the screen, one on each half. Also *side-by-side shot.* Cf. *composite shot.*

half-page spread, (in periodical publishing), an arrangement for editorial matter or an advertisement consisting of the upper or lower half of each of two facing pages.

half run, (in car-card advertising) a placement of cards in every other vehicle. Also **half service**, *half showing.*

half showing, (in outdoor and car-card advertising) half of a full showing; a 50-intensity showing. Also **half service**, *half run.*

half title, a page of a book containing only the book's basic title; ordinarily such a page is the first printed page in the book, but sometimes such a page is repeated before the main text.

halftone, *noun* 1. a process for the printing of photographs or other work requiring shading; the printing is done from minute circular surfaces, or dots, which determine the density of tone in their area, according to their diameters.
2. a picture or the like printed by this process. Cf. *halftone screen.*

halftone blowup, an enlargement from a halftone negative; since the halftone dots are also enlarged, the effect is a rather coarse one.

halftone negative, a photographic negative exposed through a halftone screen, used in preparing a halftone print or printing plate.

halftone screen, a screen through which a photograph is taken to make a halftone negative. The screen, made of two pieces of glass with finely ruled parallel lines — those of one screen horizontal, those of the other vertical — breaks up the continuous tones of the image into dots of varying sizes, the larger ones representing the denser values. Screens run from coarse (50 lines to the inch) up to very fine (300 lines to the inch), use of which is determined by the hardness and/or smoothness of the paper stock to be used in printing. Also *screen.*

halo effect, (in research) a subjective reaction to an individual feature of an advertisement or product, conditioned by attitudes regarding the whole.

handbill, *noun* a circular intended for distribution by hand, either to persons encountered on the street or to homes, offices, etc. Also *throwaway, flier.*

hand composition, (in printing) setting of type by hand rather than by machine. Also *hand setting.*

handling allowance, an allowance from a manufacturer to a distributor or retailer for handling merchandise requiring special attention, e.g., coupon redemption.

handling charge, a charge made to a manufacturer by a distributor in lieu of a handling allowance.

hand prop, (in theater, motion pictures and television) a small prop either actually handled by an actor or used to dress a stage or studio set.

hand setting, see *hand composition.*

hand tooling, hand finishing of a printing plate to bring out highlights or otherwise improve reproduction quality.

hand type, see *foundry type.*

hanging indentation, (in printing) an indentation of all lines of a paragraph except the first, which is set full measure.

hard edge, 1. (in printing) an unwanted visible edge around a vignetted illustration that is supposed to tone in gradually with the surrounding page; a technical flaw.
2. (in art) a graphic style characterized by large sections of sharply defined colors with clearly marked boundaries.

hard goods, manufactured durable goods of metal or plastic, such as hardware or household appliances.

hardware, *noun* 1. computers and other electronic or mechanical equipment used in data processing. Cf. *software.*
2. merchandise sold in a hardware store, especially domestic tools and building supplies.

hardware store, a retail store providing tools and equipment used in the repair and maintainance of the general facilities of a residence.

harlequin, *noun* any of various simple typographic ornaments.

hatch, *verb* to mark an area of a drawing with closely-spaced lines, in order to indicate modeling or shading, to indicate a material seen in cross-section, etc.

head, *noun* 1. (in publishing) a title or other display material at the top of a page, chapter, article, etc.
2. the upper end of a book.

head end, the antenna end of a cable television service at which programs are received for distribution.

headhunter, *noun, informal* an independent personnel agent used to scout, locate, recruit, and occasionally, to select management employment prospects.

heading, *noun* the largest display matter of an advertisement, setting the theme of the copy. Also *headline.*

headline, *noun* 1. the head of a newspaper article, giving its major subject. Also *hed.*
2. the head of a newspaper front page, giving the most important story.
3. see *heading.*

head of household, a person responsible for the management of a household or family; includes single (unmarried), females (usually a housewife), or males (usually the primary source of household income).

head-on location, (in outdoor advertising) a location facing oncoming traffic.

headphones, *plural noun* a device worn over both ears, used to convert electrical signals into audible sound; usually audible only to wearers. Cf. *cans.*

headquarters call, a salesman's sales call on the central buying office of a chain of retail stores.

headroom, *noun* 1. the field of vision between the head of an actor and the top of a motion picture or television screen from which he is projected.
2. the unexploited potential for additional

consumption of a category or brand of product or service. Also *sales potential.* Cf. *brand potential index, market potential.*

heads up, (of a reel of film) with the first frame outermost, ready for projection. Also **heads out.** Cf. *tails up.*

health and beauty aids, the whole category of hair and body care items, non-prescription remedies, cosmetics, etc., especially when sold in a single section of a grocery. Abbreviated *H.A.B.A., H & BA.*

heartland, see *primary marketing area.*

heavy-half users, 1. the users of a product or service that account for half or more of its total consumption, but number less than half of the total user population.
2. that half of the user population which consumes more than half of the product or service. Cf. *heavy users.*

heavy-up, *noun* a brief or temporary increase in advertising activity. Cf. *flight.*

heavy users, those users of a brand or category of product or service whose rate of consumption is significantly above average; as a rule of thumb, that one third of users who consume two thirds of product's or service's volume. Cf. *heavy-half users.*

hed, see *headline.*

HH, *households.*

hiatus, *noun* 1. a temporary interruption of a sponsored program, typically during the 8 to 13 weeks of the summer season.
2. a temporary cessation of advertising schedules, as between flights. Also *out period.*

hickey, *noun* an unwanted area on a printing plate that has escaped etching and that must be removed.

hidden camera, a format for advertisements, especially television commercials, involving use of a camera concealed from subjects who either relate their experiences with the product being advertised to an interviewer, or who are shown using the product.

hidden offer, see *blind offer.*

hi-fi, *noun* see *preprint.*

hi-fi insert, a full-page, high-quality, four-color rotogravure advertisement that is preprinted on coated stock and furnished to a newspaper in roll form for insertion during regular run. As the roll is fed into the press, editorial copy or other advertising is printed on the reverse side, and, in some cases, a column of type is imprinted on the hi-fi insert itself. Since there is no accurate cut-off on hi-fi pages, the advertisement is designed with a repeating "wallpaper" format that allows complete exposure of all pertinent copy and illustrations for any random cut-off. Also *continuous roll insert, preprint.*

high-key lighting, lighting of a photographic subject, motion picture or television scene, etc. in which the key light is strongly emphasized so that a brilliant high-contrast effect results.

highlight, *noun* 1. an area in a painting, photograph, etc. of extremely light tonal value, representing a concentration of reflected light.
verb 2. to give emphasis to an object or an area in a picture with special lighting.

highlight halftone, a halftone in which the dots have been dropped out of the highlight areas of the photograph or illustration.

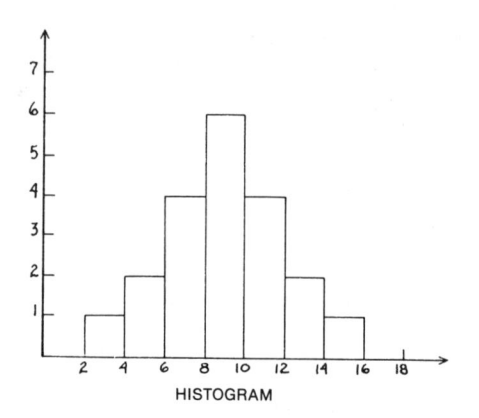

HISTOGRAM

histogram, *noun* a statistical graph in which a curve of distribution is approximated by a series of stepped bars representing the upper end of each segment of the curve.

hit, *noun* (in the entertainment business) 1. a production, program, record, etc., which succeeds in attracting large audiences.
adjective 2. noting or pertaining to such productions, etc.

hitchhike, *noun,* 1. a television or radio commercial following a show and advertising a second product by the sponsor of the show. Also **hitchhiker.**
2. a period for commericials following the end of a show.

hit it, play loudly and suddenly; an order to musicians. Also **hit.**

hold, *verb* 1. to refrain from action, as in expectation of instructions.
2. to preserve materials for possible subsequent use.
noun 3. a repeated printing of a single frame of motion picture film or animation cel, to give an effect of arrested motion. Also **hold frame.**
4. a recording tape set aside with others pending a final selection.

holding fee, a residual payment to commercial talent in a commercial not in use in a given cycle which maintains the advertiser's right to later reuse the same commercial without renegotiating terms.

holding power, the ability of a television or radio show to keep its audience; measured as a percentage of the total number of those hearing any part of the program, versus the average audience.

holdover audience, that portion of a television or radio audience for one program who were tuned to the previous program on the same station. Also *inherited audience.*

home, *noun* a household unit; used as a basic population unit in audience measurement surveys.

home center, a retail store providing a broader variety of hardware items and building supplies than traditional hardware stores and lumber yards.

home service book, a magazine whose editorial content centers on various aspects of domestic living; a shelter magazine.

home station, a radio or television station originating signals within a geographic survey area.

homes per rating point, see *gross rating point.* Abbreviated *H.P.R.P.*

homes using television, a term used by the A.C. Nielsen Co. which refers to the total percent of homes in a given area using television during a given time period. Abbreviated *H.U.T.*

home video recorder, a device for recording and replaying television programs in the home. Abbreviated *H.V.R.* Cf. *videodisc.*

hook, *noun* 1. any device in a printed advertisement intended to stimulate an immediate response or inquiry.
2. a premium for purchasers of a product.
3. an offer made on a television or radio program intended to stimulate audience response and thus measure audience size.

hooker, *noun* 1. a particularly attractive feature of a package deal.
2. see *dealer imprint.*

Hooven process, a process for the automatic typewriting of form letters, special matter such as addresses and salutations being typed in advance by hand.

horizontal arrangement, a shelf arrangement in a retail store in which a full line of a manufacturer's related products are placed in adjacent positions on the same shelf. Cf. *vertical arrangement.*

horizontal contiguity, see *contiguity.*

horizontal cume, a cumulative audience rating for television or radio programs in the same time period on successive days.

horizontal discount, a discount to an advertiser who buys television or radio time over an extended period, usually a year.

horizontal half-page, the upper or lower half of a periodical page, especially as purchased for an advertisement.

horizontal marketing system, a cooperative marketing venture between organizations involved in similar but usually noncompetitive businesses; e.g., Million Market Newspapers, Inc., a sales corporation sponsored by five independently owned newspapers. Also *symbiotic marketing.*

horizontal publication, a trade publication for persons holding similar positions in different types of business. Cf. *vertical publication.*

horizontal selling, selling to all legitimate buyers regardless of their area of industry. Cf. *vertical selling.*

hot, *adjective* (of stage or studio lighting, or of a televised image) excessively bright.

hot feed, a delay in the feeding of a television show from another station.

hot kine, kinescope film processed for immediate rebroadcast, a positive image being produced by electronic treatment of the negative.

house agency, an advertising agency owned or controlled by an advertiser.

house brand, brand owned and sold only by a single retailer, or retail chain.

household, *noun* a housing unit and its occupants who share a common access to the outside and cooking facilities, in Census terms. Also *home.* Abbreviated *HH.*

house organ, a periodical published by a company, with editorial content devoted to company activities; an *internal house organ* is edited primarily for company personnel, while an *external house organ* is intended for company customers or others outside the company.

house public relations, (in Canada) public relations activities both developed by, and for the benefit of, an advertising agency.

housewife, *noun* any female head of a household who is 16 years old or older.

housewife time, see *daypart.*

HPRP, *homes per rating point.*

H.T.N., *Hughes Television Network.*

hue, *noun* the specific color or blend of colors of the spectrum composing any actual color. Also *chroma.* Cf. *intensity, value.*

Hughes Television Network, an independent television network which provides many stations with programs, especially sporting events and specials. Abbreviated *H.T.N.*

Huston crane, a camera crane used for high-angle shots.

H.U.T., *homes using television.*

81

H.V.R., *home video recorder.*

hypermarché, *noun* a retail food outlet of much larger than supermarket size using cost cutting stock, display and inventory control methods to provide low retail prices and high turnover. Cf. *warehouse store.*

hyping, *noun* intense activity on the part of a broadcaster to increase ratings during a rating survey. Also **hypoing.**

I

I.A.E.A., *International Advertising Executives' Association.*

I.A.R.I. letter grade, a score in letter form, A being highest and E the lowest, assigned to periodical advertisements as a measure of their recollection among: all advertisements in the same issue; advertisements of comparable size; and advertisements for the same general class of products. Introduced by the Industrial Advertising Research Institute.

I.B.C., *inside back cover;* used in ordering periodical advertising space.

IBM size coupon, a coupon whose size is approximately that of one half of a dollar bill, or 2.458 by 3.250 inches.

iconoscope, *noun* an electronic tube used in television cameras for converting visual images into electronic signals. Also *ike.*

I.D., 1. see *station identification.*
2. see *identification commercial.*

identification, *noun* (in psychology) the tendency of an individual to identify himself with persons or things with whom he closely associates, or desires to emulate.

identification commercial, a radio or television commercial of ten seconds length. Also *:10, identification spot.* Abbreviated *I.D.*

identification spot, see *identification commercial.*

identity, *noun* 1. (in psychology) a person's awareness of his own personality as a single, consistent entity.
2. (in public relations) the manner in which owners or employees conceive of an organization, or the realities of such an organization. Also *corporate identity.* Cf. *image.*

idiot card, see *cue card.*

I.F.C., *inside front cover;* used in ordering periodical advertising space.

ike, *noun, informal* iconoscope.

illustration board, a heavy paperboard, finished on one side, used for wash and tempera drawings. Also *illustrator's board.*

illustrator, *noun* (in advertising) a person who uses nonphotographic means, such as paint, ink, or pencil, to create pictures for use in advertisements.

illustrator's board, see *illustration board.*

image, *noun* 1. the body of feelings, impressions, and opinions regarding a corporate entity, e.g., a business firm, held by its various publics. Also *corporate image.* Cf. *identity.*
2. (in photography, motion pictures, and television) a visual composition as rendered by a camera.

image orthicon, a highly sensitive television camera tube developed by RCA. Also *orthicon.*

imagery transfer, (in an audience survey) a television watcher's recollection of a television commercial as a whole on being re-exposed to either the audio or video component.

impact, *noun* 1. the effect of a communications medium on its audience.
2. the effect of advertising on such an audience, measured by either the extent and

degree of its awareness attainments, or the sales it produces. Also *effectiveness*.

impact scheduling, scheduling of two television or radio commercials for one brand within a short period so as to expose the same audience to the same message twice.

imported signal, see *distant signal*.

impression, *noun* a person's or household's exposure to an advertisement.

impression study, a study made by Daniel Starch and Associates to determine the kinds of impression made on the public by advertisements in periodicals.

imprint, *verb* 1. to reprint a piece of printed matter in order to add special copy.
noun 2. special copy thus added, e.g., the name and address of a local retailer.
3. a small sign on the base of an outdoor advertising structure, identifying the owner or servicing plant.

impulse buy, a consumer purchase motivated by chance rather than plan; e.g., the sight of a product on display in a retail outlet visited for other purposes can motivate such a purchase. Also **impulse purchase.**

in-ad coupon, a coupon placed in a store or chain's own retail advertisement, redeemable only at that particular store or chain. Also **in-ad.**

I.N.A.E., *International Newspaper Advertising Executives*.

in-and-out promotion, a very brief retail feature for an item, intended only to encourage the sale of other items.

incentive, see *sales incentive*.

inch, *noun* see *column inch*.

inches per second, the standard scale for measurement of the recording or playback speed of audio magnetic recording tape; 15 is standard for optimum audio quality, 7-1/2 is most often used for reel-to-reel recordings, while 3-3/4 and 1-7/8 are most commonly used for extended playback times where audio quality is a secondary concern (e.g., cassettes). Abbreviated *I.P.S.*

incremental analysis, a method for predicting the relation of varying advertising budgets to the resulting gains or losses of audience.

incremental spending, increased advertising or promotion expenditures for a product or service; motivated by investment plans, defensive needs, the desire to dispose of excess profits, etc. Cf. *investment spending*.

incumbent, *noun* one who enjoys a presumed prior claim to an exclusive privilege by virtue of current tenure; e.g., a program sponsor or an advertising agency for a specific client.

indent, *verb* (in typesetting) to set type so that a line begins inside an established margin, as at the beginning of paragraphs. **indentation,** *n*.

independent, *noun* 1. a business organization not affiliated with, or owned by, a larger organization.
2. a television or radio station carrying less than ten hours a week of network programs. Also *indie, indy*.

independent network, a program-originating U.S. commercial broadcast network not associated with "the big three" — NBC, CBS, or ABC.

independent store, 1. a retail store under individual management.
2. a single store or a branch store of a retail chain with no more than three outlets, as defined by A. C. Nielsen in its retail indices.

independent television market, 1. a market area whose local television stations have a larger combined share of viewing than that of stations from outside the area. 2. a home market for one or more independent television stations.

independent variable, (in research design and statistics) a variable subjected to controlled change in order to observe associated changes in dependent variables.

index, *noun* 1. (in statistics) any basis for calculating a set of quantities in terms of one quantity taken as a norm or as a basic figure, especially ratios where a 1:1 relationship is expressed as an index of 100. 2. (in publishing) a directory of contents in a publication. 3. hence, a subject reference publication, as *Nielsen Station Index.*

index Bristol, a hard-finished Bristol board used primarily for index cards.

index card, a ruled card used for making notes of data to be filed with other such cards of data in alphabetical or some other regular order.

index of social position, a system for assigning persons to social classes, developed by Professor A. B. Hollingshead of Yale; the basis is a combination of the occupation and educational background of the head of the household. Abbreviated *I.S.P.*

India ink, a deep black, indelible drawing ink.

India paper, see *Bible paper.*

INDICIA

indicia, *noun* an envelope marking accepted by a postal service in lieu of stamps on bulk mailings.

indie, *noun* see *independent.*

indirect questionnaire, a questionnaire in which the true questions are disguised, their answers being inferred from the responses given to other questions.

individual location, a location for a single outdoor advertisement.

industrial advertising, advertising of industrial goods and services.

industrial goods, machinery, materials, and other commodities used for production and for the supplying of services within industry rather than for direct use by the public. Also *producer goods.* Cf. *consumer goods.*

industrial product, any manufactured industrial item or commodity.

industrial store, a retail store for use by employees of a company, usually owned and operated by the firm. Also *company store, commissary store.*

indy, *noun* see *independent.*

inferior character, (in typography) a small character set below the base line for normally set type; e.g., H_2O.

in-focus, *noun* (in photography, motion pictures, or television) the condition of a subject in a camera's image when the lens has been properly adjusted to include the subject within its focused depth of field.

inherited audience, see *holdover audience.* Also *inheritance.*

in-home, *adjective* noting or pertaining to exposure to media advertising in the home.

initial, *noun* the first letter in a block of copy; sometimes enlarged beyond normal font size or otherwise distinctively treated.

initial sale, a purchase of a product or service by a buyer who has not previously purchased the product or service, but who is a prospect for future purchases.

85

inky, *noun,* see *baby spotlight.* Also *dinkie inkie, inky dink.*

Ainline, *noun,* a category of display type having an unprinted inner part, showing white against black. Cf. *outline.*

inlooker, *noun* a person who has seen at least one major portion of the editorial section of a periodical. Cf. *reader.*

in-pack coupon, a store redeemable coupon enclosed in a product's package, for potential later use by the product's buyer; may be redeemed on a subsequent purchase of the same product, or on a different product (**cross-coupon**). Cf. *on-pack coupon.*

in-pack event, a sale promotion featuring use of an in-pack premium or coupon. Also **in-pack.**

IN-PACK PREMIUM

in-pack premium, a premium item enclosed in a product's package; usually offered with the product at no extra charge.

input, *noun* coded data fed into a computer. Cf. *output.*

inquiry, *noun* a request from a potential customer made in response to an advertisement; useful in determining advertising effectiveness, the audience characteristics for different media, etc.

inquiry test, a test of advertising based on responses such as inquiries or coupon returns.

insert, *noun* 1. a separately printed section of a periodical that is bound with or tucked into its regular pages; printed either by the periodical or by an advertiser, an insert usually is printed on special stock or has color work that is superior to that of the rest of the magazine.
2. see *enclosure.*

insertion, *noun* an advertisement in a periodical.

insertion order, an order, with accompanying specifications, for an insertion.

inside panel, a panel in an array of outdoor advertising panels which is not closest to traffic.

instant, *adjective* a convenience-oriented product featuring relatively fast preparation time; especially dehydrated foods.

instantaneous-reference recording, a recording made from a live radio program for sponsor reference; an air check.

Institute of Outdoor Advertising, an organization formed in 1974 by suppliers of outdoor advertising space to serve to promote advertisers' and advertising agencies' understanding and use of the outdoor advertising medium.

Institute of Survey Research, a University of Michigan affiliated organization which provides its clients with periodic measurements of consumer economic confidence and purchase intentions.

institutional advertising, advertising intended to create good will for a company rather than to advertise goods or services.

institutional size, a large product or package size designed to meet the needs of institutions (e.g., hotels, restaurants, plants, hospitals, etc.), rather than individual consumers or households.

institutions advertising, advertising for institutions or establishments, e.g., hospitals, schools, hotels, and restaurants.

in sync, (in television and motion pictures) a state of perfect synchronization between video action and audio.

intaglio printing, a printing method in which the image areas of the printing plate have been etched below the plate surface to hold the ink from which the printing is done, as in rotogravure and steel-plate engraving; opposed to letterpress in which the printing (image) surface is raised, and offset lithography, in which the printing surface is level with the nonprinting area surrounding it.

integrate, *verb* to insert a sequence of or from a film or videotape into a television program, as for a commercial.

integrated commercial, 1. a television or radio commercial worked into the main performance of a program so that no perceptible interruption of the action takes place.
2. a commercial in which more than a single product or service is advertised.

integrated format, a television or radio program format giving two or more sponsoring advertisers exposure according to the portion of the time purchased by each.

integrated unit, see *commercial unit.*

Intelsat, *noun* International Telecommunications Satellite Consortium, an international satellite transmission system established in 1964.

intensity, *noun* 1. (in outdoor advertising) the amount and kind of advertising space purchased, with specific reference to a certain mixture of illuminated and unilluminated poster panels, in certain quantities, that are regarded as affording full coverage under local conditions; full coverage is described as 100-intensity, with less than full coverage given a proportionally lower figure.
2. see *saturation.*
3. a level or degree of light emitted by a light source.

interaction, *noun* (in statistics) an effect due to a combination of factors or predictor variables on a dependent or criterion variable, in an analysis involving a linear model; evident when the influence of two or more factors or predictor variables in combination is different from their separate influence.

intercutting, *noun* (in motion pictures or television) presentation of the same scene in a rapid series of shots taken from different angles.

interference, *noun* static or other factors that interfere with television or radio reception.

interim statement, a sworn, unaudited circulation statement by a periodical publisher, made quarterly or on special occasions.

interior monologue, a monologue heard by a motion picture or television audience but supposed to be taking place only in an actor's thoughts.

interlock, *noun* a television commercial or other sound film in its earliest edited form, consisting of audio and visual elements on synchronized but separate tracks (e.g., film and tape); used to obtain agreement at trial showings regarding editing and refinement to be incorporated in the final, integrated print.

internal house organ, see *house organ.*

internal movement, the pattern of changes in product purchasing in a certain market or group of markets.

International Newspaper Advertising Executives Association, an organization of advertising executives of daily newspapers founded in 1911; formerly Newspaper Advertising Executives Association. Abbreviated *I.N.A.E.*

International Radio and Television Society, an organization, founded in 1952, of persons in management, sales, and executive production in radio, television, and related industries. Abbreviated *I.R.T.S.*

internegative, *noun* a negative made from a color transparency or color print in order to produce a color print of the original transparency or print.

interpolate, *verb* (in statistics) to estimate values within the range of known, continuous data. Cf. *extrapolate.*
interpolation, *n.*

interpositive, *noun* 1. (in photography) an intermediate photographic or photostatic positive produced to permit further reduction or enlargement of image size beyond that possible in one original exposure.
2. (in motion pictures) a positive prepared for use in optical effects, while permitting the original negative to be preserved unchanged.

interstate commerce, commerce beyond boundaries of single states, thus subject to Federal law. Cf. *intrastate.*

Intertype, *noun, trademark* a type-casting machine that produces individual slugs, each slug consisting of a complete line of type.

interval scale, (in statistics) a measurement scale using equal separations between quantitatively ordered scale points, without a definite zero point. Cf. *nominal scale, ordinal scale, ratio scale.*

interview, *noun* any of a variety of activities and techniques practiced for the purpose of obtaining information from one or more persons by means of questions. Cf. *behavior sample interview, directive interview, free-association interview, nondirective interview, focus group interview.*

interviewer bias, (in research) nonobjective attitudes and feelings regarding a subject or hypothesis under study held by an interviewer; tends to contaminate interview findings.

in-the-market traffic, (in outdoor advertising) all traffic that originates within the market in which an outdoor advertising plant operates. Cf. *out-of-market traffic.*

intrastate commerce, commerce within the boundaries of a state, thus subject only to state law. Cf. *interstate.*

introduction, *noun* 1. the initial stage of an advertising campaign.
2. (in law) the first six months of retail sales for a new consumer product or service.
3. see *product life cycle.*

introductory offer, a special offer made to stimulate interest in a new or improved consumer product.

introductory year, the first year of a new brand or a new advertising campaign, dated usually from the time of its presentation to the public.

inventory, *noun* 1. the total space or time that a communications medium has for sale to advertisers.
2. the amount and kind of merchandise on hand, whether owned by a manufacturer, distributor, or retailer.

investment spending, increased advertising or promotion expenditures for a product or service, typically funded by temporary reductions in the profit rate in the expectation of future increases in sales and profits. Cf. *business-building test, incremental spending, payout.*

invoice, *noun* an itemized list identifying goods shipped, along with such other information as quantity, price, and size; may also serve as a bill or receipt.

involuntary attention, attention paid to advertising without deliberation or conscious effort, especially when such attention is provoked contrary to an individual's intent.

ionosphere, *noun* an atmospheric layer beginning 25 miles above the earth's surface, from which AM sky waves are reflected, especially at night.

I.P.S., *inches per second.*

iris in, (in motion pictures or television) to begin a scene by opening an iris from a completely closed position, so that the scene appears within an expanding circle. Also *circle in.* Cf. *focus in.*

iris out, (in motion pictures or television) to end a scene by closing an iris, so that the scene appears within a shrinking circle. Also *circle out.* Cf. *focus out.*

I.R.T.S., see *International Radio and Television Society.*

island display, a retail store display accessible on all sides. Also **island.**

island position, 1. a newspaper advertisement position completely surrounded by editorial matter.
2. the position of a television or radio commercial with program content directly before and after it.

isolated, a commercial with no other commercial immediately before or after it.

I.S.P., *index of social position.*

issue, *noun* all copies of a periodical published on a given date, hence bearing uniform editorial and advertising content within its various editions.

issue life, the period during which a given issue of a periodical is assumed to be read by the average reader, typically five weeks for a weekly and three months for a monthly.

italics, *plural noun* printed letters having a rightward slant, used for emphasis. Also **italic letters.**

item, *noun* 1. a unit of product or service, as conventionally sold.
2. one size and form of a product sold in an assorted variety.

iteration, *noun* (in mathematics) arrival at a solution through repeated trial; used when application of a formula is not possible.

itinerant display, (in Canada) a traveling display.

J

jacket, *noun* see *dust jacket.*

jingle, *noun* 1. music and verse combined in a commercial; typically sung, and usually characterized by a compelling rhyme scheme.
2. such a commercial, especially when music fills all available sound time.

jobber, *noun* 1. a person who buys in quantity from various sources for sale to retail stores. Cf. *distributor.*
2. see *service wholesaler.*

job lot, a large quantity of goods, usually a miscellany, sold as a whole.

job printer, a small scale commercial printer.

job ticket, a document, usually an envelope with a printed form on its face used by advertising agencies to transmit instructions regarding a production or printing job, and to serve as a record of execution.

joint venture, a cooperative business enterprise involving two independently owned business firms, established on the basis of licensing, joint ownership, or contract; in international marketing, usually involves foreign and resident national firms.

jumble display, a loosely arranged display of uniformly priced but heterogeneous objects offered for sale in a retail store.

jump cut, (in motion pictures or television) a cut between shots executed in a manner adding an improper discontinuity to continuous action.

junior page, see *junior unit.*

junior panel, 1. (in outdoor advertising) a 6-sheet poster, as opposed to the larger 24-sheet and 30-sheet posters.
2. (in transit advertising) any advertising display unit of smaller than standard poster size.

junior spread, see *pony spread.*

junior unit, a magazine advertisement produced in a single size, whose dimensions are a full page in some publications and a partial page in larger size publications with editorial matter on top or bottom and one side. Also *junior page.* Cf. *digest size.*

justify, *verb* (in typesetting) to space type so that each line is set flush left and right, aside from specified indentations, and with words and letters evenly spaced.

jute, *noun* a flexible, water-resistant containerboard made of wood pulp and waste fiber; used for boxes.

K

k, see *key*.

kC, kilocycle; see *kiloHertz*.

keep standing, (in printing) hold type or printing forms used in a completed job on file until further instructions from the customer; an order to a printer or typesetter.

Kem, *noun, trademark* a modern, elaborate device for editing sound motion picture film interlocks. Cf. *movieola*.

kern, *noun* (in typography) a portion of a letter projecting beyond its main body so as to create a possible overlap with an adjacent letter.

KEY

key, *noun* 1. (in painting or photography) the relative lightness or darkness of tonal value.
2. (in theater, motion pictures, or television) the relative brilliance of a set's lighting; typically, one speaks of a painting, photograph, or set as being in a *high key* (light) or a *low key* (dark).
3. see *keyline*.
noun 4. a black printing plate. Abbreviated *k*.
verb 5. to code an advertisement or coupon so that responses can be identified by carrier medium.

key account, 1. a major retailer, from the viewpoint of a manufacturer or a distributor.
2. a major client of an advertising agency.

key light, (in theater, motion pictures, television, or photography) the major lighting source for a scene, especially a spotlight directed to a small but critical portion of a scene.

keyline, *noun* an arrangement of all typographic and visual elements of an advertisement, brochure, mailer, etc., showing precisely the size and position of each element; normally with reproduction type proofs in position, as well as photostats of illustrations showing size and positioning. Also *key, type mechanical*.

key plate, (in color printing) the plate, usually the black plate, whose position determines the position or register of all other plates.

key station, that station of a broadcasting network that originates its major programs.

kHz, *kiloHertz*.

kickback, *noun* a portion of a fee, commission, or the like, passed by the recipient to the party who made its payment possible; e.g., a portion of an agency commission paid to an employee of an advertiser: considered unethical.

kicker, *noun* a floodlight lighting the side and rear of a photographic subject, object on a stage, etc.

kidvid, *noun, informal* television programming intended to appeal exclusively to children.

kill, *verb* to eliminate, as a scene from a show or standing type held by a printer.

kill copy, a copy of a periodical marked to show material (advertising, etc.) not to be run in the next issue.

kiloHertz, *noun* (in radio and audio) a unit of 1,000 alternations of current or sound waves per second. Abbreviated *kHz*. Also **kilocycle.** Cf. *frequency.*

kinescope, *noun* 1. a technique for making motion picture film of images on a television tube.
2. a film made in this way. Also **kine,** *telerecording.* Cf. *film transfer.*

Kleig light, powerful wide-angle light used to light stage, motion picture, and television sets.

kneaded eraser, a puttylike eraser for cleaning drawings, made so that a used area can be pressed inward and a clean area exposed.

knee shot, (in motion pictures or television) a shot of three-quarters of an actor's body, whose bottom is just above an actor's knee.

Kodachrome, *noun, trademark* 1. a multilayer film, manufactured by Eastman Kodak, for color transparencies.
2. a transparency made with this film.

Kodacolor, *noun, trademark* a color film manufactured by Eastman Kodak, for making full-color negative transparencies and photoprint positives.

kraft board, a cardboard made with unbleached sulphite wood pulp.

kraft paper, a strong brown paper made from unbleached sulphite wood pulp; used to wrap or bag retail parcels.

Krylon, *noun, trademark* a clear spray used as a fixative or protective coating on artwork, type proofs, etc.

L

label, *noun* 1. a design borne by banner fixed to a unit container of a product.
2. the banner itself.
3. the identifying features exclusive to such a design.
verb 4. to affix or design such a banner.

laboratory method, the study of respondent reactions to advertising under artificial, controlled conditions.

laid paper, a soft-textured, bulky paper showing a pattern of parallel watermark lines.

laminate, *verb* to bond or compact materials in layers, as a printed sheet to acetate for strength and permanence.

Lanham Act, the Federal Trade Mark Act of 1946, governing the application and protection of trademarks and other private marks.

lap dissolve, (in motion pictures or television) a dissolve at the end of a shot that leaves the focused image of the new shot in its place.

last-in-first-out, *adjective* noting or pertaining to an accounting system in which the inventory at the close of an accounting period is valued by the most recent price. Cf. *first-in-first-out.* Also *lifo.* Abbreviated *L.I.F.O.*

last telecast, the last date on which a commercial or program is scheduled for television broadcast. Abbreviated *L.T., L.T.C.*

late fringe, see *daypart.*

lateral recording, a recording, as on a phonograph disc, in which the grooves undulate from side to side; standard in commercial recordings.

Latin square design, (in research design and statistics) a system of randomization in which two factors are controlled; differs from a factorial design in that the influence of controlled factors is not measured, and sampling is done within the cells of the design, rather than across all cells. Also *chi square design.*

law of closure, see *principle of closure.*

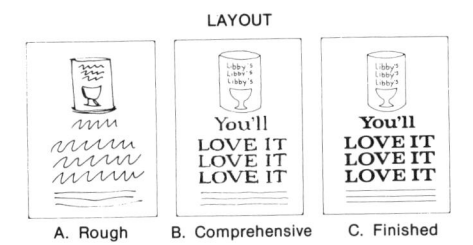

LAYOUT

A. Rough   B. Comprehensive   C. Finished

layout, *noun* any drawing intended to show the planned contents and visual appearance of a printed page, poster, advertisement, etc.

layout man, a person responsible for the visual arrangement of the various graphic and typographic elements of an advertisement.

layout paper, a translucent paper used to superimpose different versions of a sketch until a satisfactory design is produced.

L.C.L., *less-than-carload lots.*

lead, *noun* 1. a strip of lead or other metal for increasing the space between lines of type.
2. (in theater, motion pictures and television) a player in a production acting the most important role.

93

verb 3. to increase the space between lines of type with such metal strips or by some other means.

leader, *noun* 1. a line of periods, bullets, etc. used to connect widely separated typographic elements, as the chapter titles and page numbers on a table of contents. Also **leaders.**
2. a length of blank motion picture film or magnetic tape, used for holding the end of the film or tape in a takeup reel.

lead-in, *noun* 1. an introductory monologue, as to a television or radio show.
2. a television or radio program which precedes another.

leading, *noun* 1. the amount of space between lines of type, created by the use of lead strips or some other means.
2. any spacing of lines of type in excess of the minimum. Cf. *solid.*

Leading National Advertisers—Publishers Information Bureau, a service which publishes monthly reports on advertising space and revenues of national and regional magazines, as well as the space and estimated spending of advertisers using these magazines. Abbreviated *LNA—PIB.*

leading question, an interview question whose wording is calculated to influence the answer given; biased and therefore unsound.

lead-mold electrotype, a letterpress printing plate made of lead, surfaced with electrodeposited copper.

lead-out, *noun* a television or radio program which follows another, with regard to its effect on audience flows. Cf. *program following.*

learning curve, 1. (in research) a graphic depiction of the rate at which respondents produce a response which has been rewarded.
2. (in marketing) a graphic depiction of the rate at which product unit costs decline as its manufacturer gains marketing experience.

lease-back, *noun* a business technique in which the seller of something, e.g., a building, rents it from its new owner with certain options.

leased inventory, a credit technique used to obtain the first inventory of a new retail store, in which the wholesaler is the lender who collects his money, with interest, from the retailer's daily cash receipts; allows the retailer to begin business without investing in merchandise.

leave piece, a document left with a prospect by a salesman at the conclusion of a sales call. Also **leave behind.**

ledger paper, a hard-finished writing paper, used for documents and accounts.

leftover matter, typeset copy not used in an issue of a periodical; usually set in case it is needed to fill empty space. Also *overset matter, overmatter.*

leg, *noun* part of a network fed from a single station.

legend, *noun* 1. any short piece of writing or lettering meant to be read as an individual entity.
2. a piece of descriptive writing used as a picture caption or the explanation of symbols on a map or chart. Cf. *callout.*

less-than-carload lots, lots of merchandise occupying less than the space of a railroad freight car, and thus more expensive per unit owing to higher freight charges. Abbreviated *L.C.L.*

letter, *noun* 1. (in printing) a unit of type representing a character of an alphabet.
2. a written communication, usually sealed in an envelope and delivered to an intended recipient by impersonal means.

letter gadget, an object attached to or enclosed with an advertising mailing piece to arouse interest in an advertising message.

letterhead, *noun* stationery with the name of a business firm or the like, printed or engraved, used for formal correspondence. Other information, such as the address, telephone number, and principal members of the organization may also appear on the sheet.

lettering, *noun* 1. the formation of letters or words by hand, to produce a legend.
2. material so produced.

lettering man, a person who renders letters or words by hand, especially for photographic reproduction in advertisements.

letter of intent, a letter stating one's intention to enter into a business relationship, e.g., to purchase media space or time.

letterpress, *noun* any technique of printing in which the ink is carried by raised surfaces; opposed to intaglio, where recessed surfaces carry the ink, and planography, where the printing surfaces are flush with the nonprinting surface.

letterpress supplement, a newspaper supplement printed on newsprint or similar stock by letterpress rather than by the more common rotogravure process.

letterset, see *dry offset printing*.

lettershop, *noun* a firm that reproduces advertising literature and provides other services, e.g., proofreading, binding, addressing, and mailing.

letterspace, *verb* to space out the individual letters of a line of print in order to fill a justified line while avoiding awkward spaces between words and/or an improper word break.

l.f., *light face*.

liability policy, an agreement by a manufacturer insuring a wholesaler or distributor against legal action from a retailer or customer. Abbreviated *L.P.*

library music, see *stock music*.

library service, a service renting out music for broadcasting purposes.

library shot, see *stock shot*.

life, *noun* the ability of an advertisement or promotion to elicit the intended action as indicated by the continuation of such a reaction upon repeated exposures of the advertisement. Cf. *wearout*.

lifestyle, the pattern of spending used by individuals or families to express their values and means.

lifo, *adjective* see *last-in-first-out*.

L.I.F.O., *last-in-first-out*.

lift, *noun* (in television or radio) recorded or filmed material from an earlier commercial production reused in a new commercial, either for economy or to maintain uniform execution of a key sequence.

ligature, *noun* 1. a stroke linking two letters.
2. a combination of letters printed as a single character because of the tendency for the letters to touch, i.e., fi, ff, fl, ffl, as well as diphthongs and combinations of capitals.

light box, a boxlike device faced with translucent white material on one side and containing an electric light source; used to view photographic transparencies.

light face, *noun* a typeface with strokes that are thinner than those of regular or medium weight type. Abbreviated *l.f.*

Likert scale, (in research) a summated scale for attitude measurement in which respondents state their agreement or disagreement with statements in one of a range of three to seven possible positions, ranging from complete agreement, to no opinion, to complete disagreement.

limbo, *noun* (in photography, motion pictures or television) any neutral background for a shot, lacking all specific reference to places, weather conditions, etc.

limited animation, see *animation.*

limited distribution, 1. distribution of a product to one or more specific geographical areas rather than nationwide.
2. less than complete distribution of a product in the stores of an area.

limited-time station, a television or radio station sharing a channel band or frequency band with another station with an overlapping reception pattern and therefore restricted in broadcasting to certain hours when the other station is off the air; part-time station.

line, *noun* 1. see *product line.*
2. see *credit.*
3. a sentence or phrase in a script or commercial; e.g., a slogan.
4. see *agate line.*
adjective 5. (of printing) noting or pertaining to artwork or plates rendered with lines, solid areas, or hatching, etc.; not requiring halftone reproduction.

lineage, *noun* a total amount of periodical advertising space, named in the number of lines run. Also **linage.**

linear programming, a class of mathematical techniques for selecting optimum decisions that simultaneously satisfy a number of requirements; usually carried out through computers.

line extension, a new product marketed under an existing brand name, intended for use in the same category as the "parent" brand's original product, or product line, while being designed to draw new users to the brand's franchise from products competitive to the original product; e.g., "dry" and "oily" new shampoo products using the brand name of an existing shampoo are line extensions. Cf. *flanker, brand extension.*

line copy, artwork suitable for reproduction as a line illustration as compared to halftone copy.

line cut, (in printing) a plate or the like that reproduces artwork through solid areas, lines, hatchings, etc. without giving shaded effects by means of halftone dots.

line drawing, a drawing done in lines only, without shading.

line graph, see *graph.*

line length, the width of a column in a periodical.

line negative, a photographic negative of a line drawing, made without a halftone screen.

liner, *noun* any paper serving as a lining, as in a box or package.

line rate, a charge per line for newspaper space.

lineup, *noun* a group of television or radio stations broadcasting a certain network program.

Linotype, *noun, trademark* a machine for setting letterpress type in which individual matrices are assembled for the casting of entire lines of type, called slugs.

lip synchronization, 1. direct recording of sound during the taking of a motion picture or television film; so called because the actual voices of the actors are recorded. Also **lip sync,** *direct recording.*
2. matched timing of video and audio signals in a motion picture or television production involving on-camera spoken lines.

list broker, an agent who sells lists of sales prospects.

listener, *noun* a person in the audience of a radio station. Cf. *viewer.*

listener diary, a diary or log of television or radio programs seen or heard, kept by a respondent in an audience rating survey.

listening area, the geographical area of a television or radio station's coverage.

list house, an organization acting as a list broker.

lithograph, *noun* a reproduction made by lithographic means.

lithography, *noun* a planographic printing technique, based on the mutual repulsion of grease and water, in which parts of a printing plate or stone that are not to print are wetted so as to repel a greasy ink, which adheres to those parts that are to print.

litho sheet, a lithographed poster sheet.

little America method, a technique for translating the media delivery of national advertising media plans into the media of one or more local areas, in a manner that attempts to match local deliveries to those which would be obtained nationally. Also **little U.S. method.** Cf. *as-it-falls method, correct increment method, media translation.*

live, *adjective* 1. (in television or radio) presented directly from an actual performance or event: *a live program.*
2. (of the sound of a film) recorded simultaneously with the action filmed. Also **live action.**
adverb 3. (in television or radio) directly from an actual performance or event: *This program is brought to you live...*

live animation, see *animation.*

live fade, (in television or radio) a diminution of transmitted sound created in the studio rather than in the control room. Cf. *board fade.*

live matter, 1. (in printing) areas of printing plates that are to print as opposed to dead metal or nonprinting areas.
2. composed type that has been used but is to be used again.

3. the visual area in a magazine full or partial bleed advertisement wherein copy and illustrations are retained within a fixed field to avoid elements being trimmed off in the publication's binding process.

live tag, (in television or radio) a short, live message added to a recorded announcement.

live time, time during which a television or radio station transmitter is fed a live performance from another station.

live-time delay, see *clock-hour delay.*

live title, (in television) a title shot made directly by a studio camera from the set rather than being introduced on a slide or film.

living-room interview, an interview at a central location in which respondents view television in a homelike setting.

Lloyd Hall Editorial Analysis, a technique employed by Lloyd Hall Associates for analyzing the editorial content of magazines according to the numbers of pages devoted to various areas of interest over a period of time; useful in determining suitable advertising media.

LNA—PIB, *Leading National Advertisers—Publishers Information Bureau.*

load, *verb* 1. to increase an order from a retailer by offering him a premium or some other incentive.
2. to add materials to paper to improve its surface qualities.

loader, *noun* see *dealer loader.*

load factor, the estimated average number of passengers per automobile, used in estimating exposure to outdoor advertising; the Traffic Audit Bureau national load factor is 1.75.

loading deal, a deal in which a retailer receives a premium or some other incentive for a quantity purchase of a certain product. Cf. *dealer loader.*

local advertising, 1. advertising by a local merchant.
2. advertising placed at rates available to local merchants.

local-channel station, a television or radio station licensed to transmit to its own locality only.

locally-edited supplement, a Sunday newspaper supplement owned and edited by the newspaper itself; sometimes associated with other such supplements for the purpose of obtaining national advertising.

local media, communications media whose audiences are primarily drawn from the same locality as the media; these media customarily have a preferential rate for local advertisers.

local program, a television or radio program intended for a local audience only.

local rate, the advertising rate charged by a local communications medium to a local advertiser; usually lower than the national rate.

local station, a television or radio station serving a single market area, typically low-powered and broadcasting on a frequency which may be shared by other stations 100 miles or more distant.

local tag, (in television or radio) an identification of a local dealer added to a recorded commercial announcement. Also *dealer super.*

location, *noun* an actual setting used for a motion picture or television film; used especially in the phrase *on location.*

lockup, *noun* the stage at which letterpress type, plates, etc. are locked in place, ready for printing or platemaking.
lock up, *v.*

Loewy panel, an outdoor advertising panel with a structure built to a standard Raymond Loewy design, featuring light gray color molding of metal or plastic.

log, *noun* 1. any book or other record kept to note and preserve the details of a prolonged and recurring event, as the broadcasting day of a television or radio station.
2. a logarithm.

logo, *noun* 1. see *logotype.*
2. see *colophon.*

logotype, *noun* 1. a brand name, publication title, or the like, presented in a special lettering style or typeface and used in the manner of a trademark. Also *logo.*
2. see *colophon.*

L.O.H., an abbreviation for "lady of the house" used by the A. C. Nielsen Co.

long play, a phonographic recording of large size, usually 33⅓ R.P.M. and containing more than two musical selections. Abbreviated *L.P.*

long shot, (in photography, motion pictures or television) a shot of a distant subject. Abbreviated *L.S.*

loop, *noun* 1. an audio tape in loop form, spliced to its own end to permit the continual repetition of sounds.
verb 2. to add audio elements to a sound track in synchronization with a video sequence.

loose, *adjective* 1. (of artwork) sketchy in appearance, giving an impression of a subject but not its details.
2. (in television or motion pictures) noting or pertaining to a shot leaving ample visible space around a subject.

loosen up, (of a motion picture or television scene) to increase the visible space around a subject.

lose the light, to come to have insufficient light to film a motion picture or television show out of doors.

loss leader, a retail item advertised at an attractively low price in order to attract customers for the purchase of other, more profitable items.

lottery, *noun* a scheme in which making a required purchase gives a person a chance to win a prize which is awarded at random; lotteries cannot be used as promotion devices under U.S. postal regulations. Cf. *sweepstakes, contest.*

lower-case, *adjective* noting or pertaining to the small letters of an alphabet of type or lettering as opposed to capital or upper-case letters.

low-key light, a key light of low intensity.

L.P., 1. *liability policy.*
2. *long play.*

L.S., *long shot.*

L.T., *last telecast.* Also *L.T.C.*

L.T.C., *last telecast.*

lucy, *noun, informal* see *camera lucida.*

Ludlow, *noun, trademark* a designation for a type composition process in which handset type is cast into a slug for printing.

luminous, *adjective* noting or pertaining to any paint or the like used for lettering or tinting advertisements in such a way that they appear vividly under street lighting, blacklight, etc.

M

M, Roman numeral for 1000, as in cost per thousand, as used in marketing, media and printing terms. **MM** similarly represents 1,000,000.

M.A.B., *Magazine Advertising Bureau.*

machine-coated paper, an inexpensive grade of coated paper.

machine composition, any kind of typesetting other than handsetting.

machine-finish paper, a highly calendered, uncoated paper.

Madison Avenue, 1. a New York City thoroughfare which once served as the address of major advertising agencies.
2. hence, the New York City advertising agency business.
3. loosely, the advertising agency business.

mag, *noun* magnetic, as in *mag track* (magnetic film sound track).

magazine, *noun* 1. a periodical which tends to emphasize comprehensive, thoughtful editorial coverage of a subject area as much as timeliness; usually bears a superior production quality to newspapers.
2. a camera chamber holding film.

Magazine Advertising Bureau, the sales arm of the Magazine Publishers Association, devoted to promoting magazines as an advertising medium. Abbreviated *M.A.B.*

magazine concept, 1. a format for a television or radio program involving several distinct successive parts.
2. a form of broadcast advertising time sales involving purchase of a program's commercial occasions by different advertisers. Cf. *sponsorship.*

magazine plan, a plan by which advertising aimed at a certain geographic zone can be placed only in magazines for distribution in that zone.

Magazine Publishers Association, an organization of magazine publishers, founded in 1919, for the purpose of promoting magazines both as a means of improving the lives of their readers and as an advertising medium, as well as for the purpose of supplying its members with information and services; the Magazine Advertisers Bureau is its sales arm. Abbreviated *M.P.A.*

magazine supplement, a preprinted tabloid or magazine size supplement distributed in newspapers, usually in Saturday or Sunday editions.

magnetic tape, a plastic ribbon faced on one side with metallic powder which can be magnetized or demagnetized at will, using the proper devices; used to record information, such as video or audio signals.

magnetic track, a sound track recorded on a magnetic strip on the border of a motion picture film. Also *mag track.* Cf. *optical track.*

mail-ballot map, a map prepared through returns from a mail survey questionnaire.

mailing list, a list of prospective buyers, prepared for direct mail solicitation.

mail-in premium, a premium obtained by mailing in a suitable response to the manufacturer or distributor, with or without money.

mail order, a buyer's expression of intent to purchase submitted to a seller by mail.

mail-order advertising, advertising soliciting an order for purchase, using the Postal Service as a means of returning the order to the person or organization making the offer. Cf. *direct mail advertising.*

mail-order house, a retail company selling primarily through mail orders.

mail-survey map, a map of television or radio station coverage prepared with the help of solicited or unsolicited mail to the station.

main head, the principal display head of a body of printed matter, as an advertisement.

maizie, *noun* a wooly pattern created with a cucalorus.

makegood, *noun* 1. the broadcast of a television or radio commercial free of extra charge to its advertiser, to make amends for faulty presentation or for failure to present the commercial at the originally scheduled time.
2. a periodical advertisement rerun under similar circumstances.

make-ready, *noun* 1. (in printing) the process of shimming up various typographic elements in a form to compensate for their various resistances to roller pressure in order to insure even printing throughout.
2. the materials used in this process.
3. the process of preparing a press for printing, especially in four-color work.

makeup, *noun* the arrangement of typographic and illustrative elements on a printed piece as an advertisement or a complete magazine.

makeup restriction, a restriction on advertisement layout imposed by a periodical publisher to ensure that no unsalable advertising space is created by oddly proportioned advertisements.

mall, *noun* a shopping center in which several stores are located in close proximity, and are accessible to pedestrians without the necessity for crossing thoroughfares to go from store to store. Also *shopping mall.*

management, *noun* 1. the combined application of prediction and control to the affairs of an organization or an operational process.
2. those employees of an organization responsible for guiding its operations to the fulfillment of its objectives.
3. those leading executives of an organization responsible for decisions of the greatest importance to the organization.
manage, *v.*

management consultant, an agent retained by corporate management to provide ideas regarding the manner in which the organization's operations, plans, or personnel may be improved.

management supervisor, an advertising agency employee responsible for the successful management of designated accounts, and for liaison with client management. Cf. *account supervisor.*

mandatory copy, copy legally required for inclusion on a package label, in a television commercial, print advertisement, etc. Also **mandatory.**

M. and E., (in motion pictures, television, or radio) music and sound effects.

manufacturer's brand, a brand sold by a manufacturer rather than by a wholesaler or distributor.

manufacturer's courtesy store, a retail store operated by a manufacturer for the public, for the purpose of disposing of seconds, remainders, and overruns.

manufacturer's representative, a sales representative of a manufacturer, who may be either a salaried employee or a broker acting for several manufacturers on commission. Also **manufacturer's agent.**

manuscript, *noun* a draft copy of the text of a book or play, as sent by its author or editor to a publisher, producer, or typesetter. Abbreviated *MS.*

margin, *noun* 1. the difference between cost and selling price of a product; computed either as a cash figure or as a percentage of the selling price. Also *gross margin, markup.*
2. (in printing) the area between the printed area and the edge of a sheet or page.

mark, *noun* any device or expression that can be registered under the Trade Mark Act of 1946; a trademark, service mark, collective mark, or certification mark.

markdown, *noun* a reduction in price, so as to promote increased sales.

market, *noun* 1. a population, group, industry, geographical area, etc., regarded as a source of current or potential demand for a product or service.
2. a place where goods are bought and sold; e.g., supermarket.
3. the extent of demand for a product or service.
verb 4. to offer a product or service for sale.

market-by-market allocation, see *area-by-area allocation.*

market development, 1. the number of units or dollar value of all brands of a product or service category that have been sold per thousand population within an area in a stated period. Also *category development.* Cf. *brand development.*
2. loosely, a product's, service's, or category's degree or rate of usage in markets and market segments to which it is available.

market development index, the ratio between a local market development rate, and the national rate; used as an indicator of category or brand sales potential. Also *category development index, market index.* Abbreviated *M.D.I.* Cf. *brand development index.*

marketer, *noun* a person or organization that offers a product or service for sale.

market index, see *market development index.*

marketing, *noun* the knowledge and active processes of a seller directed to fulfillment of gainful exchanges; such processes include product or service development, pricing, packaging, advertising, merchandising, and distribution.

marketing concept, a management philosophy which holds that the best means to satisfy corporate objectives is to direct all corporate efforts to find ways to permit customers to satisfy their desires.

marketing director, an employee of a manufacturer or mass service organization responsible for review and approval of marketing plans; may include responsibility for sales management.

marketing mix, the levels and interplay of the constituent elements of a product's or service's marketing efforts, including product features, pricing, advertising, merchandising, distribution, and marketing spending, especially as decisions relating to these elements affect sales results.

marketing plan, 1. a strategy for marketing a product or service.
2. a comprehensive document containing background and supportive detail regarding a marketer's objectives and strategies. Also *plan.*

marketing research, research designed to supply information necessary for the effective marketing of consumer desired goods and services.

marketing research director, see *research director.*

market mapping study, a market research study which depicts key groupings of consumers or their product or service attitudes graphically. Also *perceptual mapping study.* Cf. *market structure study.*

market pattern, the pattern of concentration of purchases of a product within a general or specific market. A pattern of extensive purchasing by the market as a whole (*thick market pattern*) or of meager purchasing by the market as a whole (*thin market pattern*) often appears.

market penetration, the degree or rate of usage of a product, service, or category among current users.

market potential, sales volume for a product or service available to or desired by a supplier; influenced by category development, and often expressed in terms of share of market. Cf. *headroom, brand potential index.*

market profile, a summary of the characteristics of a market, including information on typical purchasers and competitors, and often general information on the economy and retailing patterns of the area.

Market Research Corporation of America, a consumer research organization specializing in continuous syndicated reporting of food and drug buying habits and usage patterns on the basis of diaries kept by a consumer panel. Abbreviated M.R.C.A.

market response, the sales consequences of stimulation provided by marketing spending.

market segment, *noun* see *segment.*

market segmentation, see *segmentation.*

market share, the percentage of a category's sales, in terms of dollars or units, obtained by a brand, line, or company.

Markets In Focus Enterprises, a marketing and media research firm in New York that sells syndicated studies of local patterns of media, product, and service usage.

market structure study, a market research study which seeks to isolate the critical factors (demographic, attitudinal, etc.) which determine the patterns of consumer behavior toward a category of goods. Cf. *market mapping study.*

market test, see *sales area test.*

markup, *noun* 1. the difference between the price at which a product is purchased for resale and the price at which it is sold, figured either in money or as a percentage of the purchase price.
2. any increase in price.
3. see *margin.*
4. (in typesetting) the written instructions on manuscript copy covering typeface, size, width and any other special instructions for the typesetter to follow in setting the job.

marriage split, (in periodical advertising) an arrangement among advertisers to purchase a certain space in different regional editions of a nationally distributed periodical jointly, with the advertisement of each appearing in copies delivered to their respective areas of the country.

mask, *noun* 1. a shield fitted to a camera lens to reduce or give a specific shape to the camera's field.
2. a basically rectangular but slightly rounded frame for a television picture tube.
3. any of various shields or screens used to conceal objects, prevent surfaces from being painted, etc.
4. a photographic negative or positive used in making color corrections in photoengraving.
verb 5. to shield with a mask.

mask out, *verb* to cover an area or detail so that it will not appear in a photograph.

masked-identification test, a test of advertising memorability in which respondents attempt to identify advertisers or brands in advertisements in which brand names and trademarks are effaced.

mass display, a display of a retail product

set up in a store apart from the product's usual shelf display.

mass magazine, a magazine edited for the general public.

mass medium, a communications medium intended to interest the general public.

mass merchandiser, a retail outlet or chain handling 3 or more general merchandise lines in a store of at least 10,000 square feet of space; having often evolved from discount stores, such outlets cultivate a discount image through advertising, promotion, and pricing policies.

mass publication, a periodical edited for the general public.

master, *noun* any film, videotape, disc, etc. recording of all elements of a performance in complete and final form to be used as an original for reproduction and release.

master contract, see *blanket contract.*

master control, the central control facility of a television or radio station.

master newspaper list, a complete list of U.S. daily newspapers, or of those newspapers used by an advertiser, used for the planning or ordering of advertising; usually includes rate and circulation data. Cf. *mock newspaper schedule.*

master of ceremonies, a person who provides continuity in a variety show by introducing the show itself and its various acts. Also *emcee.* Abbreviated *M.C.*

master tape, an edited audio tape or videotape complete with all elements to be recorded on quantity prints or dubs.

MASTHEAD

masthead, *noun* an area of a periodical giving the official title, the publisher, the principal staff members, and often a statement of editorial policy.

mat, *noun* 1. see *matrix.*
adjective 2. see *matte.*

mat board, cardboard available in various textures and colors for artwork.

matchbook covers, an advertising medium employing the exterior and occasionally interior faces of the safety card used on matches as a display space; usually dispensed at no charge, as either an accompaniment to a purchase of smoking materials, or by institutions such as hotels or restaurants.

match dissolve, (in motion pictures or television) a dissolve in which the principal figures or objects in the close of the preceding scene appear in the same positions in the new one.

matched sample, (in statistics) a sample identical to one or more others in significant respects.

mat knife, a knife for cutting mat board.

matrix, *noun* 1. a sheet of fibrous material used as a mold for casting letterpress plates called stereotypes; it bears an impression made by set foundry type or an original letterpress plate and is more

cheaply mailed to a number of publications than actual duplicate plates. Also *mat.*
2. a mold from which a letterpress type character is cast. Also *mat.*
3. a system for coding information densely, especially audio information; e.g., such matrix systems as SQ (CBS trademark) and QS (Sansui trademark), used to encode quadriphonic signals into a pair of stereo audio channels.
4. an array of numbers arranged in rows and columns.

matrix algebra, (in statistics) a system of mathematical axioms and operations used for work with matrices; essential in the development and understanding of multivariate statistical analysis.

matrix film, see *stripping film.*

mat service, a service that supplies newspapers with matrixes of advertising, artwork, public relations material, etc.

mat shot, (in motion pictures and television) a shot of a scene in which one figure is superimposed over another and backgrounds in a manner which results in a convincingly integrated image. Also *travelling mat shot,* **matte shot.**

matte, *adjective* not glossy; without strong highlights: *a matte finish.* Also *mat.*

matter, *noun* (in printing) composed type.

maturity, *noun* see *product life cycle.*

maximil, *noun* the milline rate of a newspaper before any discounts. Also **maxiline.** Cf. *minimil.*

maximum depth requirement, the maximum length of a periodical advertisement of less than full column length allowed to pay less than a full column space rate.

M.B.M., *market-by-market allocation.*

MBS, *Mutual Broadcasting System.*

M.C., *master of ceremonies.*

McKittrick's Directory, a quarterly guide to advertising agencies, their personnel, and their accounts. Also **McKittrick.**

M.C.U., *medium close-up.*

M.D.I., *market development index.*

M.D.R., *minimum daily requirement.*

M.D.T., *Mountain Daylight Time;* see *time zone.*

mean, *noun* a number equal to the sum of all the numbers in a set divided by the quantity of numbers in the set. Thus, 8, 6, 3, 7 added together equal 24, and since the set contains 4 numbers the mean is 6. Also *arithmetic mean.* Cf. *average, median, mode.*

measure, *noun* the character space available in the width of a single column or line of type.

mechanical, *noun* see *pasteup.*

mechanical animation, see *animation.*

mechanical binding, (in printing) a form of binding publications, with wires, plastic bands, etc., passed through perforations near the back of individual pages rather than signatures; allows pages to lie flat.

mechanical requirements, the layout and makeup specifications of a periodical, to which prepared advertising printing material must conform.

media, *noun* plural of medium; the most commonly used form of this word.

media buyer, see *buyer.*

media director, an employee of an advertising agency responsible for supervising the selection and purchase of space or time in communications media for client's advertising efforts.

median, *noun* 1. (in statistics) the point in a distribution of scores above and below which 50% of the scores fall.
2. the exact midpoint of a distribution. Cf. *average, mean, mode.*

Media Records, a research organization publishing reports of major advertisers' advertising volume in daily and Sunday newspapers, given by paper in agate lines, and total dollar (by brand, if indicated) expenditures.

media survey, a survey of the extent to which specific communications media reach specific markets and audiences.

media translation, an adaptation of a media spending plan from a national to a local level, as for testing purposes, or vice-versa. Cf. *little America method, as-it-falls method, correct increment method.*

media weight, the number and size or length of advertisements, or the total audience delivery level, produced by an advertising effort.

medium, *noun, (plural: media)* an established vehicle for providing the public with information or entertainment, especially one which sells the opportunity to advertise.

medium close-up, (in television and motion pictures) a shot taken from a range between medium and close up.

medium shot, (in television and motion pictures) a shot of a subject in the foreground, showing a substantial amount of the scene around the subject.

megaHertz, *noun* a unit of radio wave frequency equal to one million cycles per second or one thousand kiloHertz. Abbreviated *MHz, MH.*

memory unit, a part of a computer that stores information and programs for future use.

mental set, a pre-existing attitude or belief that conditions a person's responses to new situations.

merchandise mix, 1. the basic variety of stock of a distributor.
2. by item or sales, the various products and package sizes of a given brand, category, or marketer. Also *mix.* Cf. *product line.*

merchandise pack, a package of a retail product that offers a premium, which is usually enclosed. Cf. *in-pack premium.*

merchandiser, *noun* 1. an expert at merchandising.
2. a manager of a retail sales outlet.

merchandising, *noun* 1. marketing activities, including sales and promotion, designed to make retail goods available, attractive and conspicuous in a store.
2. solicitation of salesman and retailer support for a marketing effort.

merchandising allowance, see *promotion allowance.*

merchandising committee, a committee appointed by a store chain, wholesaler, or the like to decide on the acceptance of new products, manufacturer's promotions, etc. Also *buying committee.*

merchandising director, an employee of a manufacturer, advertising agency, distributor or retailer responsible for planning and implementing retail selling efforts.

merchandising service, any of various services offered, usually free of direct charge, by a communications medium to help in promoting an advertiser's products or to gather marketing information of interest to him.

meter, *noun* 1. (in television rating surveys) any of various devices for recording the periods when a television set is in use, and usually, the channel to which it is tuned. Cf. *Audimeter, Arbitron.*
2. (in research) any of various devices for the measurement of consumer and audi-

ence behavior in terms of mechanical or physiological responses.

methodology, *noun* (in research and statistics) the study and principles underlying development of research design and analysis.

metro area, *metropolitan area;* see *standard metropolitan statistical area.* Also **metro.**

metropolitan area, see *standard metropolitan statistical area.* Also **metro,** *metro area.*

metro rating area, a metropolitan television or radio coverage area as defined by the American Research Bureau. Abbreviated *M.R.A.*

MHz, *megaHertz.* Also *MH.*

microfiche, *noun* a cardlike piece of microfilm used for recording multipage documents.

microphone, *noun* a device for transforming sound waves into electrical impulses in an audio system. Also *mike.* Cf. *omnidirectional microphone.*

microwave, *noun* a radio wave less than one meter in length from one cycle to the next.

microwave link, a microwave relay television station.

middle break, station identification in the middle of a television or radio program.

middle majority, a term for the lower-middle and upper-lower classes of American society, taken together; constitutes about two-thirds of the total population.

middleman, *noun* any selling factor involved in the distribution chain between growers, fabricators, or manufacturers, and consumers; especially wholesalers.

middle-of-road, *adjective* see *format.* Abbreviated *M.O.R.*

midpoint, *noun* (in statistics) the halfway point of a number of steps into which a total range of values has been divided. Cf. *median.*

mike, *noun* see *microphone.*

mike boom, a telescoping arm for holding a microphone above a performer.

milking strategy, a marketing strategy designed to extract greatest possible profit, rather than sales potential, from a product or service; usually designed to generate funds which may be invested in other ventures believed to have greater long-range profit potential. Also *profit-taking strategy.*

millimeter, *noun* a metric unit equal to one thousandth of a meter or 0.03937 inch; standard size films are measured in millimeters of width. Abbreviated *mm.* Cf. *motion picture film.*

milline rate, a figure used to determine the cost-effectiveness of advertising in a newspaper; reached by multiplying the cost per agate line by one million, then dividing by the circulation. Cf. *tru-line rate.*

mimeograph paper, a paper, made in white and several colors, especially formulated to absorb mimeograph ink.

minimil, *noun* the milline rate of a newspaper after all possible discounts for space and frequency purchases. Also **miniline.** Cf. *maximil.*

minimum daily requirement, (obsolescent) a standard of adequacy of daily human nutrient ingestion, citing the least amount of individual vitamin and mineral intake levels deemed necessary for most people to avoid symptoms of dietary deficiency disease. Cf. *recommended dietary allowance.*

minimum depth requirement, a newspaper requirement that advertisements

have a certain proportion of depth to width, usually one inch per column.

minimum frequency, a level of exposure to or, scheduling of advertising that is believed to represent the lowest level at which the advertising will be effective in attaining its ends, while permitting the greatest degree of advertising continuity.

minute-by-minute profile, an estimate of the varying number of listeners to a television or radio program at closely spaced periods during the program; used to determine the most advantageous times for scheduling a sponsor's commercials.

mirror shot, (in motion pictures or television) a shot of an image in a reflecting surface.

misredemption, *noun* redemption of coupons presented either by persons who have not made the purchases the coupons are intended to promote, or by retailers who have not redeemed the coupons in the normal course of business with properly qualified customers.

missionary salesman, 1. a salesman employed by a marketer to make contact with prospects who currently are not purchasing his products. Also *pioneer salesman.*
2. loosely, a detailer.

mix, *noun* 1. the re-recording of separate visual and audio elements on a film or tape to produce a master.
2. the number of original performances and reruns of a television series included in a contract.
3. see *merchandise mix.*

mix-and-match sale, a sale at which the customer is allowed to select a certain number of assorted items for a fixed price.

mix down, to mix audio and video elements.

mm., *millimeter.*

M.N.A., *multi-network area rating.*

mobile unit, 1. a camera unit of a television station carried by a person or mounted on a truck for travel to the scenes of various events.
2. research facilities which can be moved to desired interviewing sites, such as shopping centers.

mock newspaper schedule, a selective list of daily newspapers of the United States, chosen for their high milline rate and coverage and arranged in the population order of their communities; used to facilitate mass purchasing of advertising space. Cf. *master newspaper list.*

mockup, *noun* any closely imitative representation of something, especially one constructed at full scale and possibly usable as the actual object modeled.

mode, *noun* 1. (in statistics) that point or value within a distribution where the greatest number of scores fall.
2. the highest point of a histogram or bar graph.

model, *noun* 1. a more or less closely imitative representation of an object, scene, etc. at reduced scale.
2. a mathematical representation of a set of relationships or principles.
3. a person retained to appear before an audience to silently demonstrate a process or merchandise (especially apparel).

modeling light, a light on a photographic, motion picture, or television subject, etc. for the purpose of giving emphasis to its general form or to prevent excessive light-and-shade contrast.

modern, *noun* any category of roman type in which the difference in thick and thin strokes is greatly emphasized and in which serifs are perfectly horizontal. Cf. *Old Style.*

moire, *noun* 1. a patterned effect in a halftone illustration, resulting from a chance relationship between the pattern of the halftone dots and some other pattern in the picture, e.g. a fine texture or a pre-existing

halftone screen.
2. a design produced by the regular interference pattern of two superimposed, regularly patterned screens.

mold, *noun* 1. an impression made from a letterpress engraving, usually on a vinyl sheet, under heat and pressure (wax and lead once used, are now obsolete materials). A printing plate is produced by treating the face of the mold, depositing a coating of copper by electrolysis, and backing with metal to the proper thickness.

molding, *noun* a trim strip of metal, wood, or plastic surrounding an outdoor advertising panel.

mom and pop store, a small, family operated retail store.

monarch, *noun* a paper size for stationery, the sheets being 7¼×10½ inches.

monaural, single channel audio, as opposed to *stereophonic* or *quadraphonic.* Also *mono.*

monitor, *noun* (in television production) a television receiver, usually without sound, placed in a television studio to permit the production and performing staff to review a performance in progress.

monitor, *verb* 1. to check the timing, program content, and commercial content of a television or radio show.
2. to supervise and control the transmission of a television or radio show in progress, from a control booth.
3. to supervise and control a recording in progress.
noun 4. a device for broadcast monitoring.
5. loosely, to periodically inspect: *monitor sales rates.*

mono, 1. see *monotone.*
2. see *monaural.*

monotone, *noun, adjective* see *black and white.* Also *mono.*

Monotype, *noun, trademark* a typesetting machine that casts individual characters and sets them in justified lines.

montage, *noun* 1. a combination of juxtaposed or superimposed images, used in photography, layout design, motion pictures and television as a means of giving a succinct impression of a complex subject, of time elapsed, etc.
2. (in radio) a blend or sequence of sounds as an effect.

month's supply, the size of a marketer's (especially retailers) inventory of a product, stated in terms of the number of months of sales at current sales rates onhand inventory alone could provide; as defined by A. C. Nielsen Co.

mood programming, (in television or radio) the scheduling of similar programs over an extended time interval, without regard to normal time blocks, in such a way that the mood established or sustained by one program will not be abruptly dispelled by the next. Cf. *block programming.*

M.O.R., *middle-of-(the)-road;* see *format.*

morning drive, see *daypart.*

mortise, *noun* an opening in a printing plate, sheet of reproducible copy, etc. into which a smaller plate or piece of type or artwork is to be fitted. Cf. *notch.*

MOS, (of motion picture films or television) noting or pertaining to a silent production or sequence.

motion picture, a sequence of photographs recorded in a manner permitting restoration of images of the subjects filmed, in motion.

motion picture film, photographic transparency film used to photograph or print motion pictures; most common formats are identified by width in millimeters, as 8mm. and super 8mm., used primarily by amateurs; and such sound-synchronized formats as super 8mm., used in low quality professional as well as amateur work; 16

mm., used for television station prints and for some commercial filming; 35mm., used for most feature films, commercial filming, and television network prints; and 70mm., used for wide screen feature films. Normal exposure and playback speeds for these formats would be as follows:

	feet per minute	frames per second
regular 8mm silent	14.5	16
super 8mm synch	14.5	18
super 8mm	14.5	24
16mm (synch)	36	24
35mm (synch)	90	24
70mm (synch)	225	24

motivation, *noun* an internal psychological state which serves as the basis for action. Also **motive.**

motivation research, psychological research into the underlying patterns of human motivations, especially buying behavior. Abbreviated *M.R.*

motive, see *motivation.*

mount, *noun* see *base.*

movieola, *noun* a relatively simple device for editing sound or silent motion picture film. Cf. *Kem.*

moving shot, (in motion pictures or television) a shot of a moving object from a camera moving in the same direction. Also *action shot.*

Moviola, *noun, trademark* a machine that reproduces film and sound in miniature for editing purposes.

M.P.A., 1. *Magazine Publishers Association.* 2. *multiple product (commercial) announcement.*

M.R., *motivation research.*

M.R.A., *metro rating area.*

M.R.C.A., *Market Research Corporation of America.*

MS., *manuscript.* Plural, **MSS.**

M.S., *medium shot.*

M.S.O., *multiple systems operator.*

M.S.T., *Mountain Standard Time;* see *time zone.*

M.S.U., (in Canada) one thousand standard units; used in Canada as an arbitrary measurement for the wholesale sale of a product in various unit sizes.

multideck, *noun* a set of tiered display shelves, open or in a refrigerated case.

multidimensional scaling, (in statistics) a group of techniques used to discover and describe patterns or structures, in any dimensional space, inherent in a set of variables.

Multigraph, *noun, trademark* a small cylinder press that prints from letterpress type by means of an inked ribbon.

Multilith, *noun, trademark* a small offset press printing from paper masters.

multi-network area rating, an audience rating given by the A. C. Nielsen Co. to network program performance in 70 cities where all three networks are represented. Abbreviated *M.N.A.*

multiple-color press, a press that can print more than one color at the same time.

multiple correlation, see *correlation.*

multiple pricing, the offering of more than one retail unit for sale at a single unit price, e.g., two for twenty-five cents.

multiple-product announcement, (in television or radio) a commercial for more than one product or service. Abbreviated *M.P.A.*

multiple-regression analysis, a statistical method for predicting variation in a dependent variable through analysis of a number of independent variables involved with it.

multiple sound track, a group of sound tracks used for stereophonic or quadraphonic audio reproduction.

multiple systems operator, an operator of a number of community antenna television systems. Abbreviated *M.S.O.*

multiple-unit sale, a sale involving more than one item.

multiplex, a system for imposing additional information on broadcast signals in a manner compatible with the original signal system; for example, use of such a system to enable reception of FM radio signals in stereo.

multistation lineup, a group of television or radio stations in a single market area carrying the announcements of an advertiser.

multivariate analysis, (in statistics) the simultaneous measurement, and assessment for interference, of statistical relationships within or between sets of variables.

musical clock, an early-morning radio program consisting of time announcements, music, and commercials.

music track, a track of a film or videotape that bears background music.

mut, *noun* see *quad.*

Mutual Broadcasting System, a former national radio network founded in 1934. Abbreviated *MBS.*

N

n, *noun* (in research) the number of respondents in a sample or subsample.

N.A., 1. *no answer.*
2. *not available.*

N.A.B., 1. *National Association of Broadcasters.*
2. *Newspaper Advertising Bureau, Inc.*

N.A.B. code, a code of standards for commercial time, program content, etc. established by the National Association of Broadcasters.

N.A.C., *net advertising circulation.*

N.A.D., *Nielsen Audience Demographic Report.*

N.A.E.A., *Newspaper Advertising Executives' Association.*

N.A.R.B., *National Advertising Review Board.*

narrow gauge, see *substandard.*

N.A.R.T.B., *National Association of Radio and Television Broadcasters.*

N.A.S.A., *Newspaper Advertising Sales Association.*

national, *adjective* noting or pertaining to products, services, or media distributed in all areas of a nation, usually the U.S.

national advertising, advertising serving a common objective, delivered to a nationwide market.

national advertising rate, a periodical or broadcast advertising rate charged by local media for advertising placed by national or regional advertisers; customarily higher than the rate for local advertising.

National Advertising Review Board, an advertising industry organization which provides self-regulatory review and approval of advertising proposed for use in any medium. Consists of 50 members: 30 advertisers, 10 advertising agencies, and 10 individuals or groups representing the public interest. Abbreviated *N.A.R.B.*

National Advertising Sales Association, an organization, founded in 1907, for the promotion and development of newspaper advertising. Abbreviated *N.A.S.A.*

National Association of Broadcasters, an association, formed in 1922, now the National Association of Radio and Television Broadcasters. Abbreviated *N.A.B.*

National Association of Radio and Television Broadcasters, an association of broadcasting networks and individual stations formed for the purpose of promoting the interests of the broadcasting industry. Abbreviated *N.A.R.T.B.*

National Association of Transportation Advertising, see *Transit Advertising Association.*

National Broadcasting Company, a national radio and television network founded in 1926. Abbreviated *NBC.*

National Business Publications, see *American Business Press.*

National Cable Television Association, an association of cable television operators founded in 1952. Abbreviated *N.C.T.A.*

National Editorial Association, the former name of the National Newspaper Association. Abbreviated *N.E.A.*

National Educational Television, an organization that provides educational tele-

112

vision programs for local stations. Abbreviated *N.E.T.*

National Industrial Advertisers' Association, an association of advertisers, agencies, and communications media formed for the purpose of promoting industrial advertising and marketing. Abbreviated *N.I.A.A.*

National Newspaper Association, an organization of small town newspaper editors, founded in 1885; formerly, National Editorial Association. Abbreviated *N.N.A.*

National Opinion Research Center, an academic research organization at the University of Chicago investigating public opinion; occasionally conducts studies for private clients. Abbreviated *N.O.R.C.*

National Outdoor Advertising Bureau, Inc., an organization, founded in 1916, for the purpose of rendering various outdoor advertising sales and administrative services to advertisers and advertising agencies. Abbreviated *N.O.A.B.*

national plan, a strategy for a nationwide marketing effort.

national rate, the rate charged by a communications medium for advertising nationwide. Also *general rate.*

NBC, *National Broadcasting Company.*

N.B.P., *National Business Publications.*

N.C.H., *Nielsen Clearing House.*

N.C.S., *Nielsen Coverage Service.*

N.C.T.A., *National Cable Television Association.*

N.D.A., *new drug application.*

N.D.I., *Nielsen Drug Index.*

N.E.A., *National Editorial Association.*

near pack, 1. a premium item offered free or for a discounted price with the retail purchase of another product, and positioned close to (but not touching) this product at the point of sale. Also **near pack premium.**
2. a promotion making use of a near pack premium. Also **near pack event.**
3. a receptacle used to hold and display near pack premiums.

negative, *noun* a developed film, photostat, or the like, having the light and dark values reversed; used for printing positives. Also **neg.**

negative correlation, see *correlation.*

neighborhood showing, a closely-spaced group of posters advertising a product or service available in the same neighborhood.

nemo, *noun* 1. a television or radio program fed to a station from outside.
2. the point of origin of such a program.

neon, see *neon light.*

neonized bulletin, an outdoor advertising display using neon tubes.

neon light, a transparent tube filled with an inert gas such as neon which, when electrified, emits a brightly colored light; usually bent tubes are used to form advertising signs. Also **neon lamp, neon tube, neon.**

N.E.T., *National Educational Television.*

net, *noun* 1. any quantity remaining from a gross amount after suitable deductions.
2. see *net cost.*

net advertising circulation, see *net circulation.* Abbreviated *N.A.C.*

net audience, the number of individuals or households reached by a communications medium over a specified period, each of these being counted only once regardless of the number of exposures to the medium.

net circulation, (in outdoor advertising) the total number of persons passing an advertisement within a given period who are facing so as to see it easily. Also *net advertising circulation.* Cf. *gross circulation.*

net controlled circulation, the number of purchased and unpurchased copies of a controlled-circulation publication that are actually distributed to its intended readership.

net cost, 1. the cost of a service provided by an advertising agency aside from the agency commission. Also *net.*
2. an advertising rate after deduction of applicable discounts, the agency commission included. Also *net, net plus.*

net effective distribution, see *effective distribution.*

net orders processed, see *net sales.* Abbreviated *N.O.P.*

net paid circulation, the net circulation of a periodical for which not less than 50% of the newsstand or subscription has been paid; the minimum is that of the Audit Bureau of Circulations.

net plus, see *net cost.*

net profit, the difference between the price obtained by the seller of a good or service, and all costs incurred by the seller for the transaction, including the cost of purchasing or producing the goods or services sold; expressed in terms of dollars or as a percentage of dollar sales, before or after taxes. Cf. *gross margin.*

net rating, the percentage of the total potential audience, to which a television or radio program, commercial, etc., is exposed, as expressed after audience duplication is deducted. Cf. *reach.*

net rating point, a single percent of the total potential audience, unduplicated; used in expressing a net rating. Abbreviated *N.R.P.* Cf. *gross rating point.*

net sales, the quantity of items sold, or the amount received for these items, after all adjustments and returns. Also *net orders processed.*

net unduplicated audience, the actual number of persons who may be exposed to advertising, regardless of how many exposures each person may have. Cf. *gross audience.*

net weekly audience, the number of persons or households that tune in at least once a week to a television or radio program which is aired more than once a week.

net weekly circulation, the number of persons who have tuned in to a specific radio or television station for at least five consecutive minutes in a given week.

network, *noun* 1. (in television or radio) a group of stations associated to broadcast certain programs simultaneously.
2. (in advertising) a group of independent and non-competing agencies that exchange ideas and services. Also *agency network.*

network affiliate, see *affiliate.*

network continuity department, a television or radio network's continuity acceptance department.

network feed, the system of lines, radio waves, etc. by which a network signal is transmitted to various regions and individual stations.

network franchise, see *franchise.*

network identification, identification of a television or radio network, made at the beginning or end of a network broadcast.

networking, *noun* the organization of television or radio stations and programs for the purpose of network broadcasting.

network option time, television or radio station air time at an affiliated station on which its network has the option to place programming. Also **network time.**

new business, prospective or recently acquired clients or accounts purchasing through a single supplier, as an advertising agency or distributor.

new business man, 1. a sales person who is responsible for making initial sales. Also *pioneer salesman.*
2. an advertising agency employee or principal responsible for developing new agency clients.

new drug application, an application for Food and Drug Administration approval to market a new medical remedy product, submitted by a manufacturer with substantion of the safety of the product for human consumption. Abbreviated *N.D.A.*

new product, 1. (in law) a product which has been in distribution, available to its ultimate consumer, for less than six months.
2. a product bearing a new brand name, or a newly introduced flanker item or line extension; occasionally used loosely to refer to an improved product of an existing brand, or a new size.

news, *noun* 1. information of interest to a public which has not been previously available.
adjective 2. noting or pertaining to such information.

newspaper, *noun* a publication, usually a periodical accepting advertising, issued in a manner that provides its public with comprehensive accounts of very recent events. Also *paper.*

Newspaper Advertising Bureau, Inc., an association of U.S., Canadian, and Philippine daily newspapers, founded in 1913 to promote the use of newspapers and supplements as an advertising medium. Abbreviated *N.A.B.*

Newspaper Advertising Executives Association, the former name of the International Newspaper Advertising Executives. Abbreviated *N.A.E.A.*

newspaper syndicate, an organization that sells photographs, columns, comic strips, etc. to a number of newspapers for simultaneous publication.

newsprint, *noun* a soft, coarse wood pulp paper used in printing newspapers.

news release, see *release.*

newsstand circulation, sales of a periodical through retail outlets, rather than by subscription; usually considered with respect to the total number of issues sold in this manner, or the percentage of this total relative to total circulation.

next to reading matter, alongside the editorial section of a periodical rather than surrounded by advertising; used in ordering advertising space.

N.F.I., *Nielsen Food Index.*

N.G., *no good;* a notation used in editing rejections, as of a recording on film or tape.

N.I.A.A., *National Industrial Advertisers' Association.*

nickeltype, *noun* an electrotype nickel plated to increase its durability on press as to number of impressions obtained during a press run.

Nielsen Audience Demographic Report, a publication of the A.C. Nielsen Co. giving data on television audiences, analyzed according to sex, age group, and other demographic characteristics, for each program or time period. Abbreviated *N.A.D.*

Nielsen Clearing House, a division of A.C. Nielsen Co. that administers the processing of store redeemed coupons for contracted clients. Abbreviated *N.C.H.*

Nielsen Company, See *A. C. Nielsen Company.*

Nielsen Coverage Service, a service of the A.C. Nielsen Co. that supplies audience data for television stations on a county-to-county basis. Abbreviated *N.C.S.*

Nielsen Drug Index, a syndicated market research service of the A. C. Nielsen Co. measuring product distribution, inventories, sales, and share of market on a bimonthly basis in drug and mass merchandiser stores, on a nationally projectable basis. Abbreviated *N.D.I.*

Nielsen Food Index, a syndicated market research service of the A. C. Nielsen Co. measuring product distribution, inventories, sales, and share of market on a bimonthly basis in retail food stores, on a nationally projectable basis. Abbreviated *N.F.I.*

Nielsen Market Section Report, a report issued by the A. C. Nielsen Co. of television audience sizes within specific market areas of the United States.

Nielsen rating, a rating of television program audience size used by the A.C. Nielsen Co., stated in terms of gross rating points either for those who have heard the program for the average minute in a quarter hour, or those who have been exposed to the program for five or more minutes (**total audience**).

Nielsen Station Index, a service of the A.C. Nielsen Co. which provides local television station program ratings. Also *Viewers in Profile.* Abbreviated *N.S.I.*

Nielsen Television Area, *obsolete,* see *designated market area.* Abbreviated *N.T.A.*

Nielsen Television Index, a biweekly report of estimated national network television audience sizes, based on Audimeter records collected by the A. C. Nielsen Co. Also *pocketpiece.* Abbreviated *N.T.I.*

night, *noun* see *daypart.*

:90, *noun* a commercial of ninety seconds length; relatively uncommon. Also **ninety.**

ninety-day cancellation, the right to cancel advertising on 90 days' notice, as in outdoor advertising.

nixie, *noun, informal* 1. an undeliverable piece of mail.
2. a small light emitting electronic tube capable of indicating any of several numbers or digits.

N.N.A., *National Newspaper Association.*

N.O.A.B., *National Outdoor Advertising Bureau.*

no answer, (in research) a term used to identify the reason for the absence of data in response to a questionnaire. Abbreviated *N.A.*

no-change rate, a media space or time rate offered to an advertiser who uses the same copy repeatedly.

nominal scale, (in statistics) a scale derived from the arbitrary assignment of numbers to things. Cf. *interval scale, ordinal scale, ratio scale.*

non A.B.C., (of a periodical) not a subscriber to the Audit Bureau of Circulation.

non-directive interview, an interview in which the respondent's answers are unrestricted and unprompted. Cf. *directive interview.*

non-duplication, *noun* the broadcasting of different programs on AM and FM stations owned by the same company, as required by the FCC.

non-food item, an item sold in a grocery but that is more commonly or historically associated with sale in another kind of store. Also **non-food.**

non-parametric, *adjective* (of a statistical procedure) noting or pertaining to a set of statistical techniques not requiring rigid or stringent adherence to distribution assumptions in hypothesis testing.

nonprobability sample, (in statistics) a nonrandom sample of undetermined bias; useless for determining cause-effect relationships or generalization of inferences. Also **non-random sample.**

non-response, *noun* (in research surveys) a missing response to a survey question, or a respondent who, for any reason, fails to respond to a questionnaire in a predetermined sample. Abbreviated *N.R.*

non-response rate, (in research surveys) the percentage of respondents who fail to respond, either totally to a questionnaire in a predetermined sample, or to an individual question in a survey.

non-serial, *noun* a television or radio series that does not present a continuous story, as an audience participation show.

nonstructured interview, an interview in which the respondent talks freely, with little or no guidance as to subject matter.

nonverbal, *adjective* without the use of written or spoken words: *nonverbal communication.*

N.O.P., *net orders processed.*

N.O.R.C., *National Opinion Research Center.*

normal curve, see *normal distribution curve.*

normal distribution, (in statistics) a distribution of the items of a single variable in a random sample that follows the pattern normally to be expected, with the mass of the items clustering around the mean.

normal distribution curve, (in statistics) a symmetrical curve, convex at its center and concave at its ends, reflecting a normal distribution of items in a sample. Also *bell-shaped curve, Gaussian curve, normal curve.*

normal lens, a camera lens with an angle of acceptance of scenes, and consequent perspective, close to that of the unaided human eye.

no-stretch paper, a photographic and photostatic printing paper stabilized to prevent stretching.

not available, a term used to identify the reason for missing data in a table. Abbreviated *N.A.*

notch, *noun* an opening cut into a side or corner of a printing plate or the like in order to receive special type or a cut; differs from a mortise in not being surrounded on all four sides by the original plate. Also *outside mortise.*

noted score, a term used by the research firm of Daniel Starch & Associates to designate the percentage of ad-noters for a certain issue of a certain periodical.

noter, *noun* see *ad-noter.*

no-television market area, a market area whose local television coverage is not adequate to provide majority viewership of home stations.

notification date, (in television or radio) a deadline for notification by an advertiser of his intention to exercise his right to a new or continuing sponsorship.

N.R., *non-response.*

N.R.P., *net rating point.*

N.S.I., *Nielsen Station Index.*

N.T.A., *Nielsen Television Area.*

N.T.I., *Nielsen Television Index.*

null hypothesis, (in statistics) the assumption, for the purposes of an objective inquiry into a circumstance involving the potential presence of chance, that effects in a population are equal.

number, *noun* 1. a musical piece.
2. (in theater, motion pictures and television) a relatively brief act or sketch, especially involving vocal music.

nut, *noun* 1. the total cost of complete sponsorship of a television or radio show.
2. see *quad.*

O

O.A.A.A., *Outdoor Advertising Association of America, Inc.*

O. and O., a broadcasting station owned and operated by a network.

O.A.T., *on-air test.*

O.B.C., *outside back cover;* used in ordering periodical advertising space.

objective, *noun* 1. a goal of a business firm or process, usually for a stated period of time.
adjective 2. noting or pertaining to an attitude of dispassionate, fair-minded evaluation; usually required of the best journalism and advertising agency service.

objective-and-task method, a method for deriving a marketing budget which sets total appropriations at that level judged adequate to cover the cost of those tasks which will, when performed, allow attainment of objectives.

objective research, see *quantitative research.*

oblong, *noun* a book with an oblong format; width greater than depth or binding edge.

observational method, any behavior research method that uses observation of subjects' actions rather than questioning to derive findings.

obtained score, the actual percentage of respondents who prove recall of a printed advertisement; the term is that of Gallup and Robinson.

O.C., *on camera.*

occasion, *noun* a television or radio time interval intended or used for a commercial announcement. Also *commercial occasion.*

occupational classification, classification of persons, e.g., periodical subscribers, in terms of their business, profession, or position within a company.

octavo, *noun* a book bound with a number of signatures of sixteen pages each; the commonest form of book. Abbreviated *8vo.*

O.F.C., *outside front cover;* used in ordering such a periodical advertising space, where available.

off, *adjective, adverb* (in theater, motion pictures, or television) away from the scene visible to the audience. Also *offstage.*

off air, see *off the air.*

off camera, outside the image field of a motion picture or television camera.

off camera announcer, (in motion pictures and television) an announcer whose voice is heard but who does not appear on camera. Cf. *off screen announcer.*

off card, (of television or radio time) at a special rate, not shown on a rate card.

offensive spending, purchase of advertising or other marketing support intended to expand one's sales. Cf. *defensive spending.*

off invoice, *noun* a deduction from an invoice from a manufacturer or wholesaler to a retailer made in exchange for the retailer's promotional efforts. Also **off invoice allowance**.

off label, 1. a special reduced retail price marked over the regular label of an item.

Cf. *price pack.*
2. an inferior grade of a brand, discount priced and specially labeled.

off mike, (of a sound) directed away from a microphone, as to give an effect of distance. Cf. *on mike.*

off scene, not visible to an audience.

off screen announcer, an announcer in a television program who is heard but not seen. Cf. *off camera announcer.*

offset, *noun* 1. any planographic printing process in which the printing surface transfers the image to a rubber surfaced roller called a blanket, which in turn does the actual printing. Also *offset lithography.*
2. an unwanted deposit of ink from the surface of a freshly printed sheet to the back of a sheet placed on top of it. Often prevented by inserting a non-printed slip sheet between printed sheets.

offset paper, a paper designed for use in offset printing; available coated or uncoated, in a variety of finishes.

offset scrapbook, a book of camera ready copy in a scrapbook format, reproduced for promotional purposes.

off shelf display, a display of merchandise in a store in a location other than the customary position for such merchandise on the store's shelves.

off the air, (in television or radio) noting or pertaining to material not broadcast, or facilities not used in the process of broadcasting. Also *off air.*

oil paint, a paint using oil, often linseed oil, as a vehicle in which to suspend pigment. Also **oil, oils.**

Old English, a black letter display type.

old-line wholesaler, a wholesaler who sells and delivers merchandise only, having no affiliates and offering no services.

OK w.c., *okay with corrections;* used in signed approvals of art, keyline, or proof material where corrections (usually minor) have been noted as needed.

oldstyle, *noun* 1. any Roman type in which all strokes are approximately even and in which serifs are slightly slanted.
adjective 2. noting or pertaining to any face of type characters, some portions of which come below the base line. Also **old style.**

oleo, *noun* (in television) a painted backdrop.

omnidirectional microphone, a device for converting sounds received from a 360° angle into electrical impulses in an audio system. Also **omni mike.**

on air test, a test of a commercial or program that uses a real broadcast of the test material on television or radio as the stimulus for a measurable audience response, such as recall, attitude or purchase interest change, interest, or audience size. Abbreviated *O.A.T.*

on camera, actually picked up, as by a motion picture or television camera. Abbreviated *O.C.*

on the air, (in television or radio) noting or pertaining to material which is broadcast, or facilities which are in the process of broadcasting. Also **on air, on.**

one-cent sale, a sale of two retail items for the regular price of one, plus one cent.

one-sheet poster, a poster consisting of a single sheet 28" by 42" or 30" by 46" used especially on subway and railroad station platforms.

one-shot, *noun* 1. a motion picture or television shot of a single subject only.
2. a television drama requiring one program only.
3. see *special.*

one-time rate, the rate charged for a single, unrepeated advertisement. Also *open rate, transient rate.*

:120, *noun* a commercial of one hundred twenty seconds length; rare. Also **one twenty.**

one way mirror, a glass partition used to separate viewers such as sponsors or researchers from research respondents in an adjacent room; by being only partially reflectorized, such a partition serves to transmit light intact into the darker of the two rooms, while reflecting light as a mirror back into the brighter room.

one-way screen, a halftone screen with lines running in one direction only instead of the customary two.

onionskin, *noun* a thin, hard-finished, translucent paper, used for tracings and carbon copies.

on mike, (of a sound) directed toward a microphone, as is customary. Cf. *off mike.*

on-pack, *noun* a piece of merchandise, premium, advertising matter, coupon, etc., attached to or part of the exterior of a product package.

on-pack premium, a premium affixed in some manner to the exterior of a product's package.

on-premises bakery, a bakery with sales facilities in a supermarket.

on speculation, without the obligation of payment; advertising may be prepared on speculation in the hope that a client will approve it. Also **on spec,** *spec.*

on the button, see *on the nose.*

on the line, (of a television image) acceptable for transmission.

on the log, entered in a log, as a log of television or radio broadcasts.

on the nose, perfect, as the focus of a television camera or the timing of a radio program. Also *on the button.*

O.O.T., (in television or radio) *out of town.*

opacity, *noun* a characteristic of paper used for printing, indicated by the degree to which print on one face shows through on the reverse side.

opaque, *verb* to block out areas of a photographic transparency in order to eliminate the details in such areas from a photographic print or printing plate.

opaque projector, a projector which can cast enlarged images of opaque, flat, still material.

open, *noun* see *opening billboard.*

open distribution, distribution of a product within a certain territory by any dealer choosing to carry it. Cf. *exclusive distribution.*

open end, 1. a termination to a television or radio program that is not determined by scheduling.
2. a conclusion to a network program or commercial that is left blank for local advertising.

open-end diary, (in research) a diary without limited choices for the making of entries. Cf. *closed-end diary.*

open-end question, an interview question which a respondent may answer as he pleases, without being confined to a predetermined choice.

open-end transcription, 1. a recorded television or radio program, usually syndicated, with free time for local announcements.
2. a recorded commercial with free time for a local announcement.

121

open face, a category of display type having open letters defined with strokes of uneven thickness that give a three dimensional effect. Cf. *in-line, outline.*

opening billboard, an introduction to a television or radio show; usually includes a mention of the sponsors. Also *open.*

open left, begin a shot with the subject to the extreme left; a direction sometimes given to a motion picture or television cameraman.

open rate, 1. the highest rate for advertising charged by a medium. Also *base rate, card rate.*
2. see *one-time rate.*

open right, begin a shot with the subject to the extreme right; a direction sometimes given to a motion picture or television cameraman.

open-side envelope, an envelope with a longitudinal flap.

operating expenses, all expenses incurred in keeping a business in operation under normal conditions.

operations research, (in marketing) the application of such mathematical methods as models to a system of variables, to project probable changes in the system resulting from changes in one or more variables. Abbreviated *O.R.*

operator, *noun* one who manages a business on a day-to-day basis.

opinion leader, any person who strongly influences the opinions or attitudes of others. Cf. *two-step-flow theory.*

Opinion Research Corporation, a research firm in Princeton, N.J., that conducts a variety of projects useful to business with relation to public, stockholder, and employee attitudes; issues the Public Opinion Index for Industry, a periodical report. Abbreviated *O.R.C.*

opportunity of exposure, the amount of reasonable expectation that an advertisement will be seen or heard.

Optak, *noun, trademark* a planographic process using an inked gelatin plate to which the image is transferred photographically, with no further chemical or mechanical action. Formerly *Aquatone.*

optical, *noun* 1. any special visual effect done with a camera or other piece of motion picture or television equipment. Also **optical effect.**
2. see *optical answer print.*

optical answer print, a print of a commercial in which all color corrections and optical effects have been incorporated; used to obtain final approvals of a commercial production. Also *optical.*

optical center, the point on a page upon which a reader's eye naturally falls when turned to the page; slightly above the geometrical center.

option time, television or radio station time reserved by, or available on demand to, a network or the station itself.

optical track, a sound track recorded by optical means on the margin of motion picture film of at least 16 mm. width. Cf. *magnetic track.*

O.R., *operations research.*

orange goods, goods that are consumed and replaced at moderate rates; usually are in fairly broad distribution, require moderate service, and have a moderate to good gross margin (e.g., dress clothing). Cf. *red goods, yellow goods.*

orbit, *verb* (of a television or radio station) to schedule an advertiser's announcements for a variety of programs or time periods.

O.R.C., *Opinion Research Corporation.*

order, *noun* 1. a prospect's agreement to make a purchase.

2. a seller's document used to record and implement the terms of a purchase.
3. a service package, product, or group of products exchanged in a sales transaction.

order book, a catalogue used as a reference in ordering merchandise.

order form, a printed, itemized list used for recording orders of merchandise.

order letter, a preliminary letter of agreement between an advertising buyer and a communications medium specifying terms of purchase of advertising space or time; sent by the buyer.

order-process department, a department of a television or radio network that prepares cost estimates and initiates contracts for advertisers.

ordinal scale, (in statistics) a measurement scale with unknown and unequal intervals between points, and no definite zero point. Cf. *interval scale, nominal scale, ratio scale.*

ordinate, *noun* (in mathematics) the vertical coordinate of a graph; the y-axis. Cf. *abscissa.*

organization chart, a table, usually of lines and boxes, used to depict lines of reporting and authority, subordinate to superior, in a hierarchical organization.

organization marketing, public relations activities of a firm in service of its marketing objectives.

organizer, *noun* 1. a printed sheet, presenting the main points of a salesman's argument, and around which his argument is organized.
2. the binder in which such sheets are carried.

original, *noun* 1. camera copy, as a photograph, drawing, painting, etc., for photomechanical reproduction. Also *finished art.*
2. the first photoengraving or film reproduction made from camera copy, as opposed to electrotypes or other duplicate materials made from such copy.

original purchase unit, (in readership surveys) an actual purchase of or subscription to a periodical.

original tape, a videotape accepted for transmission or reproduction.

originate, *verb* (of a television or radio station) to produce and transmit a program or other material, especially when fed to other stations.

origination point, see *feed point.*

orthicon, *noun* see *image orthicon.*

O.T.C., *over the counter.*

O.T.O., *one time only;* used to specify a single television or radio program or commercial announcement.

outdoor advertising, advertising outdoors, as on billboards, posters, or signs. Also **outdoor.**

Outdoor Advertising Association of America, Inc., an organization of outdoor advertising plant operators, founded in 1891, for the purpose of maintaining industry-wide standards and for furnishing its members with information and services. Abbreviated *O.A.A.A.*

outdoor plant, see *plant.*

outdoor service, maintenance of and repairs to outdoor advertising.

outdoor space buyer, an advertising agency employee who is responsible for buying outdoor advertising space.

outline, *noun* any display type having open letters defined with strokes of even thickness. Cf. *inline, openface.*

outline halftone, (in printing) a halftone of a subject with the background removed. Also *silhouette halftone.*

out-of-focus, *noun* (in photography, motion pictures, or television) the condition of a subject in a camera's image when the lens has not been adjusted to include the subject within its focused depth of field.

out-of-focus dissolve, (in motion pictures or television) a dissolve in which the camera taking one shot is slowly put out of focus, after which the camera for the next shot is slowly brought into focus. Also *defocusing.*

out-of-home audience, the portion of a television or radio audience that is away from home when exposed to a certain program or commercial.

out-of-market traffic, (in outdoor advertising) traffic originating beyond the area in which an outdoor advertising plant operates.

out of pocket, noting or pertaining to costs for services or merchandise provided to an organization by an outside supplier, rather than being developed by the organization's own production capability.

out of stock, (of something sold) not presently available, especially for retail sale, because of inadequate supply, or insufficient distribution support.

out of sync, (in television and motion pictures) a lack of synchronization between video action and audio.

out period, see *hiatus.*

output, *noun* 1. information supplied by a computer. Cf *input.*
2. the production of an organization, plant, or person.

outsert, *noun* a piece of printed material attached to, rather than inserted into, a package. Also *package outsert.* Cf. *package insert.*

outside mortise, see *notch.*

outtake, *noun* (in motion pictures) one of several takes of the same shot, usually one not planned for use in the final film. Also *trim.*

over and under, an amount of money or stock allowed as a discrepancy when calculating cash-register receipts, taking inventory, etc., in a store; allows for error, breakage, price changes, etc.

overcommercialization, *noun* (in television or radio) clutter resulting from scheduling of too many commercials.

overhang, *noun* see *extended cover.*

overlap, *noun* 1. (in motion pictures or television) a period in which two successive images appear together during a lap dissolve or the like.
2. see *extended cover.*

overlapping circulation, circulation to the same subscribers of two or more periodicals under consideration. Cf. *duplication.*

overlay, *noun* 1. any sheet, image, printed matter, etc. superimposed on an existing design or piece of art work.
2. see *snipe.*
3. a promotional theme structure lending unity to the elements of a promotion effort.

overmatter, *noun* see *leftover matter.*

overnight, *noun* a report on television program audience size delivered the day following broadcast.

overprinting, *noun* the superimposition of additional printed matter over matter already printed, usually by means of a screen or different transparent color to prevent the underlying matter from being obscured. Cf. *double print.*

overrun, *noun* 1. a number of additional copies of a magazine article, advertising page, collateral piece, etc., printed in ex-

cess of those required for general circulation, distribution or quantity ordered.
2. excessive production of items, creating a manufacturer's overstock.

overset matter, see *leftover matter.*

overshoot, *verb* (of a motion picture or television camera) to shoot an area beyond the limits of a set by accident.

overstock, *noun* inventory in excess of a supplier's needs, usually sold at a discount.

over the counter, see *proprietary pharmaceutical.* Abbreviated *O.T.C.*

overwire hanger, see *banner.*

Oxberry, *noun, trademark* (in motion pictures) a camera stand used to produce elaborate, multi-level animation effects.

Ozalid, *noun, trademark* 1. a process for reproducing drawings or the like on a sensitized paper with the use of ammonia vapor.
2. a black-on-white print made by this process.

ozzie, *noun* a pattern of concentric rings created with a cucalorus.

P

P., *page.* Also **p.**

P.A.A.A., *Premium Advertising Association of America, Inc.*

package, *noun* 1. a television or radio show or series ready for broadcast, offered to an advertiser, usually for a lump sum.
2. a television or radio program owned by a packager.
3. a combination of television or radio programs or commercial spots offered together to an advertiser, usually at a discount, by a network, or station. Also *plan, package plan.*
4. the exterior appearance of a single unit of a product.

package band, a promotion offer or other announcement printed on a band wrapped around a retail package.

package cut, an advertising illustration showing a package or carton, usually provided by manufacturer's sales representatives to cooperating distributors for retail advertising.

package design, 1. a marketing services professional specialty, consisting of the art and study of creating effective product packages.
2. the graphic design employed on a package for a unit of product.

packaged goods, products wrapped or packaged by the manufacturer, especially small items used broadly and frequently consumed; typically sold through food, drug, and mass merchandiser retail stores.

package enclosure, a premium, or less accurately, a brochure, enclosed in a package. Cf. *package insert, in-pack premium.*

package flat, see *flat.*

package insert, a piece of advertising or promotion matter placed in a package. Cf. *outsert, package enclosure.*

package outsert, see *outsert.*

package plan, see *package.*

packager, *noun* 1. an organization that owns television or radio programs offered to networks or stations for sale.
2. a person or organization that packages products, for a fee or sale. Also *packer.* Cf. *processor.*

package rate, see *plan rate.*

packer, *noun* 1. see *packager.*
2. a person or organization that packages meat products.

packer's label, a retail goods label owned by a manufacturer or packer.

pad, *verb* to add material to a commercial or television or radio program only so that it does not end too soon, or sound too empty of content.

page, *noun* 1. (in publication space buying) the printed area of a page; used as a basic space unit in advertising and advertising rate calculations.
verb 2. to turn pages, as *page through.*

page proof, a printer's proof of a completed page, with or without illustrations in place.

page size, (in publication advertising) the size of a full-page, nonbleed advertisement.

painted bulletin, a billboard on which the advertising message and illustration is painted directly. Also *bulletin.* Cf. *poster panel.*

painted display, an advertisement on a painted bulletin.

painter's guide, usually a line rendering with color overlays indicating the forms and colors for a painted bulletin.

paired comparison, (in statistics) a comparison of a number of things that have a common point or points of similarity, i.e., along one dimension, each thing being compared with, and rated with regard to, all the others on a two-by-two basis.

pallet, *noun* a flat platform used for loading, moving, and storing stacked containers, usually in warehouses; the pallet with its load is lifted and moved by forklift trucks or crane slings.

palletize, *verb* to store and move freight on pallets.

pan, *verb* 1. (in motion pictures or television) to make a shot in which the camera moves in a horizontal or vertical arc; to make a panoramic shot.
adjective 2. (of theater, motion picture or television scenes or sets) to a panorama or panoramic shot.
3. (of film) see *panchromatic*.

panchromatic, *adjective* (of black and white film) registering all visible colors in gray values falling between white and black. Also *pan*.

P and H, see *postage and handling charge*. Also **P&H**.

P and W, *pension and welfare*. Also **P&W**.

panel, *noun* 1. a permanent group of respondents for investigations of consumer opinions, attitudes, reactions, etc.
2. an outdoor advertising display board, whether regular or illuminated, usually of billboard size.

pan master, a fine-grained panchromatic black and white film or slide made from a color original, used as the source for subsequent printing.

pan shot, (in motion pictures or television) a shot in which the camera pans a scene. Also **panoramic shot**.

pantograph, *noun* a mechanical device for reproducing a line figure when the figure is traced with a stylus.

pantry audit, a consumer research survey of items actually found in respondent's homes. Also **pantry inventory, pantry check**.

paper, *noun* 1. a thin, light material usually made from wood fibers, whose surfaces are intended to carry writings or print.
2. a document written or printed on such a material.
3. see *newspaper*.
4. (informal) money or financing for credit.
verb 5. to use paper to cover a surface or wrap an object.
papery, *adj*.

paperboard, *noun* any heavy paper-like material made from wood pulp, waste paper, or straw.

papier-maché, *noun* a mixture of wood and paper fibers with a paste of clay and rosin, molded into various forms; used for making matrixes.

parallel location, location of an outdoor advertisement parallel to a street or road, or with both ends within six feet of a line parallel to a street or road.

parameter, *noun* (in research and statistics) a statistical characteristic of a population which is subjected to measurement among a random sample of the population and subsequent analysis in research.
parametric, *adj*.

parent store, a retail store that operates a number of branch stores.

partial self-liquidator, see *semi-liquidator*.

partial sponsorship, sponsorship of a television or radio program by several advertisers, each having a separate section. Also *segment sponsorship.* Cf. *magazine concept.*

participating announcement, (in television or radio) a commercial from one of several sponsors of a program.

participation, *noun* a commercial included in a program in which several sponsors participate. Also **participation announcement.**

participation program, 1. a television or radio program with a number of co-sponsors.
2. see *audience-participation program.*

part-time station, a television or radio station restricted to a limited number of hours. Cf. *limited-time station.*

pass-along audience, the number of persons who receive a periodical from the original subscriber or purchaser; does not include others in the homes of such persons. Also **pass-along readers, pass-along circulation, secondary readership.**

pastel, *noun* 1. a light colored chalk-like stick used in a drawing; such drawings require a fixative.
2. such sticks as an artistic medium.

pasteup, *noun* an assemblage of type proofs, art work, etc. pasted on paperboard, used for reproduction by an engraver. Also *mechanical.*

P.A. system, see *public-address system.*

P.A.T., *Product Acceptance Test.*

patch, *noun* a section of a printing plate or keyline corrected or revised by new material stripped in or pasted over the original material.

patent, *noun* 1. a grant by a government of exclusive right to produce, or to license the production of, an invention for a certain period; in the U.S. the period is 17 years.
verb 2. to obtain this right with regard to an invention.
adjective 3. noting or pertaining to the body of law covering such protections, which include trademarks and product designs.

patent medicine, see *proprietary pharmaceutical.*

patronage dividend, a check or credit voucher from a wholesaler to a retailer, made as part of a profit-sharing system.

patronage rebate, a check or credit voucher from a wholesaler to a retailer as a credit for large-quantity purchases or as a promotion allowance.

pattern plate, 1. a reinforced electrotype plate made from original engravings or other electrotype plates.
2. a molding plate used as a master for the reproduction of other printing plates.

payback, *noun* see *payout.*

payload, *noun* 1. any freight or cargo that will bring revenue to the carrier.
2. merchandise returned to a wholesaler by way of a truck primarily engaged in distributing merchandise to retailers; so called because the return trip is, in a sense, productive.

payout, *noun* 1. a profit return on an investment, especially an investment of marketing expenditures. Also **payback.** Cf. *investment spending.*
2. see *breakeven point.*
pay out, *v.* 3. to return such a profit.

pay television, home television programming for which the viewer pays, usually by the program or by the month; distributed by cable or broadcast decoder. Also *premium television.*

P.B.S., *Public Broadcasting Service.*

P.C.A., *Program Cumulative Audiences.*

P.D., *public domain.*

P.D.T., *Pacific Daylight Time;* see *time zone.*

P.E., *printer's error.*

pedestal, *noun* a motion picture or television camera mount on which the camera rests directly, without being cantilevered from a boom.

penalty cost, the differential efficiency of media coverage provided by national media versus the equivalent local media; a factor in preparing media plan translations for test markets.

pencil test, (in motion pictures) a rough version of an animated sequence prepared prior to the rendering of finished artwork.

penetration, *noun* 1. the effectiveness of advertising in reaching and persuading the public.
2. the percentage of homes in a geographical area that own a given product, such as a television or radio set.

penny-saver, *noun* an envelope mailed third class with a sealed top flap but an ungummed end flap permitting postal inspection. Also *postage-saver.*

pension and welfare, a portion of a talent residual returned to the talent union's pension and insurance benefit investment trust. Abbreviated *P and W.*

percentage-of-sales method, a method for determining marketing budgets based on a predetermined percentage rate of spending relative to anticipated dollar sales.

percent composition, see *audience profile.*

perception, *noun* the ability of the human mind to receive sensory impressions and give them meaningful interconnection and interpretation.

perceptual mapping, see *connotative mapping.*

perceptual mapping study, see *market mapping study.*

per diem, a cost, allowance, or fee calculated on a daily basis, as for services or travel and entertainment expenses.

perfect binding, a form of binding in which the binding edge of signatures are scuffed and then glued to the backbone or binding edge of a periodical or book, thus eliminating wire staples.

perforate, *verb* to pierce a sheet or multiple sheets with small, closely-spaced dots or slits to facilitate tearing, as in printed advertising pieces having reply forms, coupons, etc.

performance allowance, a rebate of a portion of the purchase price of goods provided to retailers who agree to perform cooperative merchandising services such as advertising or display; paid after the retailer provides proof of his efforts.

performing-rights society, an organization of composers, authors, publishers, etc. that licenses performances on behalf of its members.

per inquiry advertising, advertising for which the proprietor of a communications medium is paid according to the number of inquiries or completed sales that result. Abbreviated *P.I.*

periodical, *noun* a publication that appears at regular intervals, as a newspaper or magazine.

Periodical Publishers' Association, an organization, founded in 1900, for the purpose of aiding good relations within the periodical publishing industry and for checking the credit standing of advertising agencies. Abbreviated *P.P.A.*

perishable, *adjective* (of food) readily deteriorated under normal conditions of atmosphere and temperature.

personal influence, all patterns of personal, face-to-face interactions of prospects which bear directly on their purchase decision; includes personal sales contacts, opinion leader influences, and word-of-mouth advertising.

personal interview method, a research method in which a sample of respondents are interviewed individually, face-to-face.

personality, *noun* 1. see *format*.
2. a person selected for use in an advertisement due to the public recognition and reputation he enjoys.

personal sales, sales made on the basis of a face-to-face contact, personal telephone call, personal letter, etc., from a salesperson to a prospect.

person marketing, activities directed to modify public attitudes and behavior regarding a specific person, such as a political candidate, celebrity, or prospect for a position.

persons using television, a measure of audience size that refers to the total number of persons viewing television at those times reported. Also **persons viewing television.** Abbreviated *P.U.T.*

perspective, *noun* 1. the illusion of depth created in a flat visual presentation such as a picture, stage set, or moving image, by use of a system of vanishing points or lines to which depicted objects or lines regularly diminish or converge as receding.
2. (in audio) the effect of space given by the placing of sound sources and microphones.

persuasiveness, *noun* the ability of advertising to influence audience or prospect attitudes, especially purchase intent, in the manner intended by the advertiser. Cf. *believability*.

phantom section, a drawing or rendering showing the exterior of an object as if it were transparent, so as to reveal interior detailing. Also *ghosted view*.

phosphor, *noun* a substance in the screen of a color television receiver's picture tube which emits light of a single color when scanned by the tube's electron beam.

photoboard, *noun* a set of still photographs made from a television commercial, accompanied by the script, and printed on a single sheet of paper; used primarily for record-keeping or merchandising purposes.

photocomposition, *noun* non-metal typographic machine composition using characters on photographic grids to produce letterform images on photographic film or paper.

photocopy, *noun* 1. a photographic copy made directly on sensitized paper, especially automatically.
verb 2. to make such a copy.

photoengraving, *noun* 1. the process of making letterpress printing plates by photochemical means.
2. a picture printed from a plate made by such a process.

photogelatin process, a collotype process for reproducing black and white or color photographs, without halftone screens.

photogenic, *adjective* noting or pertaining to physical characteristics, especially facial features, which allow a person to be an attractive photographic subject. Cf. *telegenic*.

photogram, *noun* a positive photographic print of objects in silhouette form made by placing the objects on the paper and exposing it to light.

photograph, *noun* 1. a fixed, two-dimensional image registered on a light sensitive surface, usually of paper or film.
verb 2. to register such an image.

photography, *noun* the art of registering and fixing visual images by means of a camera on light-sensitive photographic film.

photogravure, *noun* 1. a gravure printing process using a photochemical etching method.
2. a print made from this process.

photolettering, *noun* a technique for supplying reproducible display copy in the form of a photographic positive of letters developed on film or paper; the letters are enlarged to the desired size in printing the positive.

photomatic, *noun* a television commercial produced from filming a sequence of still photographs; usually used only for testing purposes. Cf. *animatic.*

photomontage, *noun* a single photographic print composed of portions of other photos or pictures. Also *montage.*

photo-offset printing, lithographic printing using plates prepared by a photochemical process.

Photopolymer, a classification of plastic material capable of receiving an image from film when exposed to light; the term is now applied to a family of lightweight, flexible plates consisting of a photopolymer surface bonded to a backing of thin metal or inert plastic. Used for both direct printing and for molding duplicate reproduction products, such as newspaper mats.

photoprint, *noun* a photographic print; a positive on paper or the like.

photo proof, see *repro proof.*

Photostat, *noun, trademark* 1. a type of high contrast photographic negative or positive made on paper.
verb 2. to copy as a Photostat. Also *stat.*

physical distribution, marketing activities intended to move products physically from manufacturer to purchaser.

physical inventory, a record of saleable stock on hand at a given time, with its sale or replacement value.

physical plant, see *plant.*

P.I., *per inquiry advertising.*

pi, *noun* (in printing) an accidental mixing or scrambling of metal type characters or slugs. Also *pied type.*

P.I.B., *Publishers' Information Bureau, Inc.*

pica, *noun* (in printing) 1. a unit of type height equal to one sixth of an inch.
2. any type font one pica, or twelve points, high.
3. a typewriter font one pica deep and with ten characters per inch of breadth.
4. a unit of width measure one sixth of an inch as in newspaper column widths.

pick it up, respond to cues more quickly; an instruction to a performer.

pickup, *noun* 1. the element of a television camera that converts visual images into electrical signals.
2. the stylus, cartridge, arm, or head of a phonographic record player or audio tape player that converts signals from a disc or tape into electrical signals in an audio system.
3. the quality of the picture and sound picked up from a performance.
4. merchandise acquired by one wholesaler from another to replenish his own supply.
5. see *pickup material.*

pick up, 1. to receive an image or sound, or a recorded signal, from a transmission or recording.
2. to respond to one's cue in a theatrical performance or the like.
3. to use pickup material in an advertisement.

131

pickup material, advertising material created for one advertisement and used in some form in a different advertisement. Also *pickup*.

picture-line standard, the standard number of horizontal electronic scanning lines on a television image; in the United States, 525.

picture tube, an electronic tube in a television receiver that converts electrical impulses into visible images.

piece count, a count of the number of boxes or other containers delivered to a retailer rather than the number of actual items within the boxes, or cases.

pied type, see *pi*.

piggyback, *noun* (in television or radio) a presentation of two unrelated commercials by the same sponsor one immediately after the other; the commercial occasion for such a paired announcement is usually purchased as a single unit.

piggyback commercial, a commercial used in a piggyback configuration. Also *split commercial*.

piggyback coupon, (in periodical publishing) a pop-up coupon so inserted as to lie across advertising of other advertisers on the page following.

pigment, *noun* the coloring substance in paint, ink, etc.

pilot, *noun* (in television or radio) a sample show from a proposed series, used as a demonstration to prospective sponsors.

pilot study, a small-scale trial research study, as of consumer attitudes, conducted to provide a basis for judging the promise of a large-scale survey on the same lines. Also **pilot survey**.

pioneer salesman, see *new business man, missionary salesman*.

pipeline, *noun* the amount of a product which a manufacturer has sold but that has not yet been purchased by consumers; hence, wholesaler and retailer inventories.

Pipeline, Inc., a marketing research firm selling syndicated estimates of clients' product movement through drug wholesalers.

pitch, *noun* 1. *informal* a salesman's presentation to a prospect, intended to solicit an order.
2. *informal* an advertising agency presentation to a new business prospect.
3. a musical note used to tune a musical instrument or musical group into harmony.

pix, *noun, informal* pictures, especially photographic prints.

plan, *noun* 1. see *marketing plan*.
2. see *strategy*.
3. see *package*.

planogram, *noun* a graphic depiction of the ideal manner in which a product or product category's retail shelves should be stocked by item; typically prepared by manufacturers for use by their sales forces.

planography, *noun* any printing technique, e.g., lithography, in which the printing surface is flush with the non-printing surface; differs from letterpress, in which the printing surface is raised, and intaglio printing, in which the printing image is below the surface.

plan rate, the advertising rate offered by a medium for a television or radio package plan; always lower than card rate. Also *package rate*.

plans board, an advertising agency management committee for review of creative strategies, and approval of proposed advertisements.

plans committee, a management committee or organization for determining company policy and making long range general plans for sales, advertising, expansion, etc.

plant, *noun* 1. see *plant operator.*
2. the outdoor structures in an area operated by such an organization. Also *outdoor plant.*
3. the physical site and furnishings of an enterprise. Also *physical plant.*
4. a production facility, as a factory.

plant operator, 1. a company that owns and maintains outdoor advertising facilities. Also *plant.*
2. a person who manages a production facility.

plastic plate, a letterpress plate formed of plastic with raised characters, used for making castings rather than for printing; supplied to a newspaper by a mat service in place of a matrix. Also **plastic.**

plate, *noun* 1. a flat sheet of material, flexible or rigid, made of metal or plastic, whose surface will accept an image capable of being reproduced by ink onto another surface, such as paper.
2. a book illustration, especially a large and relatively important one.

plated stock, high gloss, smooth paper that has been pressed between polished metal sheets.

platen, *noun* 1. any element in a printing press that presses the sheet to be printed against the printing surface.
2. the roller of a typewriter.

plate size, the size of a printed advertisement; must take into account the publication's mechanical requirements and other restrictions.

platter, *noun, informal* a phonographic record.

play, *verb* 1. to operate a device which can recreate recorded signals, as on records, tape, or film.
2. to perform a dramatic role.
3. to perform a musical piece, or on a musical instrument.

noun 4. a dramatic composition, or a stage performance of same.

playback, *noun* 1. an audition of an audio or video recording, as for editing or criticism, usually soon after it is made.
2. the set of answers given by respondents to interviewer questions in a survey. Also *protocol.*

plow-back method, a method for determining an advertising appropriation based on the use of all anticipated net profits from a specific period; used especially in aggressive advertising of new products. Cf. *investment spending.*

plug, *noun* 1. a television or radio commercial.
2. a free on-air mention of a product, service, or personality that has advertising value.

ply, *noun* 1. a thin layer in a sheet of material built up of such layers.
2. a unit of thickness used in specifying Bristol board and other heavy papers or cardboards.

P.M., *noun* 1. see *push money.*
2. *informal* a newspaper published only in afternoon editions.

P.M.A., *primary marketing area.*

P.M.B., *Print Measurement Bureau.*

P.N.R., *proved name registration.*

pocketpiece, *noun, informal* see *Nielsen Television Index.*

point, *noun* 1. a unit used in measuring the height of printing type; in the U.S., equal to one-twelfth of a pica or one seventy-second of an inch.
2. a measure of cardboard thickness, equal to one one-thousandth of an inch.
3. see *gross rating point.*
4. a period used as a punctuation mark, as in "decimal point."

133

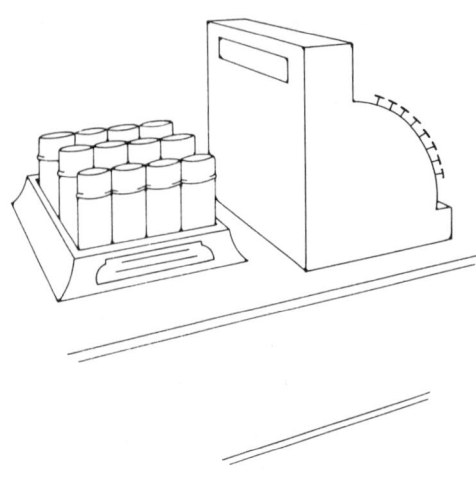

POINT OF PURCHASE

point-of-purchase, the place at which a customer encounters a retail item that he may buy. Also *point-of-sale*.

Point-of-Purchase Advertising Institute, Inc., a nonprofit organization, founded in 1938, of makers of point-of-purchase advertising displays, and of the advertisers and retailers who use them. Abbreviated *P.O.P.A.I.*

point-of-sale, see *point-of-purchase*.

pole piece, an advertising display in a retail store, mounted on a pole for greater visibility. Also *spectacular*.

political advertising, the process of use of advertisements to influence elections and government, by persuading voters and government officials to behave voluntarily in a recommended manner.

Pollard-Alling, *noun, trademark* a brand of addressing machine printing through an inked ribbon with aluminum plates.

polyphase method, an audience measurement method in which listeners, after being favorably tested for adequate ability to recall television or radio programs, are asked to maintain diaries on their broadcast media program selections.

pony spread, a periodical page arrangement in which an advertisement occupies a portion of each of two facing pages. Also *junior spread*.

pony unit, a reduced size version of a standard advertisement. Also *junior unit*.

pool, *noun* see *commercial pool*.

pool car, a railroad freight car carrying a single brand of merchandise for more than one retailer in an area.

pool out, to develop one or more commercials for use in a commercial pool.
pool-out, *n.* a commercial so developed.

pool partner, a commercial which is used in a commercial pool; usually in reference to a two commercial pool, or a newly developed commercial.

P.O.P., *noun* display material used at the point of purchase.

P.O.P.A.I., *Point-of-Purchase Advertising Institute*.

pop-in, *noun* (in television or radio) a brief commercial making one point about something advertised; a program may have several.

pop-off, *noun* (in television) a sudden departure of something from on camera to off camera in a show.

pop-on, *noun* (in television) a sudden emergence of something on camera in a show.

population, *noun* (in statistics) the whole number of persons or things under study; usually represented by a sample. Also *universe*.

pop-up, *noun* a special die-cut folder so made that when opened part of it rises from the center fold.

pop-up coupon, a tear-off perforated coupon stitched into the binding of a periodical as a separate, small space unit. Also *preclipped coupon.*

portfolio test, a test of periodical advertising using a dummy magazine which contains the advertising being tested as well as other advertising that is used as control.

position, *noun* 1. (in marketing strategy) the consumer perception of a product's or service's benefit or benefits, in comparison to its competition, which its manufacturer attempts to create and encourage. Also **positioning,** *product position.*
2. the placement of an advertisement in a publication in terms of page number, side, etc., or of a commercial in a program. Also **positioning.**
position, *v.*

position request, a request by an advertiser for a certain location in a periodical or on a television or radio program, if available; has less force than a positive demand for a preferred position.

positive, *noun* a photographic image in which the tonal values imitate those of the subject, light for light and dark for dark. Also **pos.** Cf. *negative.*

positive correlation, see *correlation.*

post, *noun* 1. (in research) the condition of a subject or respondent in an experiment after a test treatment has been applied. Also *post-test.* Cf. *pre.*
adjective 2. noting or pertaining to such a condition.

postage and handling charge, a charge presumably made to cover the costs of postal delivery and preparation for such shipment of an order made by mail; made in addition to the purchase price of the item. Abbreviated *P and H.*

postage-saver, see *penny-saver.*

postal card, a card sold by the U.S. Postal Service, having a printed indicia and sent as first class mail. Also **post card.**

post choice, *noun* a term used in tests of the persuasiveness of advertisements, being the percentage of a sample audience that chooses a certain brand of product after exposure to an advertisement for the brand. Cf. *pre-to-post.*

poster, *noun* a printed paper advertisement, pasted or tacked up in a public place. Also *bill.*

poster frame, a framed panel used for holding a poster on or in a bus, terminal, station, store, etc.

poster panel, a billboard on which advertising is displayed in printed paper sheets rather than being painted. The standard poster panel is approximately 25 feet long and 12 feet high, and takes a poster of 10 to 30 sheets. Cf. *painted bulletin.*

poster plant, an outdoor advertising plant specializing in posters and poster panels.

poster showing, an outdoor advertising showing consisting of posters.

posting, *noun* the physical placement of an outdoor advertisement.

posting date, the date at which an outdoor advertising showing is scheduled to begin; a five-day period (**posting leeway**) is customarily allowed for the plant to erect or paste up all locations purchased.

posting period, the length of time purchased by an advertiser for display of outdoor or transit advertising; usually 30 days.

postmark advertising, an advertising slogan or design printed by a postage meter.

post-sync, *noun* later addition of sound to a motion picture or television film recorded without sound.

post-test, *noun* see *post.*

posture, *noun* the relative agressiveness of an advertising campaign, or personality.

potential audience, the number of persons or households capable of exposure to a medium by virtue of ownership, presence, or use of the medium in question.

potentiometer, *noun* a device for manually regulating the rate of electrical flow; especially one used to control the level of sound produced by an audio system. Also **pot.**

pounce pattern, a method of preparing large painted bulletins from relatively small art masters using projection and tracing.

powderless etch, an etching process for letterpress printing plates that eliminates the need for "dragon's blood," the red powder commonly used to protect areas not to be etched.

power, *noun* the wattage supplied by an amplifier, as for a broadcast signal.

powerhouse, *noun, informal* see *clear-channel station.*

pp., *pages.*

P.P.A., *Periodical Publishers' Association.*

P.R., *public relations.*

practical, *adjective* (on a theater, motion picture, or television set) actually usable: *a practical door.*

P.R.D., *product research and development.*

pre, noun 1. (in research) the condition of a subject or respondent in an experiment prior to the application of a test treatment. Also *pre-test.* Cf. *post.*
adjective 2. noting or pertaining to such a condition.

preamplifier, *noun* a device for strengthening and controlling a weak electronic signal to a level that an amplifier can receive. Also *preamp.* Cf. *amplifier.*

precancelled stamp, a postage stamp bearing the cancellation mark of a post office when sold; used for third class, fourth class, and bulk rate mail sent from the post office designated.

pre-choice, *noun* a term used in tests of the persuasiveness of advertisements, being the percentage of a sample audience that uses a certain brand of a product before exposure to an advertisement for the brand. Cf. *pre to post.*

precision sample, see *probability sample.*

preclipped coupon, see *pop-up coupon.*

predate, *noun* 1. an edition of a daily newspaper bearing the following day's date. Also *bulldog edition.*
2. a Sunday edition of a newspaper printed the previous Saturday morning.

predesignated sample, (in research) a sample of respondent homes or persons chosen before a survey begins.

preempt, *verb* 1. to take precedence with regard to television or radio time regardless of prior commitments; a speech from the President, or coverage of a major emergency, may preempt previously scheduled broadcasting.
2. to make a preemptive claim.
preemption, *n.*

preemptible, *adjective* (of television or radio broadcast time) noting or pertaining to a commercial occasion sold at a discount but subject to preemption pending its later sale at a higher rate.

preemptive claim, an advertising claim making first use of a benefit or support for a benefit that competitors could also advertise but presumably will not rather than appear imitative.

preferred position, a location for an advertisement in a periodical or television or radio schedule that an advertiser demands and for which he is charged a higher than usual rate. Cf. *run-of-paper, fixed position.*

premiere, *noun* (in theater, motion pictures, or television) the first public performance of a show or commercial. Cf. *preview.*

premium, *noun* 1. something offered free or at reduced price as an inducement to buy a different item or items.
2. an extra charge or higher total cost, as for a preferred advertising position or for special treatment of advertisements. Also *premium price.*
adjective 3. noting or pertaining to a product's pricing level when such prices are deliberately maintained at a higher level than most competitive products.

Premium Advertising Association of America, Inc., a New York association, founded in 1911, of users of premiums in sales promotion; conducts surveys relating to the use of premiums. Abbreviated *P.A.A.A.*

premium container, a container for a retail product which, being reusable after the original contents are gone, functions as a premium.

premium pack, a package of a product offering a premium, usually in either in-pack or on-pack form.

premium price, see *premium.*

premium rate, (in television or radio) an extra rate charged for a preferred position.

premium television, see *pay television.*

prepack display, a display case or bin that arrives at a retail store containing the merchandise it is to display, already in place. Also **prepack shipper.**

preprice, *verb* to mark a retail item with its retail price before delivery to a store.

preprint, *noun* 1. a printing of periodical advertising matter on separate sheets before actual publication; done by an advertiser for special purposes, e.g. to serve as retail displays or in order to merchandise his advertising support to retailers.
2. a color newspaper advertisement (e.g., spectacolor) printed on one side of rotogravure stock which is then supplied pretrimmed to the newspaper, which does its own printing on the reverse side.
3. see *hi-fi insert.*

preprint order form, a form listing wholesaler's items constantly in stock, used by a retailer in making out his orders.

pre-production, *noun* (in motion pictures, television or radio) planning and organizational activities in preparation for a production.

prescore, *verb* 1. to record the background music of a film before shooting begins.
2. to record any audio element of a film before shooting begins.

presentation, *noun* a formal face-to-face exposition of factual information, plans, visual material, etc. regarding a subject or a proposed course of action.

press, *noun* 1. (in printing) any machine for transferring words and images to paper or other sheet material through the medium of ink. Also *printing press.*
2. loosely, journalists and journalism.
adjective 3. noting or pertaining to printing machines, their products, or journalists.

pressing, *noun* an issue of a record pressed from a master original.

press proof, a proof of a page, book signature, etc. made on a press that will be used for printing the actual edition of the finished publication.

press release, see *release.*

press run, see *run.*

pressure-sensitive, *adjective* noting or pertaining to any adhesive backing that holds firmly to a surface that it has been pressed against, protected by a paper covering that is peeled off at the time of application; used on decals, posters, etc.

prestige advertising, see *institutional advertising.*

pre-sunrise authority, special authority to a daytime station to begin broadcasting before sunrise. Abbreviated *P.S.A.*

pretest, *verb* 1. to test before use, as an advertisement on an audience sample.
noun 2. see *pre.*

pre-to-post, (in research) 1. any observations, especially measurements, of behavior of subjects or respondents preceding and following a test treatment.
2. measures of respondents' change in desire for or purchase intent for a product or service before and after exposure to an advertisement for the product or service in question, or a competitor. Also **pre-to-post purchase intent, pre-to-post choice.**

preview, *noun* (in theater, motion pictures, or television) an exposure of a show or commercial to a select audience before the production is publicly available. Cf. *premiere.*

preview light, a green warning light on a television camera, indicating that the camera is about to transmit.

price, *noun* 1. the amount of money a seller receives or asks in exchange for a product or service; from the prospect's or buyer's viewpoint, the cost of the product or service. A key variable in the determination of a marketing strategy and marketing mix.
verb 2. to determine the amount of money a seller requests or receives in exchange for a product or service.

price cut, 1. a reduced retail price marked on an item.
2. a reduction in price for goods or services.

price marking, marking of a retail price either on a package or on the box in which such a package comes.

price pack, a retail package announcing a temporary reduction from the standard retail price, used as a promotional inducement to purchasers. Also **price-off pack,** *cents off.*

primary audience, 1. the potential audience for a single advertising message.
2. the persons or places to which a periodical is sold or delivered for use.
3. the persons to whom the editorial content of a periodical is directed. Also *primary readership,* as in #2.
4. the total number of primary readers of a periodical.

primary circulation, the recorded circulation of a periodical, based on subscription and newsstand sales figures.

primary household, a household including a subscriber or purchaser of a periodical.

primary marketing area, 1. the principal area of editorial and advertising coverage of a newspaper.
2. the principal area of sale for a product, service, or category whose sales are sharply skewed regionally. Also *heartland.* Abbreviated *P.M.A.*

primary reader, a person residing in a primary household who has looked at the content of a periodical.

primary readership, see *primary audience.*

primary service area, (in AM radio broadcasting) the area in which a station's signal is strong, with the ground wave not subject to objectionable interference.

prime, *noun* see *daypart.* Also **prime time.**

Prime Time Access Rule, any of three successive rulings of the Federal Communications Commission limiting television network feeds in order to stimulate local prime time broadcasting. Cf. *Westinghouse Rule.*

principal, *noun* 1. a proprietor, partner, or major officer in a business.
2. one who is represented by a broker or agent, as a manufacturer.

Principal Register, the main Federal Government register of trade marks, etc., kept under the provisions of the Trade Mark (Lanham) Act of 1946; marks ineligible for registration may be eligible for inclusion in the Supplemental Register.

principle of closure, (in psychology) the theory that a subject will tend to complete, in his mind, an object, action, etc. that he perceives as incomplete. Also *law of closure.* Cf. *Cloze procedure.*

print, *verb* 1. to reproduce words, pictures, etc. on paper or other sheet material in ink with the aid of machinery.
2. to process paper, etc. with machinery in the course of such reproduction.
3. (of type or the like) to mark on paper, etc. with ink.
4. to make a photographic positive, blueprint, etc.
noun 5. printed words: *a clause in fine print.*
6. something registered on paper or the like by photographic means for use as a positive or blueprint.

printed bulletin, an outdoor advertisement using printed material in a space used for painted bulletins.

printed-word media, all media for advertising prepared by printing, e.g., periodicals, posters, shopping bags, or matchbooks. Also **print media.**

printer's error, (in printing) any type error or undesirable feature of a proof or the like that is deemed to be the fault of the printer and is therefore not charged to the publisher or author in correction. Abbreviated *P.E.* Cf. *author's alteration, editorial alteration.*

printing broker, a person who locates printing facilities needed by a client, e.g., an advertising agency, for a fee included in the price quoted.

printing depth, the minimum depth to which a plate or cylinder must be etched or engraved in order to print properly.

printing press, see *press.*

Print Measurement Bureau, a Canadian organization of periodical publishers, advertisers, and advertising agencies formed to assure the provision of standardized periodical readership figures. Abbreviated *P.M.B.*

Printon, *noun, trademark* a plastic-based paint.

prism shot, a photographic image taken through an image multiplying prism so as to reproduce the same image many times.

private brand, a wholesaler's or retailer's own brand.

private label, a wholesaler's or retailer's label bearing his private brand.

prize broker, one who arranges barters of merchandise given as prizes on television or radio shows in return for mentions of the brand names of the merchandise on the shows. Also *barter broker.*

probability, *noun* (in statistics) the percentage of times, in a given number of occurrences, that certain results should appear if the sample chosen is truly random and if the occurrences under study are subject to chance alone.

probability sample, (in statistics) a sample in which all population members in the universe being measured have an equal chance to be included, and therefore projectable to the universe. Also *precision sample.*

problem-solution, *noun* a format for advertisements involving depiction of a con-

139

sumer problem and demonstration of the manner in which the advertised product can solve the problem. Also **problem-solution advertising.**

processor, *noun* one who converts raw material into a refined or finished product. Cf. *packer.*

process letter, a letter whose body is printed so as to imitate typing.

process plate, (in four color printing) a photoengraved plate that prints one of four separated colors in reproducing the original full color illustration in yellow, red (magenta), blue (cyan), and black.

process printing, use of two or more halftone printing plates in order to obtain a range of colors and tones in printed illustrations.

process screen, see *rear screen projection.*

process shot, (in motion pictures or television) a shot combining separate film images into a single scene by superimposition. Cf. *mat shot.*

produce, *verb* 1. to create the physical material (film, printing plates, magnetic tape, etc.) which will be used by a medium as an advertisement. Cf. *producer, production.*
2. to manage the development of a planned public event, especially entertainment.
3. to ready a good for market.
noun 4. fresh vegetables and fruit sold at retail.

producer, *noun* 1. a person who develops and manages the financing, staffing and production of a play, motion picture, television show, etc.
2. an advertising agency employee responsible for the production of commercials; includes such functions as selection of a production supplier, cost control, and quality control. Also *production director.*
3. a processor or packer.

producer goods, see *industrial goods.*

product, *noun* a physical item, especially one to which value has been added, offered for sale; consists of a *tangible product* (a physical object or service package seen as the thing to be sold), an *extended product* (the unseen services and ancillary features such as packaging which accompany a tangible product), and the *generic product* (the essential benefit sought by the buyer in the product).

product acceptance test, a test of the absolute or relative rate or amount of acceptance of a product by consumers. Abbreviated *P.A.T.*

product copy, 1. (in television or radio) all copy, sets, etc. used for a specific program.
2. portions of the prose in an advertisement devoted to product descriptions and claims.
3. a product which imitates the appearance or features of another successful product.

production, *noun* 1. the process of converting the contents of a manuscript, illustration material, general design, layout or storyboard, etc. into a printed book, magazine, advertisement, script, commercial, etc.
2. the process of converting the narrative contents of a script, set designs, etc. into a stage, motion picture, television, or radio performance.
3. a show, especially with regard to the lavishness of effort and expense in producing it: *a big production.*
4. those processes of a firm which ready a good for marketing.

production director, a person in charge of production, as for a publishing house, advertising agency, or television station. Cf. *producer, production manager.*

production manager, 1. the person responsible for the development of advertising materials (usually print) for an advertising agency.
2. (in printing) the person responsible for the final reproduction in print for a periodical, book or collateral printed piece. Cf. *production director, producer.*

140

product life cycle, a marketing theory that products or brands are like organisms in following a sequence of stages from conception to expiration. In the introductory stage, sales are derived primarily from first time trial purchases. In the growth stage which follows, sales increase from new trial while repeat purchases serve as a base. In the mature stage, sales level out as new trial is offset by cessation of purchase, while rates of repeat purchase fluctuate. In the declining stage, sales diminish as cessation of purchase becomes the dominant mode.

product line, 1. an array of forms and sizes of a product or products sold under a single label or brand, or sold by a single manufacturer. Also *line.* Cf. *merchandise mix.*
2. see *assortment.*

product manager, see *brand manager.*

product position, see *position.*

product protection, protection of an advertisement granted by any communications medium from physical or temporal proximity to competitive or distracting advertisements. Also *protection.* Cf. *commercial protection, competitive separation.*

product research, 1. research into consumer attitudes toward competing products' features.
2. research into the physical properties and characteristics of product formulations or designs either employed by competitors or being considered for future use.

product research and development, a corporate process and personnel group using product research to further corporate marketing objectives. Also *research and development.* Abbreviated *P.R.D.*

product usage information, information regarding the consumers of product types and brands, usually categorized demographically or psychographically.

professional magazine, a magazine for members of a profession or related group of professions.

profile, *noun* see *audience profile.*

profit-taking strategy, see *milking strategy.*

program, *noun* 1. a show presented by a television or radio station during a certain time period on a specific day or date.
2. a set of standing instructions for a computer.
verb 3. to arrange for a show to be presented by a television or radio station.
4. to arrange a schedule of shows or commercials for a network, station, or advertiser.
5. to prepare standing instructions, as for a computer.

program analyzer, a machine for recording audience reactions to television or radio programs.

program basis, an estimate of the actual cost of a television show, taking into consideration the length of commitment discounts earned by the show, based on the number of times it is telecast, but not any discounts earned by an individual sponsor. Used by the A. C. Nielsen Co.

program billboard, see *billboard.*

program compatibility, appropriateness of advertising to a television or radio program, and vice-versa.

program coverage, the number of persons or households, or percentage of a population, that are able to receive a given television or radio program from one or more stations.

Program Cumulative Audiences, a report, issued five times a year by the A.C. Nielsen Co., on the four-week cumulative home audiences for specific television programs, along with frequency distributions over the same period for each. Abbreviated *P.C.A.*

program delivery rating, the percentage of households within a given area estimated to be tuned in to a television or radio program at a given moment.

program following, the television or radio program following another. Cf. *lead-out*.

program opposite, a competing television or radio program on another network or station.

program profile, 1. a graphic summary of audience reaction to a television or radio program in terms of minute-by-minute viewing levels or other measures.
2. the demographic or psychographic characteristics of a program's audience.

program rating, see *rating*.

program station basis, the percentage of television or radio sets in a coverage area tuned in to a given program at a given moment, taken as a basis for a rating (**program station rating**) of the program's success against all individual competition. Abbreviated *P.S.B.* Cf. *rating*.

progressive proof, an engraver's set of proofs of a color advertisement or illustration, used as a printer's guide, containing a separate proof of each color plate (yellow, red, blue, black) and a combination proof of two or more colors on a single proof in printing sequence, the final proof containing all 4 colors showing final reproduction. Also **progressive, prog.**

projectall, *noun* a television projector for use with opaque slides.

projected audience size, 1. the number of persons or households predicted for the audience of a commercial, or television or radio program.
2. the size of an audience as estimated on the basis of a sample.

projection, *noun* 1. (in statistics) the process of estimating unknown figures on the basis of existing ones, usually with known probability for error.
2. a figure estimated in this way.
3. (in psychology) the attribution of one's feelings and attitudes to another. Cf. *identification*.
4. the process and images created by use of a projector.

projection television, television whose images are projected on a large screen.

projective technique, a psychological technique for determining underlying attitudes, topics of concern, etc. in which a subject is encouraged to give his spontaneous associations in response to ambiguous pictures, shapes, phrases, etc. submitted to him.

projector, *noun* a machine for casting images on a neutral surface by means of a strong light shining through or creating reflections from a motion picture film, slide, etc.

promo pl. **promos,** *noun* a brief announcement urging the audience of a television or radio program to remain tuned for the next program, or another future program. Also *promotion spot*.

promote, *verb* to create interest in something offered for sale by means of a promotion. Also *push*.

promotion, *noun* 1. a usually temporary effort to create extra interest in the purchase of a product or service by offering values in excess of those customarily afforded by such purchases; includes temporary discounts, allowances, premium offers, coupons, contests, sweepstakes, etc. Also *sales promotion*.
2. loosely, any effort to encourage the purchase of a product or service.

promotion allowance, an allowance made by a manufacturer or his agent to a wholesaler or retailer who agrees to promote the product purchased under allowance. Also *merchandising allowance.*

promotion drive, see *drive period.*

promotion period, see *drive period.*

promotion spot, see *promo.*

prompt, *verb* in the performing arts, to remind a speaker or performer of cues, dialogue, or similar matter.

proof, *noun* 1. an impression on paper of type, an engraving, or the like, for the purpose of checking the correctness and quality of material to be printed.
2. see *proof-of-purchase.*

proofing, *noun* 1. the act or process of making printer's proofs.
2. the act or process of proofreading type against original copy for correctness.

proof-of-purchase, evidence that a consumer has purchased a product or service, as a receipt, label, package or portion thereof, etc.; usually furnished to manufacturers, often by mail, in compliance with the terms of a sales promotion.

proofread, *verb* to read a printer's proof or document for the purpose of checking the correctness of the typesetting or page makeup, and of adding corrections and alterations.
proofreader, *n.*

PROOFREADER'S MARKS

    Take out
    Left out, insert
    Insert space
    Turn inverted letter
    Broken letter
    Push down space

    Move left
    Move right
    Align type
    Straighten line
    Insert period
    Insert comma
    Insert colon
    Insert semicolon
    Insert apostrophe
    Insert quotation marks
    Insert hyphen
    Insert inferior figure
    Insert superior figure
    Set in small capitals
    Set in italic type
    Set in roman type
    Set in bold face type
    Let it stand
    Out, see copy
    Spell out
    Start paragraph
    No paragraph

proofreader's marks, marks used by a proofreader on a manuscript or type proof to provide instructions for corrections.

prop, *noun* any object appearing in a photograph or on a theater, motion picture, or television set in order to give realism to the set or the action.

propaganda, *noun* communications intended to influence belief and action, whether true or false information is contained in such communication. In **white propaganda,** the information source is identified; in **black propaganda,** information sources are not disclosed.

proprietary pharmaceutical, a product containing a drug sold at retail without a doctor's prescription. Also *over the counter, patent medicine.*

prospect, *noun* a person who can be considered eligible for the purchase of a product or service by virture of circumstance and interest.

protected rate, a cost for goods or services which a supplier agrees to maintain for a purchaser, despite later cost increases for other purchasers.

protection, *noun* 1. a duplicate film or videotape master, held in case of damage to the master used for reproduction.
2. see *product protection.*

protection mold, see *safety shell.*

protection shell, see *safety shell.*

protocol, *noun* see *playback.*

prove, *verb* to pull a proof from type, engraving, etc.

proved name registration, proven recall of a printed advertisement elicited by the display of the brand name, as used by Daniel Starch & Co. Abbreviated *P.N.R.*

proven recall, a respondent's recall of the content of advertising that is demonstrated by a repetition of the content.

PRSA, *Public Relations Society of America.*

P.S.A., 1. *public-service announcement.*
2. *pre-sunrise authority.*

P.S.B., *program station basis.*

P.S.T., *Pacific Standard Time;* see *time zone.*

psychogalvanometer, *noun* (in research) an instrument used to measure respondent's galvanic skin response. Also *galvanometer.* Cf. *galvanic skin response, arousal method.*

psychographic, *adjective* (in research) noting or pertaining to the study of the personalities, attitudes, and life styles of individuals and groups, especially in quantitative terms; based on the belief that such readily measurable, descripive characteristics serve as better predictors of behavior than demographic characteristics.

psychographics, *plural noun* the application of psychographic research.

P.U.A.A., *Public Utilities Advertising Association.*

public, *noun* (in public relations) a group of persons, especially one that is interested in or affected by an action or an idea. Cf. *market, audience.*

public address system, an audio system used to deliver messages to masses of people, usually by non-broadcast means. Also *P.A. system.*

publication, *noun* 1. the state of being published: *to get into publication.*
2. any format published, especially a periodical.

publication-set, type or other printing materials for an advertisement set or prepared by the periodical in which it is run rather than supplied in some form by the advertiser or his agency. Also *pub-set.* Cf. *composition-set type.*

Public Broadcasting Service, a government-funded service for the distribution of programs to non-commercial television stations. Abbreviated *P.B.S.*

public domain, the realm of all publications, art works, songs, etc. that are not copyrighted, and can therefore be appropriated by anyone.

publicity, *noun* information regaring a person, corporation, product, etc. released on his or its behalf for non-paid use by media.

publicity director, an advertising agency or advertiser employee responsible for obtaining publicity for clients or the employer. Also *public relations director.*

public opinion, (in public relations) a range of viewpoints regarding an issue held by that group of persons who are interested in the issue.

public relations, 1. activities of persons or organizations intended to promote understanding of and good will toward themselves or their products or services. 2. the degree to which such entities have obtained understanding and good will from their publics. 3. a management staff function which seeks to assess and favorably influence public opinion of a person, good, or organization by delivering messages to such publics without incurring direct media costs. Abbreviated *P.R.*

public relations director, see *publicity director.*

Public Relations Society of America, an organization of public relations practitioners formed in 1948 to provide professional development and placement services for members. Abbreviated *PRSA.*

public service advertising, advertisements placed by a medium without charge in the interest of promoting the general welfare and good will of its audience.

public service announcement, a non-commercial announcement for the information of the public. Abbreviated *P.S.A.*

Public Utilities Advertising Association, a world wide association of public utility companies formed to foster advertising and public relations practices among members which will serve industry goals. Abbreviated *P.U.A.A.*

publish, *verb* to prepare and openly distribute multiple copies of a document, especially one that is printed and sold to readers or advertisers, or both.

publisher, *noun* a person or organization who bears final responsibility for the content of a publication.

Publishers' Information Bureau, Inc., a firm which publishes syndicated monthly reports on the advertising schedules and expenditures, by product or service, of advertisers in consumer magazines. Abbreviated *P.I.B.* Cf. *Leading National Advertisers — Publishers' Information Bureau.*

publisher's interim statement, a sworn circulation statement issued by a periodical publisher belonging to the Audit Bureau of Circulations at optional intervals between the regular publisher's statements.

publisher's representative, a person who solicits the purchase of advertising space from advertisers on behalf of a periodical publisher. Cf. *representative.*

publisher's statement, a notarized statement of total circulation, geographic distribution, etc., provided for every issue between regular audits; required by the Audit Bureau of Circulations and by the U.S. Postal service for second class mailing.

pub-set, see *publication-set.*

puffery, *noun* product-related copy in an advertisement not intended to be taken as a factual claim by an audience, whether by virtue of extreme exaggeration or a humorous context.

pull, *verb* 1. to print a proof for examination, especially on a small press intended only for proofing.
noun 2. the degree of demand for a product or service from purchasers. Cf. *push.*

pull back, (of a motion picture or television camera) to dolly away from a closer position to a subject.

pulling power, the effectiveness of an advertisement in persuading the public to buy a product, make inquiries, send in coupons, or take some other positive action.

pulp, *noun* 1. any disintegrated fibrous material, as wood or cloth, for making paper.
verb 2. to reduce to pulp, as for making paper or cardboard.

pulp magazine, 1. a magazine printed on coarse, cheap paper.
2. a popular magazine appealing to an unsophisticated mass audience, e.g., one concerned with crime, celebrities, or romance.

Pulse, Inc., The, a New York based media research firm which has measured spot radio audience sizes by means of personal interviews since 1941, with findings for sale on a syndicated basis.

punch card, a card for storing information in the form of an arrangement of punched holes, which engage the machinery of a sensing device.

punch marks, perforations at the side of a motion picture film, used as a warning that a reel is about to end.

purchase-privilege premium, a self liquidator or semi-liquidator premium.

purchaser, *noun* a person who purchases a product or service for its consumer, usually at retail. Cf. *consumer.*

pure program rating, an estimate of television or radio audiences for a program during a survey period, excluding any program preemptions that have occurred.

push, *verb* 1. *informal* see *promote.*
noun 2. the force employed in convincing wholesalers and retailers to purchase a product. Cf. *pull.*

push money, a special reward given by manufacturers or service sources to agents' or dealers' employees, for encouraging the sale of their own goods rather than a competitor's; usually paid on each sale, whether pushed or not. Abbreviated P.M. Cf. *allowance, deal.*

P.U.T., *Persons Using Television.*

pylon, *noun* 1. a support for an outdoor advertising display.
2. a tall outdoor sign.

pyramid makeup, a newspaper page makeup in which advertisements are positioned from bottom to top, in diminishing sizes so that they form steps from the bottom to the top outside. Cf. *double pyramid.*

Q

q and a, *question and answer.* Also *q & a.*

QC, *quality control.*

Q rating, a rating of the percentage of television and radio listeners who are aware of a given program and who regard it as a favorite.

Q-sort, a research procedure in which a respondent sorts printed statements into piles that represent the degree of truth the respondent finds in the statements.

quad, *noun* 1. (in typesetting) a measure of indentation, equal to one em *(em quad or mut)* or to a half-em *(en quad or nut).*
2. a non-printing piece of metal used by a printer to justify or letterspace a line in a type form.
3. see *quadriphonic.*

quadriphonic, *adjective* noting or pertaining to audio signals recorded in a manner permitting their playback as four separate information channels; used to better simulate the experience of live music. Also *quad.* Cf. *monaural, stereophonic.*

qualified circulation, the readership eligible to receive a controlled circulation periodical.

qualified issue reader, a person who qualifies for examination on his reactions to a periodical advertisement by giving evidence of having read the issue in which the advertisement appeared. Also **qualified reader.**

qualified respondent, a person who has met the standards established for respondents in a consumer or audience research project.

qualified viewer, a person who qualifies for examination on his reaction to a television commercial by giving some evidence of having watched the show on which the commercial was presented.

qualitative research, research involving differences of kind or condition rather than of amount or degree; usually used to broaden insight and develop hypotheses. Also *subjective research.*

quality control, an organizational process and personnel responsible for maintaining product or service quality at a designated standard level. Abbreviated *QC.*

quantitative research, statistical research involving differences of amount or degree rather than kind or condition; usually used to reach conclusions. Also *objective research.*

quantity discount, 1. a discount for large purchases, made either at one time or over an extended period.
2. see *frequency discount.*

quantity prints, 1. multiple film prints of a commercial prepared in order to permit its simultaneous airing on a number of networks or stations.
2. multiple glossy prints of a still photograph, made from an original negative, and used for mailings, sales kits or the like; usually 8 x 10 inches.

quarter, *noun* a fourth of a fiscal or calendar year.

quarter binding, a book binding using one material for the back and another for the boards.

quarter showing, (in transit advertising) a placement of car cards in one fourth of the available vehicles or one fourth of those required for a full service. Also **quarter run, quarter service.**

quartile, *noun* (in statistics) any of four parts into which the whole population of a sample is divided, the parts being arranged in some meaningful numerical order.

question and answer, 1. a format for copy for advertisements, in which consumers pose questions answered by advertisers or spokesmen.
2. a format for meetings, in which a spokesman presents material only in response to questions.

quintile, *noun* (in statistics) any of five parts into which a whole population of a sample is divided, the parts being arranged in some meaningful numerical order.

quota, *noun* 1. (in sales) a goal, expressed either in receipts expected or as a percentage of another figure.
2. (in statistics) a number or proportion to be reflected by one element in a population sample; intended to produce a suitably balanced sample.

quota sample, (in statistics) a sample in which the characteristics of those represented are selected in predetermined proportions, often based on census data. Cf. *random sample.*

R

®, *registered;* a symbol used to identify a registered trademark. Also **R**.

R.A.B., *Radio Advertising Bureau, Inc.*

rack, *noun* a system of shallow shelves, hanger hooks on pegboard, or hoppers for the storage and display of retail merchandise. Cf. *shelf.*

rack focus, (in motion pictures or television) to change the focal plan of the camera within a shot, so as to shift emphasis from a subject in the foreground to a subject in the background, or vice-versa.

rack folder, an advertising folder intended for display in a rack.

rack jobber, a service wholesaler who, by exclusive agreement with a retailer, prices and stocks a department of specified footage (usually of non-food items in a grocery store). Also **rack merchandiser.**

rack sale, the sale of newspapers from unattended open racks or boxes, payment dependent on the honesty of the takers.

R.A.D.I., *radio area of dominant influence.*

radio, *noun* 1. a mass communications medium consisting of audio signals carried by radio waves created by licensed broadcasting stations to listeners interested in the information or entertainment contained in such signals; often a medium for advertising.
2. electromagnetic waves used to transmit audio and video signals to properly equipped receivers.

Radio Advertising Bureau, Inc., a trade association of radio stations and radio networks established to promote the effectiveness and popularity of radio as an advertising medium. Abbreviated *R.A.B.*

radio area of dominant influence, a term used by The Pulse, Inc. to describe counties where most of the radio reception is of programs from home stations. Abbreviated *R.A.D.I.*

Radio Expenditure Report, a syndicated quarterly report on national expenditures for advertising time, by advertiser. Abbreviated *R.E.R.*

radio rating point, a unit of radio audience size equal to one percent of the radio owning households in the area under study.

ragged, *adjective, adverb* (of typesetting) with no attempt to make the ends of a column of type flush; used especially in the specification "ragged left" or "ragged right" in manuscript mark up. Cf. *justify.*

rag paper, any of various high quality book or typing papers composed wholly or in part of textile fibers. Also **rag bond, rag.**

railroad showing, an outdoor advertising poster at a railroad station. Also *station poster, transportation display poster.*

raincheck, *noun* (in retailing) a slip given to a customer entitling him to later buy an item temporarily out of stock at the present reduced price.

rain lap, (in outdoor posting) pasting sheets from the bottom row of paper up, thus covering the top edge of the bottom sheets with the sheet above; done to prevent rain from peeling the sheets from the board.

R. and D., *research and development.* Also *R. & D.*

random, *adjective* noting or pertaining to a subject characterized by randomness.

random access unit, a computer attachment permitting withdrawal of information as needed from a larger mass of data.

random-digit dialing, (in research) dialing of telephone numbers with a random set of digits after the exchange digits are dialed, to obtain interview respondents; gives access to unlisted as well as listed numbers. Abbreviated *R.D.D.*

randomization, *noun* (in statistics) any process used to assure that a sample will be selected at random from the total population.

randomness, *noun* (in research) 1. a characteristic of any phenomenon which is devoid of measurable regularity.
2. an equalized probability of any member of a population being selected for a sample.

random sample, (in statistics) a sample taken from a population each member of which has an equal chance of being selected. Also *unrestricted sample.* Cf. *quota sample.*

range, *noun* (in statistics) the difference between the highest and lowest measurements in a study.

rank, *noun* the relative status that one thing has with relation to another, e.g., that of one advertisement with relation to another as regards the effectiveness of each. As a rule, 1 denotes the highest rank, 2 the next, etc.

rank order correlation, (in statistics) establishment of the relationship of variables that are scored according to rank rather than by quantity.

rate, *noun* 1. the amount, per unit of space or time purchased, charged by a communications medium, as a newspaper or television station, to an advertiser.
verb 2. to estimate media audience size based on a research sample.

rate base, 1. (in periodical publishing) a minimum guaranteed circulation used as a basis for determining advertising space rates.
2. a minimum audience size guaranteed by a medium in return for a stated advertising rate.

rate book, 1. a book giving advertising rates for a number of communications media.
2. a sales representative's manual of prices for products or services he sells.

rate card, a card giving the advertising rates and other pertinent information for a communications medium.

rate class, (in television or radio) the type of rate in effect during a given time period.

rate differential, the difference in rates charged by local media for local and national advertisers.

rate holder, an advertisement placed primarily to earn a discount for quantity or frequency from an advertising medium.

rate protection, guarantee of continuation at a former rate, made to an advertiser having a contract with a communications medium that raises its rates while the contract is in effect.

rating, *noun* any figure establishing the popularity of a television or radio program or the exposure obtained by the advertising it carries, usually measured as a percentage of the homes able to receive a program that actually do receive it. Also *program rating.* Cf. *program station basis.*

rating point, see *gross rating point.*

rating scale, (in research) a scale of degrees used to measure a respondent's attitudes regarding a subject under investigation, as product preference, purchase intent.

rating service, an organization that conducts surveys of television and radio audience listening habits, exposure to commercials, etc.

ratio scale, (in statistics) a measurement scale with known and equal intervals between points, and a known true zero point. Cf. *interval scale, nominal scale, ordinal scale.*

raw stock, (in radio, motion pictures, or television) magnetic tape or film not previously used or exposed.

R.D.A., *recommended dietary allowance.*

R.D.D., *random-digit dialing.*

reach, *noun* see *cumulative audience.*

reach and frequency, a criterion for evaluating the level of cumulative audience exposure of an advertising effort on the basis of the percentage of all persons or households who are exposed to the advertising (**reach**), and the average number of exposures for each (**frequency**), over a stated period of time. Gross rating points are equal to the product of reach and frequency.

reach-in case, an upright refrigerator for retail display of perishable foods that is directly accessible to customers. Cf. *coffin case.*

reader, *noun* a person who has read material in question, as a periodical or advertisement.

reader confidence, the loyalty of a regular readership to a periodical.

reader impression study, a study conducted by the research firm of Daniel Starch and Associates to determine the significance of a periodical advertisement to ad-noters.

reader interest, interest in a product's or service's periodical advertising on the part of readers, measured either by the numbers interested in one advertisement for the product or service or by the number of readers of one periodical interested in advertising for that product or service as opposed to that for others.

reader response, actions taken by readers of a publication, especially letters or orders prompted by a print advertisement.

readership, *noun* the total number of persons that read a periodical; the primary and pass-along audiences together.

readership study, 1. a survey of the characteristics of the readership of a periodical. 2. a survey of the attention given to a periodical or any of its elements by its readership.

readers per copy, a ratio of a publication's readership to its circulation; usually stated as an average number of readers per copy.

reader traffic, the pattern of attention shift from one part of a periodical to another on the part of its readers.

reading, *noun* see *read-through.*

reading days of issue exposure, the total readership of a periodical multiplied by the average number of days the average individual reader is exposed to its contents.

reading notice, a brief, all text newspaper advertisement set in the form of editorial matter but labeled "advertisement" to prevent deception.

reading time, the average time spent by the average reader of a periodical on any given issue.

read-most, *noun* a category used by the research firm of Daniel Starch and Associates to designate persons who read more than half of an advertisement in a periodical.

read-through, *noun* a preliminary reading aloud of a script by a cast of performers before actual rehearsals. Also *reading.*

ready, *adjective* use the shot or shots planned for this time; an instruction to a television cameraman or technical director.

real time, the time required for a television or radio performance according to the script, without lengthening or shortening.

ream, *noun* a unit of 500 sheets of paper, of a given size, depending on the type of paper, on which the weight of the paper stock is based. See *basis weight*.

rear-screen projection, (in motion pictures and television) projection of images from the side opposite the audience onto a translucent screen, in order to create a background scene. Also *process screen*, **rear projection.** Abbreviated *R.P.*

reason-why, *noun* an advertising statement or advertisement offering specific, objectively stated arguments in support of claimed benefits.

rebate, *noun* any refund of payment, as one by an advertising medium to an advertiser on account of a discount earned beyond that originally anticipated.

rebroadcast, *verb* 1. to repeat a broadcast, as to present it at a more favorable time in a time zone different from that of the original.
noun 2. see *repeat*.

recall, *verb* 1. to remember the content of a program, periodical, or advertisement.
noun 2. the content or extent of such recollection. Cf. *day-after recall*.
3. a request for a return of a product for service or replacement, usually from manufacturers to owners.

recall method, a method for testing the effectiveness of advertising through the ability of respondents to recall advertisements.

receipt, *noun* 1. a voucher provided by a seller to a buyer, confirming the terms of a sale.
2. the condition of a purchaser in possession of goods ordered, as *in receipt*.
receipts, *plural noun* 3. the amount of a store's sales for a stated period of time.

receiving clerk, a clerk who tallies and checks merchandise entering a store.

recent reading technique, a technique, employed by Target Group Index, for analyzing magazine readerships by asking respondents if they have read any issue of a certain magazine in the last week or month.

recognition, *noun* 1. the agreement by a communications medium to regard an advertising agency as bona fide, competent, and ethical, and thus entitled to discounts. Also *agency recognition*.
2. (in research) remembrance of prior exposure to an advertisement provoked by a repeated exposure.

recognition method, an aided-recall method for determining whether a respondent in a survey has been exposed to an advertisement; the respondent is exposed to the advertisement in question, then told where he may have been exposed to it before.

recommendation, *noun* the approval of an advertising agency by a communications medium for recognition by its members.

recommended dietary allowance, a standard of adequate daily amounts of selected nutrients, as vitamins, minerals, and protein, required by most persons of stated ages and sexes to maintain health; established separately by the Food and Drug Administration and the National Academy of Sciences. Abbreviated *R.D.A.* Cf. *minimum daily requirement*.

record, *noun* 1. a phonographic disc containing recorded audio signals in concentric grooves.
verb 2. to store information, as of an audible performance, for later reproduction or other use.

Recordimeter, *noun, tradmark* a device used by the A.C. Nielsen Co. to record, for national audience composition research, the times that a television set is in use; unlike the Audimeter, it cannot distinguish between stations.

recording, *verb* 1. the storage of audio and/or visual signals in any of various forms for later reproduction on suitable machines.
noun 2. a disc, tape, etc. on which such signals are stored.
3. a recorded performance.

Red Book, 1. *Standard Directory of Advertising Agencies.*
2. *Standard Directory of Advertisers.*
3. In larger metropolitan areas, a telephone directory listing commercial enterprises, as well as containing classified advertising.

redeem, *verb* to fulfill the requirements of a consumer promotional offer, as a coupon or trading stamps, in a prescribed manner resulting in receipt of goods at reduced price, or gratis.
redemption, *n.*

redemption, *noun* 1. the cashing in of coupons or trading stamps in order to obtain discounts or premiums.
2. the percentage of coupons or trading stamps issued that are cashed in. Also *redemption rate.*

redemption center, a place where premiums are made available in exchange for trading stamps.

redemption rate, see *redemption.*

red goods, goods that are quickly consumed and have a high rate of replacement; usually are broadly available, require little service, and are priced with low gross margins (e.g., food products). Cf. *orange goods, yellow goods.*

reducing glass, a double-concave lens mounted in a frame and used for reducing the apparent size of artwork, etc., to judge its effect at reduced scale.

reduction print, a film print reduced from the dimensions of the original, as of 35mm to 16mm.

re-etch, *verb* to etch a halftone plate further in certain areas, so as to sharpen contrasts or highlights, in order to achieve a closer match to copy.

reference group, (in psychology) a population group with which an individual identifies himself, whether or not he is really a member of the group.

reference media, publications of statistical and other useful information issued periodically for commercial use.

reflection button, a small glass or plastic reflector, used in combination with others to create letters or designs in unilluminated outdoor advertisements.

refund, *noun* 1. a return of some or all of an amount of money exchanged for the purchase of goods or services, issued by the seller.
verb 2. to issue such a return.

region, *noun* a geographical area of the country, usually including several states, designated for analytic or administrative purposes. Cf. *unit, zone.*

regional, *noun* 1. see *regional feed.*
adjective 2. of or pertaining to a region of the country.

regional announcement, see *sectional announcement.*

regional chain, a chain of retail stores in a specific geographical area.

regional channel station, an AM radio station broadcasting to an entire region rather than to an urban area after sundown, but allowed less power than that of a clear-channel station.

regional edition, an edition of a national periodical distributed within one geographical area; its advertising space can be purchased separately.

regional feed, (in radio and television) 1. a signal feed from a national network to a region.
2. a feed of a special announcement to a group of network affiliated stations in a region. Also *sectional feed.*

regional network, a television or radio network broadcasting to one region of the country.

register, *noun* 1. (in printing) the correct superimposition of each color plate of a color illustration; the print is said to be *in register* if properly printed and *out of register* if not.
verb 2. to cause a trademark, patent, copyright, etc., to be recorded by a government agency in order to establish a claim to its exclusive use.

register mark, (in printing) a mark at the corner of or outside each plate used in a color printing process; if the marks of the various plates are perfectly superimposed, the print is in register.

registration, *noun* the process, especially when completed, of registering or obtaining a register.

regression analysis, (in statistics) an analytic procedure for relating a dependent variable to one or more independent variables, in order to develop an equation that allows estimation of the dependent variable. Also **regression.** Cf. *correlation.*

regular, *adjective* (of a poster panel or billboard) without illumination.

regular audit, an audit of a periodical's circulation conducted at established regular intervals.

related, *adjective* 1. (of advertisements) published by two or more advertisers in such a way as to support one another's message.
2. (of retail items) generally used together and thus appropriate to sell or promote together.

related display, a retail display of dissimilar but related items.

relay station, a television or radio station whose sole purpose is to receive and pass on the signal from a station at which programs originate in order to expand its coverage area. Also *satellite station.* Cf. *translator.*

release, *noun* 1. a document of informational material on a recent or current event, as within a business organization, distributed to broadcast stations, newspapers and magazines for public relations purposes. Also *news release, press release.*
2. a legal contract assigning a person's rights to use of his name, likeness, ideas, or property to another party in return for a stated consideration.

release print, a print of a motion picture or television film intended for distribution.

reliability, *noun* (in research) the consistency of a test design, measured by its ability to repeatedly produce similar results under similar conditions (*test-retest reliability*), and by the ability of one part of the design to produce results compatible with those from the remainder (*split-half reliability*).

relief, *noun* projection of letters, designs, etc. from a background surface.

relief printing, printing from inked surfaces that are raised from the base of the plate, as in letterpress printing. Also *relief.* Cf. *intaglio printing.*

remainder, *noun* a unit of product, especially a book, remaining unsold at the regular price after demand for the product at that price level has expired; usually sold at a discount. Cf. *overstock.*

reminder advertising, 1. advertising in the form of brief allusions to a product or service that is assumed to be familiar to the reader or listener.
2. advertising intended to remind pros-

pects of the benefits of a product or service, or the immediacy of their need for such benefits.

remnant space, magazine advertising space sold at a discount to ensure that it will be occupied; commonest in regional editions.

remote, *noun* a television or radio broadcast originating in a location or studio other than the one broadcasting it. Also **remote pickup.**

renewal, *noun* 1. (in outdoor advertising) an extra poster used to replace one that is damaged.
2. a renewed periodical subscription.

renewal right, (in television or radio) the right of an incumbent to renew sponsorship of a show before it is offered elsewhere. Cf. *first refusal.*

rep, *noun* (informal) see *sales representative.*

repeat, *noun* 1. a repeated broadcast of a television or radio program.
2. a periodic broadcast of a specific, single show over a number of years. Also *rerun, rebroadcast.*

repetition, *noun* reiteration of an advertisement, slogan, or theme to strengthen its impression.

replacement medium, a local communications medium used in place of a national medium, as for advertisement testing or market expansion in the area.

Report on Syndicated Programs, a periodic report of the A.C. Nielsen Co. on the market clearance status and audience size of syndicated television programs. Abbreviated *R.O.S.P.*

reported spending, see *traceable expenditure.*

reportorial, *adjective* noting or pertaining to a style or format for advertisements imitating the factual, objective editorial voice.

representative, *noun* 1. a person who solicits the purchase of advertising space or time on behalf of a medium; usually prefaced by the kind of medium sold, as *radio representative.* Also *rep.*
2. a salesperson for an agent.

representative sample, (in statistics) a form of quota sample in which percentages of various elements of a population are included that are regarded as representative of the whole population. Cf. *quota sample.*

repression, *noun* (in psychology) the placement in the unconscious of memories, desires, etc., considered unacceptable or threatening. Cf. *suppression.*

reprint, *noun* a number of proofs or copies of an advertisement printed in addition to those reproductions printed in a publication. Cf. *overrun.*

reproduction, *noun* a duplicate of an original image prepared by mechanical means.

reproportion, *verb* changing only one of two dimensions when enlarging or reducing flat copy. (Normally employed when adjusting ads to fit various newspaper column widths without changing column linage.)

repro proof, (in printing) a proof intended for photographic reproduction on a printing plate or the like; a camera-ready proof. Also *reproduction proof, slick.*

R.E.R., *Radio Expenditure Report.*

rerecording, *noun* a recording made from other recordings, as to obtain a desired volume of sound or a mixture of separately recorded sounds.

rerun, *noun* see *repeat.*

resale price maintenance, maintenance of a minimum retail price agreed upon with or imposed by a manufacturer.

Resale Price Maintenance Act, a federal law of 1937, often called the Miller-Tydings Act, enabling manufacturers complying with state fair trade laws to be exempt from federal antitrust legislation prohibiting such pricing practices.

rescale, *verb* see *resize.*

research, *noun* 1. a process of systematic, scientific investigation designed to develop information or products of use to marketers.
2. a group of employees within an organization responsible for conducting such investigations.
verb 3. to conduct such investigations.

research and development, see *product research and development.* Abbreviated *R. and D., R. & D.*

research director, an advertising agency or advertiser employee responsible for procurement, analysis, and dissemination of information on factors influencing the market for goods. Also *director of research, marketing research director, consumer research director.*

residual, *noun* a royalty paid to a performer or other person by a television or radio station or advertiser for a broadcast of a program or commerical; rates usually as established by union contract (S.A.G. or A.F.T.R.A.). Also *re-use fee, talent payment, S.A.G. fee.*

resize, *verb* to alter the dimensions of an advertisement for use in a periodical space other than that for which it was originally designed. Also *rescale.*

resolution, *noun* the clarity of a televison image as received by a set.

respondent, *noun* a person who makes solicited answers to questions in a survey.

respondent set, 1. (in research) the body of attitudes held by a survey respondent regarding matters relevant to the survey, e.g., to being questioned, or to the product or advertising that is the subject of the survey.
2. the total number of people who respond to a consumer promotion offer, as a premium or refund; used to calculate such promotion costs when multiplied by the individual cost of such offers.

response, *noun* 1. (in audience surveys) the percentage of persons in a predesignated sample who provide useful information. Also *response rate.*
2. an action prompted by an advertisement. Cf. *reader response, return.*

restock, *verb* 1. (of a retailer) to order additional amounts of a product in order to maintain stock at a satisfactory level.
2. to stock a product again that has been allowed to go out of stock.

restricted, *adjective* 1. (of sales items) not to be legally sold in certain geographical areas.
2. to be sold in certain geographical areas only under special legal restrictions.

retail, *adjective* noting or pertaining to the sale of goods to the general public. Cf. *wholesale.*

retail cooperative, a cooperative wholesale purchasing organization owned by retailers.

retailer, *noun* a person who sells goods to the general public, especially goods purchased from a manufacturer or wholesaler. Also *dealer.*

retailer-owned wholesaler, a wholesale organization owned by a retail cooperative. Also *cooperative wholesaler.*

retailer's service program, a program of services provided by a wholesaler to enable independent retailers to compete with chain stores.

retail man, a manufacturer's or broker's representative who services products, arranges displays, and offers sales assistance at retail stores.

retail rate, a television or radio station time rate for local retailers.

retail trading zone, the area including and beyond the boundaries of an urban area whose inhabitants patronize the merchants of the urban area; established by the Audit Bureau of Circulations.

retouch, *verb* 1. to alter a photograph by hand to emphasize or introduce desired features or eliminate undesired ones.
2. (in platemaking) to alter film negatives or positives to correct imperfections or achieve desired reproduction.

retoucher, *noun* a person who is employed in altering photographic materials.

return, *noun* a direct response by a member of the public to an advertiser in consequence of a sales offer, contest, or coupon promotion. Cf. *response.*

return card, 1. a self-addressed postcard sent with advertising to encourage customer inquiries or orders.
2. the name and address of a sender used as corner card copy in the upper left corner of the front of an envelope or the like. Also **return card copy.**

return flat, a narrow theatrical flat set at an angle and used either to block audience views past the main flat or to give a three-dimensional quality to the main flat.

returns per thousand circulation, a figure used in gauging the effectiveness of an advertising campaign in a given communications medium by the percentage of direct responses to an advertisement.

re-use fee, see *residual.*

reverb, *noun* an echo-like sound effect produced by use of a reverberator.

reverberator, *noun* a mechanical (spring loaded) or electronic (delay circuit) device used to give sounds an echo-like effect. Cf. *echo chamber.*

reversal film, (in photography or motion pictures) film stock producing positive transparencies when developed after exposure, rather than negatives.

reverse, *noun* 1. the mirrorlike inversion of the elements on a printing plate or the like in relation to their order on the surface printed from it.
2. a photographic print in which values are inverted from the state in which they appear on a negative, as white type reversed out of a dark background.

reverse plate, a printing plate in which a legend or the like is left unprinted while the surrounding area is printed, contrary to the usual practice.

reverse shot, (in motion pictures or television) a shot of a subject from a direction diametrically opposite to that of a previous shot. Abbreviated *RevS.* Also **reverse-angle shot.**

revise, *noun* 1. a revised printer's proof, incorporating corrections already ordered. *verb* 2. to make corrections, as on a proof.

revolutions per minute, the standard measurement of the rate of rotation of a revolving machine part, as of a phonographic turntable; 33 and 45 revolutions per minute are the current standard speeds for recording and playback of phonographic discs. Abbreviated *R.P.M.*

RevS, *reverse shot.*

ribbon mike, a directional microphone of high sensitivity. Cf. *omnidirectional microphone.*

ride gain, to monitor sound levels in recording or transmission. Also *ride the needle.*

rider, *noun* an emendation to a manuscript which is indicated on a separate piece of paper.

ride the needle, see *ride gain.*

ride the showing, to survey an outdoor advertising showing from the street to see it as motorists and pedestrians do. Also **ride the boards.**

right of first refusal, see *first refusal.*

ring, *noun* (in retail selling) the amount of a sale as recorded on a cash register.

ripple dissolve, (in motion pictures or television) a move from one shot to the one following in which the new image appears as one or several wavy blurs obscure the previous image; often used to set apart imaginary sequences or flashbacks.

riser, *noun* (in television) a small platform or the like for raising a camera or an object in order to improve a shot. Cf. *apple, half apple.*

river, *noun* a conspicuous chain of white space running accidentally down a page of print, because of poorly positioned word spacing from line to line; may distract the reader.

roadblock, *verb* to simultaneously present the same commercial on all television or radio stations in a given geographical area.

Robinson-Patman Act, an act of Congress, enacted in 1936, that forbids unfair trade practices such as price and payment discrimination in interstate commerce.

rock format, see *format.*

role-playing technique, an interview technique in which a respondent is encouraged to imagine the part he would play in an imaginary situation as a way of determining his attitudes.

roll, *verb* 1. to play a film or videotape.
2. see *roll-out.*

roll-in, *noun* (in television) an insertion and integration of a commercial into a broadcast. Cf. *cut-in.*
roll in, *v.*

rolling split, (in periodical advertising) a cumulative purchase of space in syndicated newspaper supplements on a market-by-market basis in such a way that full national advertising coverage is obtained.

rolling store, a truck from which food sales are made, especially in rural areas.

roll-out, *noun* regional or national expansion of marketing of a new product or service from its area of introduction, as one or more test markets. Also **roll.**

roll over, *informal* to capitulate on the resolution of an issue, as in *roll over and play dead.*

roll-up, *noun* (in sound motion pictures) a two second interval of filmed images preceding the start of the audio track at the beginning of a film.

Roman, *noun* 1. the standard text type, with verticals truly vertical. Cf. *italics.*
2. any type face having relatively thick verticals and thin serifs connected to the principal strokes of the letters with brackets.

R.O.P., *run-of-paper.*

R.O.P. color, *run-of-paper color.*

R.O.S., *run-of-schedule.*

R.O.S.P., *Report on Syndicated Programs.*

roster recall method, a method for testing audience recall of television or radio programs that uses lists of the programs that are given the respondents.

rotary press, a press printing from a rotating cylindrical surface using curved plates. Cf. *cylinder press.*

rotate, *verb* 1. (in outdoor advertising) in a longer than 30 day schedule showing, to move an advertisement from one outdoor board location to another in order to give it wide exposure.
2. to move older retail items to the front of the stock of such items in order to sell them first.
3. to feature a retail item in a store at intervals in order to maintain its rate of sale at a satisfactory level.

4. to present a series of advertisements in a regular order of repetition.

rotogravure, *noun* 1. an intaglio printing process using a copper cylinder into which the printing image is etched.
2. a newspaper supplement with a magazinelike format printed by this process. Also **roto.**

rough, *noun* a rough layout, showing the general conception only of a design. Also *visual.*

rough cut, (in motion pictures or television) a rough assemblage of shots selected for the final print, in the proper sequence but without further editing. Cf. *fine cut.*

round robin, a network of television or radio stations each of which may originate a program or portion of a program.

rout, *verb* to grind down nonprinting metal below the printing surface of a letterpress printing plate.
router, *n.*

route list, a list of local retail stores, with notes regarding volume of business and operating methods, especially for the use of salesmen.

R.P., *rear-screen projection.*

R.P.M., *revolutions per minute.*

R print, an inexpensive color print suitable for use in comprehensive layouts though not suitable for use for print reproduction. Also *type R print.* Cf. *C print, dye transfer print.*

rubber cement, a nonstaining rubber-based adhesive used extensively in mounting artwork.

rubber plate, a letterpress printing plate used in the flexographic printing process for printing on corrugated board, cartons, etc.

rule, *noun* (in printing) a straight, type high border or divider line, either plain or decorative, used around advertisements to separate or visually enhance them.

run, *noun* 1. (in printing) the total number of copies of printed jobs, newspapers, magazines, collateral pieces, etc. that are printed as ordered. Also *press run.*
2. the total number of presentations of a television film in a given geographical area.
3. the total number of occasions of a television or radio commercial that an advertiser has purchased.
4. see *showing.*

run-around, *noun* a block of type, where a portion is set to less than full measure in order to leave space for an illustration, a large initial, etc.

rundown, *noun* (in motion pictures or television) a producer's list of the intended order of shots and effects to be used in a production.

run in, (in typesetting) to set a piece of copy as a direct continuation of the previous copy, without beginning a new paragraph. Also *run on.*

running head, a head on a book page that gives information regarding the chapter, the contents of the page, etc.

running shot, (in motion pictures and television) a shot of a subject in motion from a camera maintaining a constant position relative to the subject.

running text, the main text on a printed page, as opposed to its display lines.

running time, the time that a television or radio program or commercial is expected to take on actual presentation.

run-of-paper, *adjective* 1. (in periodical space buying) noting or pertaining to advertising positions allocated at the publisher's discretion, with or without regard to advertisers' position requests. Some publishers honor preferred-position demands,

and some treat all space orders as run-of-paper. Abbreviated *R.O.P.*
noun 2. the status of an advertisement positioned at the publisher's discretion. Also **run-of-book, run-of-press.**

run-of-paper color, 1. color advertising run anywhere in a newspaper that is convenient. Abbreviated *R.O.P. color.*
2. color advertising run in the main section of a paper rather than in a supplement.

run-of-schedule, *noun* the status of a television or radio announcement for which a specific day, or a specific hour, has not been reserved. Abbreviated *R.O.S.* Also *floating time.* Cf. *fixed time.*

run on, see *run in.*

run out, (in typesetting) to set the first line of an indented paragraph full measure while indenting the remainder; creates a hanging indentation.

run-through, *noun* a preliminary rehearsal of a motion picture or television performance with all elements present.

rural route, a rural postal route serviced by a government carrier. Cf. *star route.*

rural station, a station having exclusive coverage of a rural area.

rushes, *plural noun* (in motion pictures or television) rough, unedited prints of motion picture film shot the previous day, shown for evaluation and selection. Cf. *dailies.*

S

saddle stitch, a type of pamphlet or magazine binding using staples along the center fold between the pages.

safety, *noun* the distance between a magazine's page edge and printed copy (type and/or illustrations) not intended to be trimmed off in a full or partial bleed advertisement.

safety shell, a thin copper replica of an original printing plate from which duplicates may be obtained in case of injury to, or loss of, the original. Also **safety mold,** *protection shell.*

S.A.G., *Screen Actors' Guild.*

S.A.G. fee, see *residual.*

sale, *noun* 1. a transaction involving the exchange of a good or service for money or credit.
2. an offer of products or services for purchase at temporarily reduced prices, made by a retailer.

salable sample, a product sample of trial size which is sold at a nominal price at retail.

sales, *plural noun* 1. a marketing process which involves the personal development and maintenance of prospects for purchases as a means of meeting marketing objectives.
2. a commercial profession or a craft which seeks to personally develop and maintain buyers for goods one wishes to sell.
3. the amount of goods exchanged by an individual or organization over a stated period of time.
sales, *adj.*

Sales Areas-Marketing, Inc., a marketing research firm owned by Time, Inc., selling syndicated reports of food product movement through chain store warehouses. Abbreviated SAMI.

sales area test, a test market conducted in a geographical area where sales results can be obtained speedily or conveniently, as a sales district. Cf. *market test, test market.*

sales audit, a periodic measurement of dollar and unit movement of products through retail stores; commonly accomplished by establishing store inventories at the opening and closing of the audit, and intervening receipts of merchandise.

sales call norm, an organization's estimate of the number or length of sales calls a salesperson should make over a stated period of time, by account or in total.

sales contest, a contest open to a company's sales personnel or to prospects, structured to reward superior performance or unusually large purchases. Cf. *sales incentive.*

sales control, continuous and systematic inspection of a firm's sales results in order to develop effective plans.

sales effectiveness test, a test of the effectiveness of a communications medium or advertising campaign in selling a product.

sales force, a group of employees of an organization responsible for personally developing sales and sales prospects.

161

sales forecast, an estimate of expected sales.

sales incentive, a reward in excess of salary or commission provided to a salesperson in return for achieving a stated sales goal. Cf. *sales contest, salesman's premium.*

sales letter, a letter on a company's letterhead mailed to a prospect for a sale.

sales life, the period during which an item available for retail sale is likely to retain its original quality and may thus be sold. Also *shelf life.*

sales management, the planning, coordination, and control of sales operations and the recruitment and supervision of salesmen.

sales manager, an employee of a marketer responsible for sales management.

sales meeting, a meeting sponsored by an organization with members of its sales force, for informational, training, and motivational purposes.

salesman's premium, a reward to a salesman for extraordinary effort or for leadership in the amount sold. Cf. *sales incentive.*

sales portfolio, a manual of information carried by a salesman for reference or display.

sales potential, see *headroom.*

sales promotion, see *promotion.*

sales promotion department, 1. the department of a manufacturing or wholesaling company responsible for the planning and implementation of all promotional activities.
2. a department of an advertising agency responsible for devising promotion plans for clients.

sales quota, a figure, usually either the number of unit sales to be made or the sales revenue to be received, set as a goal for a salesman or agent in a stated future period.

sales service, a service, usually offered by a retail-owned wholesaler, that provides sales visits to retailers on behalf of and for a fee paid by manufacturers.

same size, *reproduce at the same size as the picture submitted;* an instruction to a photographer, platemaker, etc. Abbreviated *S.S.*

SAMI, *Sales Areas-Marketing, Inc.*

sample, *noun* 1. (in statistics) a group of individuals, regarded as representative of a whole population, that are selected for study or questioning.
2. a small quantity or single portion of a product, distributed gratis or at a reduced price to induce the recipient to buy the product steadily.

sample area, (in research) the geographical area within which a respondent sample is obtained.

sample cell, see *cell.*

sample reel, see *demo reel.*

sampling, *noun* 1. (in statistics) the taking of a sample.
2. (in retail merchandising) the distribution of samples.

sampling error, (in statistics) the deviation between the observed characteristics of a sample and the characteristics of the population from which it is drawn; inherent in all samples and inversely related to sample size. Also *sampling variation.*

sampling variation, see *sampling error.*

sandwich board, an advertising poster suspended from the shoulders of a person walking in the street; usually there is one board in front, one in back.

san serif

sans serif, 1. the style of type without serifs. Also *gothic.*
adjective. 2. noting or pertaining to a typeface designed without serifs.

satellite, *noun* 1. see *relay station.*
2. a relay station placed into orbit around the earth. Also **satellite station.**

satellite store, 1. a small store close to and competing with a large one.
2. a store close to but not part of a shopping center.

saturation, *noun* 1. see *chroma.*
2. an amount of advertising well above the normal levels of frequency and coverage.

saturation showing, (in outdoor advertising) a showing well above 100- intensity.

save, *verb* (in photography, motion pictures, or television) to stop or preserve a process or action.

S.A.W.A., *Screen Advertising World Association.*

S.C., in a *single column;* used in ordering periodical advertising space.
2. *small capitals;* used in specifying type.

scalability analysis, an interview technique used to determine the tendency of a respondent to exaggerate reactions, in which stimuli of different degrees or kinds are presented successively and respondent reactions noted. Also *scalogram technique.*

scale, *verb* 1. to enlarge or reduce type, artwork, etc. photographically for printing at the proper size.
2. to compute the fit of manuscript copy to type area for a given type size.
noun 3. see *scale rate.*

scale rate, 1. (in printing) a standard rate of payment for typesetting, platemaking, etc.
2. (in talent payment) a rate of payment for residuals as specified by union contract, rather than as negotiated. Also *scale.*

scalogram technique, see *scalability analysis.*

scan, *verb* 1. to make repeated and closely spaced traverses of an image with a beam of light, or with electrons, in order to transform the tonal values of the image into electrical impulses that can be reproduced as a television image or as halftone separations that will print as a four-color process reproduction.
noun 2. (in television) the time taken by such a traverse; in the United States, one sixtieth of a second. Also **scanning rate.**

scatter plan, a broadcast advertising media plan calling for a series of advertising announcements presented at random during a number of television or radio programs. Cf. *sponsor, magazine plan.*

scenario, *noun* the outline of a play, film, television show, etc. Also *synopsis.*

scene, *noun* 1. the locale, or visual image of such a locale, appearing in a dramatic action.
2. a sequence of a play, motion picture, television show, etc., occurring in a single place and over a continuous period of time.

schedule, *noun* 1. a list of things occurring in a temporal sequence, stating the time at which each is to occur. Also *timetable.*
2. a list of things having a common association in a general plan, as one of advertising to be used in a communications medium or of media to be used in a campaign.

scientific marketing, a style of marketing characterized by use of scientific research, testing, and analytic methods as a means of minimizing risks and maximizing business opportunities.

scoop, *noun* a circular floodlamp of 500 watts or above, used in motion picture and television production. Also *basher.*

score, *noun* 1. a quantitative result of a statistical investigation.
2. a linear indentation in a sheet of paper or other material, made to ease and direct folding.
3. a musical piece in document form, used to guide individual musicians in its performance.

Scotchprint, *noun, trademark* (in printing) a repro proof pulled on special dull-finish, non-shrink stock, from original letterpress engravings; used for camera copy.

scrambled merchandising, a practice of retailers who offer for sale product lines not conventionally carried by stores of their kind.

scrap, *noun* visual material derived from clippings, labels, etc., used to roughly illustrate an intended visual or scenic treatment.

Scratch-and-Sniff, *noun, trademark* a microencapsulation process, used to convey a specific scent to readers of print media; such scents are released by scratching a properly treated area of paper or scratching a tape affixed to the printed piece which breaks the microscopic sized plastic "scent bubbles," thus releasing the aroma.

scratchboard, *noun* a piece of clay-or chalk-coated cardboard overlaid with a surface of ink; the scraping-away of portions of the ink can create an engravinglike design, usually white on black.

scratch track, a sound track used as a rough guide to the sound of a final recording.

screen, *noun* 1. a surface onto which the image of a slide, motion picture or a television program is projected.
2. (in printing) the number of rows of dots per linear inch in a halftone, ranging from 55 in ordinary newspaper work to 300 for the finest offset and gravure work.
3. see *halftone screen*.
verb 4. to project photographic images.

5. to sort or eliminate, as sales prospects or research respondents.

Screen Actors' Guild, the national union of motion picture actors. Abbreviated *S.A.G.*

Screen Advertising World Association, an organization promoting motion pictures as an advertising medium. Abbreviated *S.A.W.A.*

Screen Extras' Guild, a Hollywood, Cal., union of motion picture extras founded in 1945. Abbreviated *S.E.G.*

screening, *noun* (in motion pictures or television) a viewing of filmed or videotaped material, for editing or approval purposes.

scrim, *noun* (in theater, photography, or motion pictures) a fine, translucent cloth used to diffuse light, either as a backdrop on a stage or over a light.

script, *noun* 1. a complete sequential account of dialogue, actions, settings, etc. prepared by the author of a play or show.
2. a typeface resembling handwriting.

script girl, (in motion pictures and television) a director's assistant responsible for script preparation, prompting, recording of studio activity, and other affairs. Also *continuity girl.*

scriptwriter, *noun* a person who writes scripts for television or radio programs.

S.D., *standard deviation.*

S.E., 1. *sound effect.*
2. *standard error.*

seal of approval, a symbol granted by a publication, especially a magazine, for use in advertising, stating that the magazine has tested the product advertised and found it satisfactory.

seasonal, *adjective* noting or pertaining to a product, service, or category normally purchased only at a certain time or times of the year.

seasonality index, a measurement expressing the variation in sales of goods or services, for a brand or category, from an even distribution throughout the year as influenced by seasonal factors; e.g., suntan lotions have an extremely high summer seasonality index.

second, *noun* a unit of product of substandard quality, sold at a discount. Cf. *remainder, overstock.*

secondary audience, 1. see *pass-along audience.* Also *secondary readership.*
2. the readers of a publication other than those for whom its editorial content is intended.

secondary service area, the area within which the signal of a television or radio station is inferior but receivable.

secondary source data, information obtained from a published study by another person or group.

second cover, the front inside cover of a periodical. Abbreviated *2C.*

section, *noun* 1. see *district.*
2. (in television) any of three classifications of rates for spot television announcements; section I spots are sold at the highest rates and have the highest degree of preferential treatment; section II and III spots are progressively more preemptible and less costly.

sectional announcement, see *regional announcement.*

sectional center, (in periodical publishing) the central area of a region for which a regional edition is published; defined in the U.S. by the first three digits of the U.S. Postal Service zip code.

sectional feed, see *regional feed.*

sectional magazine, a magazine intended to appeal to people in one geographical area.

security deposit, a deposit made with a wholesaler by a retailer to assure his credit.

see-fee television, pay television charged for by the program.

seen/associated, *adjective* noting or pertaining to ad-noters who claim to have seen a given advertisement and to have recognized the advertiser; used by the research firm of Daniel Starch and Associates.

S.E.G., *Screen Extras' Guild.*

segment, *noun* 1. an identifiable subgroup of purchasers or consumers within a market who share a common characteristic or special need. Also *market segment.*
verb 2. to divide a market by a strategy directed to gaining a major portion of the sales to a subgroup in a category, rather than a more limited share of purchases by all category users.

segmentation, *noun* 1. a marketing strategy which designates a market segment as a target prospect group. Also *market segmentation.*
adjective 2. noting or pertaining to such a strategy.

segment sponsorship, see *partial sponsorship.*

segue, *noun* (in television or radio) a continuous transition from one piece of music or audio effect to another.

selected take, (in motion pictures or television) an approved film or videotape of a scene or shot.

selective, *adjective* (of a periodical) of interest to a certain type of reader rather than to the public generally.

selective attention, (in psychology) attention on the part of an individual to those types of things that please or interest him most, rather than equally to all things to which he is exposed. Cf. *selective perception, selective recall.*

selective clubbing, an offer to prospective subscribers of a certain number of magazines from a list at a reduced rate.

selective distribution, 1. wholesale distribution only of items that have a markup of no less than a predetermined rate and yet are competitively priced.
2. wholesale distribution of items only to retailers who spend no less than a predetermined dollar amount or who meet certain standards in their operations.

selective magazine, a magazine published for persons with special interests. Also *special interest magazine.*

selective merchandising, merchandising that eliminates competing and redundant items.

selective perception, (in psychology) perception conditioned by preexisting attitudes and experience, or motivated by interest. Cf. *selective attention, selective recall.*

selective recall, (in psychology) degree of memory of things experienced that is influenced by preexisting attitudes, subsequent experiences, etc. Cf. *selective attention, selective perception.*

self-administered questionnaire, a questionnaire whose information is entered by the respondent without the aid of an interviewer.

self-concept, see *self-image.*

self-cover, *noun* a pamphlet or the like whose cover is of the same paper as that of the remaining pages.

self-image, (in psychology) a person's beliefs regarding what he is to himself, or others, or what he aspires to be. Also *self-concept.*

self liquidator, *noun* 1. a premium having a cost fully covered by the purchase price for which it is offered. Cf. *purchase-privilege premium, semi-liquidator.*
2. a display unit provided by a manufacturer in return for payment by a retailer covering its cost.
self-liquidating, *adj.*

self-mailer, *noun* a direct-mail piece folded and printed in such a way that no envelope or wrapper is required for mailing.

self-service, *adjective* noting or pertaining to any retail operation in which the customer himself selects and removes the items he purchases.

sell, *verb* 1. to encourage a sales transaction.
2. to complete a sales transaction.
noun 3. (in advertising) a portion of an advertisement devoted to encouraging a sale of the product or service advertised.

sell-in, an effort to attain distribution and build inventory for a product at retail. Cf. *sell through.*

selling agent, a self employed person or independent business organization who negotiates the sale of goods or services without taking title to such goods or services. Cf. *agent.*

selling idea, an advertising execution element that compellingly summarizes or expresses a creative strategy. Cf. *slogan.*

sell-off, *noun* resale to another advertiser of advertising space or time for which one has contracted.

sell through, an effort to increase the rate at which a product is sold through retailers. Cf. *sell in.*

semantic differential, (in research) a scale which can be used by a respondent to indicate his reaction to a question in terms of a position between two paired, opposed or opposite terms or adjectives.

semi-liquidator, *noun* a premium offered with a retail item that is not fully self-liquidating. Also **semi-self liquidator,** *partial self-liquidator.* Cf. *purchase-privilege premium, self liquidator.*

semi-self-service, *adjective* noting or pertaining to a retail operation where not all departments are self-service.

semi-spectacular, *noun* (in outdoor advertising) a painted bulletin to which special lighting, animation, or three-dimensional features have been added but that does not have the elaboration of a true spectacular. Also *embellished painted bulletin.*

sentence completion, (in psychology) a method for determining preexisting attitudes or information by having a respondent complete partial sentences.

separation, *noun* 1. (in television or radio) a time period maintained between competing commercials.
2. the isolation of the three primary colors from full color copy by means of camera filters in preparing four color (including black key) film negatives; used in producing process printing plates.

separation negative, any of the negatives produced in making a color separation.

sepia, *noun* 1. (in photography or motion pictures) a type of monotone film or photographic printing paper yielding brown tones instead of gray to black.
adjective 2. noting or pertaining to the brown tones characteristic of such photographs.

serial, *noun* (in motion pictures, television, and radio) a series of dramatic episodes forming a continuous story and presented at regular intervals.

serial correlation, see *autocorrelation.*

series, *noun* a number of television or radio programs presented at regular intervals and united by title, cast, story theme, etc. Cf. *serial, non-serial.*

serif

serif, *noun* (in typography) a cross-stroke at the end of a main stroke of a letter, used to improve recognizability of the letter and as a decoration.

serigraph, *noun* a print produced by serigraphy.

serigraphy, *noun* the art of color printing by means of a squegee through a series of stencil-like silk or fine wire screens, (one for each color) each of which is treated to admit only a specific image to the areas of the print. Also **silk screen.**

service, *noun* 1. an act or deed by one person serving to benefit another.
2. a business organization which performs such acts in exchange for financial compensation, as a sale or fee.
3. those acts performed by a seller of products to maintain the utility of products sold.

service charge, 1. a charge by a wholesaler for services other than delivery of goods.
2. a charge by a retailer for services not automatically provided the customer, e.g., deliveries, credit, and check cashing.

service fee, a fee paid by an advertiser to an advertising agency, either in the form of a retainer for general services or of special compensation for unusual services.

service magazine, see *women's service magazine.*

service mark, an identifying mark for the services provided by one organization; can be registered under the Trade Mark Act of 1946.

service store, a store in which selection and purchasing of goods is done through the assistance of clerks.

service wholesaler, a wholesaler who has salesmen who call on retailers and who offers various services in connection with his merchandise. Also *jobber.*

S.E.S.A.C., *Society of European Stage Authors and Composers.*

session, *noun* (in radio, motion pictures, or television) a meeting of performing talent, as actors, singers, announcers, etc., with production personnel for the purpose of creating some form of record of a performance, whether on film, tape, or phonographic record.

session fee, a payment made to performers by an advertiser as compensation for performance at a session; rates as usually established by union contract. Cf. *residual.*

set, *noun* 1. the flats and other objects forming the scene in any part of a theatrical, motion picture, or television performance.
2. a device for receiving a television or radio program.
3. (in psychology) the disposition of a person to respond in a specific way to certain stimuli.
verb 4. to arrange type in the proper order for printing.

setback, *noun* the distance between the center of an outdoor advertisement space and the line of travel it faces.

set designer, a person who designs and supervises the construction of theatrical, motion picture, or television sets.

set flat, see *flat.*

sets in use, obsolescent (in a rating survey) the percentage of television or radio sets within a coverage area that are in use during an average minute of a given time period. Abbreviated *S.I.U.* Also *tune-in.*

set-up *noun* a configuration of camera, subjects, and lighting, as in photography, motion pictures, or halftone printing.

S.F.X., *sound effects.*

shade, *verb* 1. to eliminate false signals and exaggerated contrast from a television image.

noun 2. a color in shadow, or appearing to be.

shaded, *adjective* noting or pertaining to display type having certain strokes, repeated so that a three-dimensional effect is produced.

shadow box, a boxlike frame for the display of retail items.

share, *noun* 1. (in a rating survey) the percentage of the television or radio audience in a coverage area that is tuned to the program being rated.
2. the percentage of total retail purchases, in terms of dollars or units, for a given category of product that is enjoyed by any one brand in that category. Also *share of market, share of retail sales, brand share.*

shared identification, television station identification superimposed as a legend during a commercial. Also **shared I.D.**

share of market, see *share.*

share of mind, the percentage of all brand awareness or brand advertising awareness for a given category of product or service that is enjoyed by any one brand in that category; usually elicited on an unaided basis.

share of retail sales, see *share.*

share point, a share, as of market or audience, equal to one percent of the total.

sheet, *noun* 1. a piece of paper for a printing press and plate.
2. (obsolescent) an outdoor advertising poster sized 26 inches by 39 inches.

sheet-fed press, a printing press that prints individual sheets rather than a roll or web of paper.

sheetwise, *adjective* noting or pertaining to printing in which each side of a sheet is printed on a separate press run. Cf. *work-and-turn.*

shelf, *noun* 1. a retail store's physical facility for displaying products above the floor in areas open to customers; usually, a long, narrow series of horizontal tiers. Cf. *rack*.
2. in current availability, as *off the shelf*.

shelf card, a display card set up on a shelf in a retail store.

shelf display, an arrangement of goods on a shelf so as to create a display.

shelf extender, a traylike extension to a retail store shelf, used for special displays or as a means of increasing the regular shelf display. Also *extender*.

shelf life, see *sales life*.

shelf marker, a tag giving the price of a retail item; usually placed in, or hung from a channel strip.

shelf pack, a container for retail items of sufficiently small size to permit it to be placed on a shelf with ordinary clearance height.

shelf space, the amount of space occupied by a type of merchandise in a retail store; measured in terms of square feet, linear feet, or number of facings.

shelf strip, a strip of paper printed with an advertising message, attached to the front edge of a shelf. Cf. *channel strip*.

shelf talker, a printed advertising message hung over the edge of a retail store shelf.

shelf tape, a printed adhesive tape attached to the front edge of a retail store shelf.

shelter magazine, see *home service book*.

shipment, *noun* 1. a collection of products sold as a unit, and transferred to the buyer together.
2. the amount of products sold by a supplier and transferred to customers.

shirt-board advertising, advertising printed on the white cardboard used to stiffen commercially laundered shirts.

shoehorn, *verb, informal* to add copy or visuals to an advertisement, especially one that is already crowded or pressed for time.

shoot, *noun* 1. (in motion pictures or television) a session where performances are recorded or filmed, as for a commercial.
verb 2. to record or film such a session.

shooting schedule, a schedule of shots for a motion picture or television show, giving the actual chronological sequence of shots as they are to be taken rather than as they are to be assembled for the completed film.

shop, *noun* 1. a small store.
verb 2. to personally examine product's or service's features, prices, appearance, etc. on a comparative basis.

shopper, *noun* 1. a retail customer involved in examining, rather than purchasing, merchandise.
2. see *shopping newspaper*.

shopping center, a unified cluster of establishments offering a variety of goods and services, principally catering to the automobile trade; usually located away from closely-built urban areas. Cf. *mall*.

shopping goods, retail goods customarily purchased after careful consideration of competing brands.

shopping mall, see *mall*.

shopping newspaper, a newspaper primarily edited for local shoppers, containing advertisements, information about stores, information on local events, etc. Also *shopper*.

shopping service, a survey service for a wholesaler or store chain in which the prices of competing stores are checked and reported.

short, *adjective* with less merchandise than is required to meet demand.

short rate, an extra rate charged an advertiser who has not earned a previously anticipated discount for media space or time purchased.

short-term subscription, a periodical subscription of less than one year.

shot, *noun* 1. a still photograph.
2. (in motion pictures or television) a single, continuous filming by a camera, either from one position or a moving position. Cf. *take.*

shoulder, *noun* the nonprinting area of a piece of letterpress type from which the printing surface is raised.

shoulder shot, (in motion pictures and television) a shot of a person from the shoulders upward.

show, *noun* 1. a performance designed to entertain an audience. Cf. *program.*
2. (informal) a place where such a performance is held.
3. a special, short term display of merchandise to prospects, often in cooperation with other merchants. Cf. *trade show.*
verb 4. to display merchandise.

showing, *noun* 1. a number of outdoor advertisements offered as a unit. Cf. *intensity.*
2. a number of transit advertisements, especially car cards, offered as a unit. Also *run.*

shrinkage, *noun* 1. a measured loss of sales items or of weight in sales items, due to natural causes, pilfering, etc.
2. the reduction in size during molding and drying of a matrix from which printing plates are cast; requires overdimensioning of the original if final agate line size is to be retained.

shutter, *noun* (in photography and motion pictures) a device in a camera which admits light to the film which it covers for brief intervals.

shutter speed, (in photography or motion pictures) the time interval that a camera shutter exposes film; one of the three key variables in determining proper film exposure, the other two being f-stop and film speed.

S.I., *sponsor identification.*

S.I.A., *Storage Instantaneous Audimeter.*

side bind, see *side stitch.*

side-by-side shot, see *half-lap.*

side position, 1. (in transportation advertising) a car-card position above the side windows of a vehicle; the common position.
2. the position of advertising posters on either side of the exterior of a public-transit vehicle.

side-stitch, *verb* to bind a magazine, pamphlet or booklet by stapling or sewing the folded sheets next to the edge of the fold, on the outside. Also *side bind.* Cf. *saddle-stitch.*

sign, *noun* 1. a posted notice or advertisement, usually of a permanent nature, used to provide information as to location or identification. Cf. *poster.*
verb 2. to communicate by means of a sign language, as the standard manual system.
3. to identify a person or organization by means of a recognizable symbol.

signage, *noun* a series of signs of varying content but sharing a common design system.

signal, *noun* an information bearing impulse (radio wave, light wave, etc.) transmitted between a sender and one or more receivers; for example, the series of waves broadcast by a television or radio station.

signal area, see *coverage.*

signal grade, any of several degrees of signal strength in various parts of a television or radio station coverage area.

signal-to-noise ratio, (in communications research) the ratio of relevant to irrelevant material in a communication of any kind, as measured by the effect on persons receiving the communication; a term borrowed from electronics.

signature, *noun* 1. see *logotype*.
2. a musical theme identifying a television or radio program, or advertiser's product or service.
3. a separate physical portion of a book, made by printing, folding, trimming, and binding a sheet so as to form a number of pages.

significant difference, see *statistical significance*.

sign-off, *noun* the formal conclusion of a broadcasting day.

sign-on, *noun* the formal beginning of a broadcasting day.

silent, *adjective* (of motion pictures or television) noting or pertaining to moving visual images recorded, projected, or broadcast without benefit of a sound accompaniment.

silhouette, *noun* 1. an outline figure, usually of undifferentiated black against a white background.
verb 2. to show a figure, as in a photograph, without a background.

silhouette halftone, see *outline halftone*.

silk-screen, see *serigraphy*.

silver print, 1. a photographic reproduction whose principal lines have been traced in ink that is then bleached to remove the photographic image; used to make accurate line-cut representations of a scene.
2. a photographic print whose emulsion is sensitized by silver salts.

SILVTR, *silent videotape recording;* used as a notation or direction on commercial production material.

Simmons Research Associates, Inc., a New York research firm specializing in communications media and product usage research; it issues a syndicated series, the Simmons Selective and Mass Media Studies.

simple correlation, see *correlation*.

simulation, *noun* 1. a mathematical, computer-assisted projection of the interaction of a number of variables, used to show the probable results of various courses of action in the light of known and projected data.
2. an operation designed to artificially model a real situation.

simulcast, *noun* a broadcast on a television station and radio station at the same time; often used to permit video material to be accompanied by high fidelity, stereophonic audio.

S.I.N., *Spanish International Network*.

single rate card, a rate card for a local communications medium having no separate local and national rate.

single system, any system for recording visual and audio components of a motion picture or television show on the same film or tape at the same time.

single truck, (obsolescent) a full-page newspaper advertisement.

siphon, *verb* to relay a free television broadcast via pay television.

sit com, see *situation comedy*.

site furnishing, the appurtenances and decorations of a commercial setting.

situation comedy, a television or radio show whose comedy is based on a series of humorous situations. Also *sit com*.

S.I.U. *sets in use.*

six-sheet poster panel, an outdoor-advertising poster panel 5'4" high by 11'7" wide.

16mm, see *motion picture film.*

:60, *noun* a commercial of sixty seconds length. Also **sixty.**

size, *noun* 1. a preparation made from glue or starch for filling the pores of paper to give it a coated finish.
verb 2. to fill the pores of paper with such a preparation.

skew, *noun* 1. a concentration in excess of the average, as of sales or scores.
verb 2. to result in, or seek, such a concentration.

skewed distribution. (in statistics) a distribution of frequencies that deviates from a normal distortion in having a single mode that differs markedly from the mean.

skid, *noun* a low platform for holding printed sheets or a display of merchandise.

skin pack, see *blister pack.*

skip-print, *noun* (in motion pictures) a film print in which the rate of action has been accelerated by deleting frames at regular intervals.
skip print, *v.*

skytyping, *noun* skywriting made with closely spaced and precisely calculated puffs of smoke, rather than with solid trails of smoke, by a number of airplanes flying in formation.

sky wave, an AM radio wave emitted toward the sky by a transmitter and reflected by the ionosphere; such signals become stronger at ground level after sunset. Cf. *ground wave, daytime station.*

skywriting, *noun* the process of producing messages, symbols, etc. in the sky with trails or closely grouped puffs of smoke emitted by an airplane. Cf. *skytyping.*

slate, *noun* (in motion pictures and television) a board identifying each take recorded for a production, featured at the opening of the action and used to cue its commencement.

slice of life, a form of television or radio commercial presenting a realistically enacted, dramatic simulation of a personal life situation. Also **slice.**

slick, *noun* a proof pulled on glossy (coated) paper, clean in appearance and suitable for reproduction. Also **enamel proof.**

slide, *noun* a photographic transparency mounted on glass or in a metal, plastic or cardboard frame so that it may be projected on a screen; usually made from 35mm film.

slide commercial, a television commercial with a video sequence composed wholly or in part of a slide or slides, rather than film.

sliding rate, a media rate for advertising that diminishes per unit of space or time as the number of units purchased increases. Also **sliding scale.**

slippage, *noun* 1. those people who purchase a product with the intent of claiming a promotion reward for such a purchase (e.g.: refund, coupon, or premium) who fail to fulfill this intent.
2. the ratio between such purchases, and the purchases of those people who claim such a reward; usually stated as a percentage of total purchases. Also **slippage rate.**

slip-sheet, *verb* to interleave freshly printed sheets of paper with porous sheets of non-printed paper to prevent the printed sheets from offsetting on each other.

slogan, *noun* a sentence or phrase used consistently in a series of advertisements to express the central message.

slop print, (in motion pictures or television) a rough print of an optical, used for review and editing purposes.

slow motion, (in motion pictures or television) a reduction of the apparent speed of moving things that are filmed, as to show clearly their motion or to create a special effect.

slug, *noun* 1. a solid line of letterpress type, as one produced on a Linotype machine.
2. a nonprinting lead rule of six points thickness or more.

small caps, capital letters smaller than those normal for a given type font.

small store, a retail store with annual sales of $100,000 or less, as defined by A.C. Nielsen Co. in its retail indices. Also *mom and pop store.*

smiley rating, (in research) a rating device in which one of an array of drawings of faces expressing a spectrum of feelings (e.g., frowns to smiles, hence "smiley") is selected by a respondent to illustrate his reaction to a question.

S.M.S.A., *standard metropolitan statistical area.*

smudge, *verb* 1. to damage a piece of artwork, photographic film or print, or a freshly printed sheet in a manner that results in a blurred spot, as a fingerprint.
2. to blur a well-focused advertising idea by excessive manipulation.

Smyth sewing, a form of bookbinding in which the pages of a signature are sewn together along the gutter and the signatures sewn to the back of the book.

snack counter, a restaurant for light meals at which the customers sit at a counter rather than at tables.

snap, *noun* (informal) see *snapshot.*

snappy, *adjective* (of a photograph) with high contrast and yet with full range of tones.

snapshot, *noun* a still photograph. Also *snap.*

sneak, *noun* (in motion pictures or television) a slow fading-in or -out of sounds or images.

snipe, *noun* a set of sheets containing a retailer's name or address, usually pasted at the bottom of an outdoor poster in individual geographical locations. Also *overlay.*

S.N.R. *subject to non-renewal.*

S.O., *standing order.*

soap opera, a daytime television or radio serial, often of a melodramatic nature, intended to appeal chiefly to homemakers and originally sponsored by soap manufacturers. Also *daytime drama,* **soaper.**

social class, (in sociology) a level of a division of society into a hierarchy of power, prestige, and affluence groups, from lower to middle to upper classes, or finer divisions; operationally, measured by such factors as occupation, income, place of residence, associates and affiliations, education, etc. Also **social status,** *status.* Cf. *lifestyle.*

S.O.F., *sound on film;* used as a notation or direction on commercial production material.

soft goods, textiles or merchandise made from textiles.

software, *noun* programs, charts, and other material used in connection with data processing; the elements of computer programming other than the computer and its auxiliary equipment. Cf. *hardware.*

solid, *adjective* (of printing type) individual type lines set vertically as closely as possible; unleaded.

Sonovox, *noun* an electronic device for articulating nonhuman sounds as words. Cf. *synthesizer.*

sore-thumb display, a small but conspicuous store display.

S.O.T., *sound on tape;* used as a notation or direction in commercial production material.

sound, *noun* 1. the audible product of an audio system.
2. the public impression created by a radio station, or the programming format it employs.

sound effect, any sound produced for a dramatic performance or the like, other than one by the human voice or a musical instrument. Abbreviated *S.E., S.F.X.*

sound man, 1. a person responsible for producing sound effects.
2. a person responsible for recording the audio portion of a motion picture or videotape.

sound on film, sound recorded on film rather than on discs or tapes. Abbreviated *S.O.F.*

sound on tape, sound recorded on magnetic tape rather than on discs or film. Abbreviated *S.O.T.*

sound stage, see *stage.*

sound track, the audio portion of a film or videotape. Also *track.*

source credibility, the believability of a person who provides information to those who receive it; usually influenced by the informant's perception of the informer's expertise with respect to the information in question, and his trustworthiness.

S.P.A., *special purchase allowance.*

space, *noun* 1. the portion of a publication's pages, or outdoor or transit display areas, that may be purchased for advertising.
2. the distance between typographic elements.

space allocation, the shelf space allotted to a product or group of related products in a retail store.

space buyer, an employee of an advertiser or advertising agency who buys periodical space.

space discount, a discount for purchase of a certain quantity of periodical space.

space position value, (in outdoor advertising) the value of advertising in a certain location, given the presence or absence of competing advertising, the orientation of the billboard or poster, the distance from which it is first seen, and the speed of traffic.

space schedule, a schedule of advertising space to be bought, specifying the media, the dates of appearance, the size of advertisements, and the cost, submitted by an advertising agency to a client.

space spot, any of a number of low-cost newspaper advertising spaces sold in specified quantities, to appear at unspecified intervals over a specified period.

Spanish International Network, a network of Spanish-language television and radio stations in the U.S. Abbreviated *S.I.N.*

spec, *adjective* 1. see *on speculation.*
verb 2. to specify in giving an order or instructions.

special, *noun* a single radio or television program which temporarily replaces those programs which usually appear in the time period of its broadcast; often a spectacular. Also *one-shot.*

special canvass, an intensive round of sales visits to a chain or association of retail stores intended to obtain support for a new brand or promotion.

special display, any retail merchandising display other than that ordinarily mounted for a product on a shelf. Cf. *display, shelf display.*

special effect, (in motion pictures or television) any visual effect, as an illusion, created by optical or electronic means.

special-interest magazine, see *selective magazine.*

special opening, a specially-prepared beginning or ending, identifying sponsors, for a radio or television program.

special purchase allowance, an allowance granted by a manufacturer or wholesaler to a retailer, made in addition to a basic merchandising allowance for the purchase of goods within a stated period. Abbreviated *S.P.A.*

specialty store, a store specializing in the sale of one kind of product, often together with other products used with this basic product type.

Spectacolor, *noun, trademark,* a production technique allowing four-color newspaper advertisements preprinted on coated stock to appear in the same format in the editorial sections of all issue copies; uses electronic scanning cues to assure trimming of the roll at a uniform point, without resort to a "wallpaper" design. Cf. *hi-fi insert.*

spectacular, *noun* 1. a large and elaborate outdoor advertising display with vivid color, special lighting effects, animation, or the like.
2. a television, motion picture, or stage show elaborately cast and produced.

speed, *noun* 1. the operating rate of a reproducing device, as revolutions per minute, frames per second, etc.
2. see *film speed.*

Speedaumat, *noun, trademark* an addressing machine using embossed plates and an inked ribbon.

Speedball, *noun, trademark* any of various broad-nibbed pens creating strokes of various thicknesses, used primarily for lettering.

spending split, the percentage or dollar amounts allocated by a marketer's plans to each of the key marketing spending elements, that is, advertising, consumer promotion, and trade promotion. Cf. *marketing mix.*

spiff, *noun* see *push money.*

spill-in, *noun* transmission into one market area of a television or radio signal from another.

spill-in circulation, circulation within a given urban area of a newspaper published outside the area.

spill-in coverage, coverage of a certain market by a communications medium based outside the market.

spill-out, *noun* transmission of a television or radio signal beyond its own market area.

splice, *verb* to cement or tape two sections of film or tape together.

splicer, *noun* a machine which can aid in splicing film or tape.

split commercial, see *piggyback commercial.*

split focus, (in motion pictures or television) a focus intended to give two subjects, at different distances from the camera, equal prominence.

split frame, see *composite shot.*

split-half reliability, see *reliability.*

split run, (in periodical printing) a press run that carries two or more different forms of an advertiser's message in different copies or issues, to test the effectiveness of one advertisement against another or to appeal to regional or other specific markets.

split screen, see *composite shot.*

spoilage, *noun* 1. printed matter spoiled in printing or binding; considered inevitable and allowed for in advance when ordering

printing amount.
2. the rate at which any perishable product deteriorates prior to sale.

spoils, *plural noun* unsalable goods; reimbursement is normally claimed by the purchasing retailer or wholesaler.

spokesman, *noun* a person actively endorsing a course of action desired by an advertiser in an advertisement, especially a personality familiar to the audience. Cf. *testimonial.*

sponsor, *noun* 1. an advertiser or other party that pays part or all of the expenses of a television or radio program.
2. a wholesaler who supplies and services a voluntary chain.

sponsor identification, 1. (in research) an identification by a respondent of a sponsor or his products and services with a television or radio program he sponsors; established by telephone interview during or just after the program. Abbreviated *S.I.*
2. (in television or radio) an identification announcement of a sponsor at the beginning or end of a program.

sponsor relief, withdrawal from sponsorship of a television or radio program during an off-season period.

sponsorship, *noun* ownership of the advertising rights of a sponsor.

spot, *noun* 1. see *occasion.*
2. see *spot announcement.*
3. loosely, a commercial, especially for television.
4. a spotlight.
verb 5. to buy broadcast commercial time on a market-by-market basis on individual stations.
spot, *adj.*

spot announcement, (in television or radio) 1. a commercial broadcast between programs and related to neither. Cf. *commercial.*
2. a commercial broadcast carried by an individual station, rather than a network.
3. see *wild spot.*

spot carrier, a syndicated program that is available to a sizable number of sponsors.

spot color, (in periodical advertising) color applied for emphasis to areas of a basically black and white advertisement.

spot display, any retail display created to be conspicuous.

spot drawing, a small drawing in an advertisement or periodical page that is otherwise basically text. Also *vignette.*

spot programming, the purchase of television or radio program time market-by-market from individual stations. Also *spotting.*

spot radio, 1. spot programming via radio.
2. radio station advertising as a medium.

spot schedule, a schedule of local purchases of television or radio spot time.

spotted map, a map of a locale, such as a city, town, or market, marked to show the locations of a set of outdoor advertisements. Also *spotting map.*

spot television, 1. spot programming via television.
2. television station advertising as a medium.

spotting, *noun* see *spot programming.*

spotting map, see *spotted map.*

spread, *noun* 1. two facing pages in a periodical or book.
2. an advertisement printed across two such pages.
3. see *make up.*

spread posting date, (in outdoor advertising) separated posting dates for a single showing, in which individual boards are posted at different times.

square-finish halftone, a halftone illustration trimmed square or rectangular as opposed to a vignetted or outline halftone.

squeeze track, 1. a sound track whose variations of pitch are determined by variations in its playing time.
2. a 16mm sound film with an optical sound track, prepared by direct, integrated reduction from separate 35mm optical sound and video film elements.

S.R.D.S., *Standard Rate and Data Service, Inc.*

S.R.P., *suggested retail price.*

S.S., *same size;* used as instructions to a photographer or printer.

stability, *noun* (in statistics) the relative freedom of the characteristics of a sample from chance deviation from the characteristics of the whole population; insured mainly by taking a large sample.

stabilization curve, (in statistics) a graphed curve illustrating the degrees of stability to be expected with various sample sizes.

stage, *noun* 1. a raised area used for theatrical and musical performances, public speaking, etc., before an audience.
2. an interior area used only for filming a motion picture or television performance. Also *sound stage.*
verb 3. (in engraving) to protect an area of a plate from etching by means of an applied lacquer or shellac.
4. to produce an event intended for an audience.

stage business, see *business.*

stage direction (in theater, motion pictures, or television) a note on the movements to be made by an actor, inserted into a script.

stage flat, see *flat.*

stage left, to a performer's left as he faces an audience; camera left is performer's right.

stage right, to a performer's right as he faces an audience; camera right is performer's left.

staggered schedule, a schedule of advertisements in a number of periodicals that calls for their insertion on different dates.

staging plan, see *floor plan.*

standard, *noun* 1. (in marketing or research) a numerical goal or goals intended to result from a planned course of action; failing their attainment, it is anticipated that new plans will be developed.
2. a bannerlike sign bearing an identification of an advertiser.
3. a vertical member used to support a sign. Also *upright.*

standard art, low-cost artwork supplied in varied bulk, ready-made, to advertisers. Also *syndicated art, stock art.*

standard colors, ink or paint colors adopted by a medium as acceptable for use by advertisers at no extra charge for custom-ordered colors.

standard deviation, (in statistics) a figure used to indicate the dispersion of the elements of a sample, equal to the square root of the squares of the deviations from the mean for the sample as a whole divided by the number of elements in the sample minus one. Abbreviated *S.D.*

Standard Directory of Advertisers, a periodical published by the National Register Publishing Company listing leading advertisers, their advertised products or services, and the positions of key marketing and advertising employees. Also *Red Book.* Cf. *Standard Directory of Advertising Agencies.*

Standard Directory of Advertising Agencies, a periodical published by the

National Register Publishing Company listing advertising agencies, their accounts, and key employees' positions. Also *Red Book.* Cf. *Standard Directory of Advertisers.*

standard error, (in statistics) a figure reflecting the expected variation of a particular figure, e.g., a mean or percentage, from sample to sample. Abbreviated *S.E.*

standard highway bulletin, a painted bulletin 41'8" long by 13' high.

standard metropolitan statistical area, a federally-designated urban area consisting of counties meeting certain standards for population, urban character, and economic and social integration with the county or counties serving as the urban center. Abbreviated *S.M.S.A.*

standard newspaper, a newspaper of the standard size, normally 21½" in depth 14½" wide, with eight columns totaling 2400 agate lines, or six columns totaling 1800 agate lines. Cf. *tabloid newspaper.*

standard order blank, an order form for media space and time purchases.

Standard Rate and Data Service, Inc., a Chicago-based firm that issues a number of advertising price and production requirement reference volumes for periodical, television, radio, and transit advertising. Also **Standard Rate.** Abbreviated *S.R.D.S.*

standard streamliner bulletin, a painted outdoor advertising bulletin 14' to 15' high by 46' to 48' wide.

standby, *noun* 1. a television or radio performance substituted or held ready to be substituted for a scheduled one in case of emergency.
2. a television or radio performer serving a similar function.

stand by, *be ready to go on the air;* an instruction to persons in a television or radio studio.

standby space, unscheduled periodical advertising space, offered to an advertiser at a discount with the understanding that his advertisement will appear only when the space happens to be available.

stand-in, *noun* (in theater, radio, motion pictures, or television) a person who acts in place of another performer in a production, as a temporary replacement, stuntperson, etc.

standing order, an order for a certain quantity of something, as merchandise or advertising space, filled at automatic regular intervals on repeated occasions. Abbreviated *S.O.*

standing type, type held for future use. Also **standing matter.**

stand of paper, (in outdoor advertising) the sheets of paper needed to compose a complete poster advertisement.

staple, *noun* any grocery item frequently purchased and consumed in large quantities.

Starch, Daniel, and Associates, a Mamaroneck, N.Y. research firm specializing in syndicated sales of measures of consumer response to and recognition of periodical advertising.

star commercial, a television or radio commercial presented in a program by the star of the program. Cf. *cast commercial.*

star route, a rural postal route serviced by a private carrier.

stat, *noun, verb* see *Photostat.*

Stat Can, *Statistics Canada.*

state farm paper, a periodical for farm families in a certain state of the Union.

station, *noun* a facility licensed by the Federal Communications Commission to broadcast original television or radio signals. Cf. *relay station.*

178

station break, a period between two television or radio programs, used for network or station identification, commercials, etc.

station format, see *format.*

station hour discount, a term used by the CBS television network for a discount based on sponsorship hours per week of time purchased.

station identification, identification of a television or radio station by its call letters or channel number and its location. Also **station I.D.**

station log, see *log.*

station poster, see *railroad showing.*

station-produced program, a television or radio program prepared completely by a station.

station representative, a person who solicits the purchase of commercial time from advertisers on behalf of a television or radio station.

statistical significance, observed differences between sets of numbers or test results not produced by sampling errors, and therefore representing real differences. Also **statistically significant difference,** *significant difference.*

statistics, *noun* mathematical techniques used in the description and analysis of quantifiable data and their interrelationships.

Statistics Canada, the Canadian government agency for collection of population statistics. Abbreviated *Stat Can.*

status, *noun* see *social class.*

steel engraving, an engraving on a steel plate.

stencil, *noun* 1. a sheet of paper or the like from which certain portions have been removed so as to form designs, letters, etc.; ink, paint, etc., run over the stencil passes through these areas to mark the surface over which it is laid.
2. a fibrous, waxed sheet used in mimeographing, etc.; a stylus, typewriter, etc., removes the wax so as to leave designs or lettering, and ink can pass through these areas to a sheet of paper beneath.

step, *noun* (in statistics) any of a number of arbitrary divisions of a continuous range of data, made for the sake of simplicity and often presented as a bar graph.

stereophonic, *adjective* of or pertaining to use of two simultaneously recorded, parallel audio channels to create the auditory illusion of a sound stage.
Also **stereo.** Cf. *monaural, quadraphonic.*

stereotype, *noun* 1. a printing plate cast from a matrix.
2. a generalized image or impression of a class of persons or things alien to oneself and one's social group.

stet, *verb* let it stand; an instruction to a typesetter or printer to ignore an alteration called for in a proof.

still, *noun* 1. a photograph of a scene being enacted in a play, motion picture, television show, etc.
2. a photograph of a performer, used for publicity purposes.
3. a slide or other nonmoving image used in a television show.

still man, a photographer of stills.

sting, *noun* an emphatic piece of background music used to give accent to a motion picture or television play. Also **stinger.**

stitching, *noun* 1. bookbinding with thread.
2. loosely, bookbinding with staples.

stock, *noun* 1. paper used for printing.
2. merchandise in retail inventory. Also *store.*
3. a share of corporate ownership.

stock art, see *standard art*.

stock cut, a ready-made decorative or explanatory cut, kept in stock by a printer or type house for multiple sale.

stock footage, film bearing stock shots.

stock music, recorded music kept in a library for repeated use on television or radio programs. Also *library music*.

stock shot, (in motion pictures or television) a shot of special effects, scenes, actions, etc., that is kept in a library for repeated use in cases where special filming of such subjects is unnecessary. Also *library shot*.

stockturn, *noun* see *velocity*.

stock turn, see *turnover*.

stone, *noun* (in printing) 1. a table, formerly with a stone top, used for laying out type galleys, etc.
2. (obsolescent) a smooth-faced stone from which lithographs are printed.

stoneman, *noun* a printing shop employee who lays out type galleys, etc.

stone proof, see *flat proof*.

stop action, see *freeze frame*.

stop motion, apparent motion in a television or film sequence created by moving an object slightly between frames that are taken at isolated moments rather than at normal camera speed. Cf. *animation*.

Storage Instantaneous Audimeter, a high-speed Audimeter used by the A.C. Nielsen Co. Abbreviated *S.I.A.*

store, *noun* 1. a place where retail sales are transacted. Cf. *shop*.
2. see *chain*.
3. see *stock*.
verb 4. to ensure that an item or information is kept available.

store audit, 1. an audit of store accounts to establish profit or loss.
2. see *sales audit*.

store bulletin, a communication from the main office of a store to its personnel.

storecast, *noun* a radiolike presentation of music, advertisements, etc., through loudspeakers in a retail store.

store check, an examination of the stock carried by a retail store by persons not on the store's staff, and usually not a salesperson; done as a means of sales or marketing management intelligence gathering.

store count basis, see *distribution*.

store-distributed magazine, a magazine sold primarily at retail stores, especially supermarkets.

store-door delivery, delivery of merchandise directly to a store by a manufacturer or his employees. Cf. *warehouse delivery*.

store engineering, a branch of design concerned with the proper layout and functioning of retail stores, often provided as a service by wholesalers.

store panel, a group of stores used at intervals for market research investigations.

store protection, measures taken, especially by a manufacturer, to protect retail stores against unfair competition.

store redeemable coupon, a coupon issued by a manufacturer for his product, capable of being redeemed at any store where such a product is sold.

store security, the combination of means taken to protect a store against crime.

store supplies, goods purchased for the purpose of operating a store rather than for sale to the public.

store test, a test of retail product sales rates, using a panel of cooperating retail stores, usually in a single market, under controlled conditions.

storewide, *adjective, adverb* 1. in all stores of a chain.
2. in all departments of a store.

STORYBOARD

storyboard, *noun* a presentation panel containing illustrations of the various shots proposed or planned for a television commercial, with notes regarding filming, audio components, and the script, arranged in consecutive order.

straddle show, a network television or radio show that begins during and runs beyond network option time.

strategy, *noun* 1. (in management) a plan for attaining objectives.
2. (in advertising) see *creative strategy*.

stratified sample, (in statistics) a sample representing all the categories into which the total population has been divided, each of which is separately measured.

stratify, *verb* (in statistics) to divide a population into a number of nonoverlapping categories, each of which is represented proportionately or disproportionately to its actual importance, in a sample.
stratification, *n.*

stretch, *verb* to slow down the action of a motion picture, drama, or television or radio program in order to extend the running time.

strike, *verb* to dismantle a theatrical, motion picture, or television studio set.

string-and-button envelope, an envelope whose flap is secured by an attached string that is wrapped around a paper button, secured by a grommet, on the main body of the envelope; used mainly for interoffice communications. Also **string and button.**

strip, *verb* 1. to remove a developed photographic emulsion from its base in preparation for the photoengraving of a printing plate or the like.
2. to mount a photographic negative, piece of camera-ready copy, etc., on a sheet containing similar material before reproduction on a printing plate or the like. Also **strip-in.**
noun 3. a row of lights used on a motion picture or television set.

stripping film, any of several thin film or paper materials used to correct tones in photographic prints.

strip programming, running of a television or radio series at the same hour on each weekday.

strip show, a radio serial consisting of brief individual episodes.

strobe, *noun* a high-speed electronic flash, often used to stop the action or give multiple exposures, on a single photograph, of rapidly moving objects. Also **stroboscopic flash.**

studio, *noun* 1. the workplace of an artist.
2. an enclosed space for the taking of still photographs or the production of motion pictures or of television or radio programs. Cf. *stage*.
3. a firm which specializes in producing artwork, photographs, or commercials.
4. a place from which television or radio programs originate.

studio audience, (in radio or television) a group of persons present in a broadcasting studio so as to be entertained by the program performers. Also *audience*.

studio program, a program originating in a television or radio studio. Cf. *remote pickup.*

stuntperson, *noun* (in motion pictures or television) an on-camera performer who performs physically difficult or dangerous acts, sometimes as a stand-in. Also *stuntman, stuntwoman.*

S.T.V., *subscription television.*

style, *noun* a general category into which a typeface falls, e.g., roman, italic, condensed, extended, boldface, etc.

stylist, *noun* a person who arranges materials such as food, hair, or apparel into attractive or suitable visual compositions. Cf. *designer.*

stylus, *noun* 1. a small armature with a point inserted into phonographic record grooves for play; converts undulations in the groove into vibrations the cartridge behind the armature holding the stylus point converts into electrical impulses.
2. a pointed implement used by an artist to incise lines in plates, clay, etc.

subhead, *noun* 1. a secondary head or title for a newspaper article or the like. Also **subcaption.**
2. a display line within the body of a text, serving as a subtitle for the portion of the text that follows.

subjective research, see *qualitative research.*

subject to non-renewal, (of a television or radio announcement) available only if an incumbent does not exercise renewal rights. Abbreviated *S.N.R.*

subliminal advertising, advertising presented below the threshold of perception, as a split-second announcement on television; now unlawful.

subscriber, a person who has contracted for the purchase of delivered copies of, or programs from, a medium, such as a periodical or pay television.

subscriber study, a demographic or psychographic study of the subscribers to a periodical, usually commissioned by the publisher.

subscription, *noun* a medium's contract with a subscriber.

subscription television, pay television on a monthly fee basis. Abbreviated *S.T.V.*

substance number, (in printing) a number equal to the basis weight, in pounds, of a paper stock.

substandard, *adjective* (of film) narrower than the width commonly adopted as standard, i.e., 35mm for motion picture and 16mm for television film. Also *narrow-gauge.*

suggested retail price, a retail price suggested, but not imposed, by a wholesaler. Abbreviated *S.R.P.*

sulfate paper, a strong wood-pulp paper, not extensively bleached, used mainly for bags, containerboard, etc.

sulfite paper, wood-pulp paper whitened through bleaching.

Sunday supplement, any of various non-news sections included with a Sunday newspaper, as comics, or television schedules, and especially general interest magazine sections.

super, *verb* 1. see *superimpose.*
noun 2. graphic material that is superimposed.

superboard, *noun* (in television) a board bearing light colored lettering against a dark surface for superimposition on a person, scene, etc. being televised; used to explain what is being shown.

supercalendered, *adjective* see *calendered paper.*

superette, *noun* a small self-service food store operated in the manner of a supermarket; must have an annual business of $75,000-$375,000 according to U.S. Department of Commerce.

super-imp, *noun* a composite image created by the superimposition of one camera image over another.

superimpose, *verb* to place over, as one camera image on another so as to create a composite image. Also *super*.
superimposition, *n*.

superior character, (in typography) a small character placed well above the base line; e.g., x^3y, the 3 being the superior character.

supermarket, *noun* a large, departmentalized self-service food store, often with a large variety of nonfood items; a warehouse supplying the store regularly and a large parking lot for patrons are generally regarded as characteristics of a true supermarket.

supplement, *noun* any of various separate publications added to the main editorial section of a newspaper. Cf. *Sunday supplement*.

Supplemental Register, a register for certain marks not eligible for entry in the Principal Register under the Trade Mark Act of 1946.

supplier, *noun* 1. any person or organization furnishing merchandise to a retail store. Cf. *vendor*.
2. a motion picture firm or graphic arts firm; film or art studio, engraver, printer, etc. who prepares material for an advertising agency or advertiser.

support, *noun* see *advertising weight*.

suppression, *noun* (in psychology) the deliberate and conscious avoidance of memories, desires, etc. considered unacceptable or threatening. Cf. *repression*.

surprint, *noun* 1. the single printing by photographic reproduction of two or more superimposed images from separate negatives so that each negative registers in position with the others.
2. a sheet printed from such a process. Cf. *double print*.

survey area, the geographical area covered by a research survey.

survey sheet, see *flysheet*.

sustaining advertising, advertising for the purpose of maintaining the demand for a product rather than creating or increasing it.

sustaining program, a television or radio program supported by a commercial station or network, without sponsorship by an advertiser; usually scheduled in the public interest. Also **sustainer**.

swash letter, a display capital letter having a stroke (swash) that is decoratively extended.

swatch, *noun* a sample of cloth, paint, etc. used for matching colors.

sweat, *verb* to bond two pieces of metal, as a printing plate and a base together with solder under heat and pressure.

sweep report, a report on all radio or television markets, published by an audience-research organization on the basis of comprehensive local surveys made during certain months (**sweep months**), typically November, March, and May.

sweepstakes, *noun* a promotional scheme involving the giveaway of products and services of value to a randomly selected group of those who have submitted qualified entries; to prevent infringement of lottery laws, such schemes typically do not require qualifying entrants to provide a monetary consideration, such as a purchase. Cf. *contest*. Also **sweeps**.

swell allowance, 1. a deduction from the face amount of an invoice presented by a wholesaler to a retail grocer as a compensation for anticipated decay of canned or jarred food.
2. a refund in compensation for cans or jars of food not sold because of decay.

swells, *plural noun* canned and jarred food that has decayed and is thus unsalable, often detectable by the swelling of lids by internal gas.

swish, *noun* see *whip pan.*

switcher, *noun* 1. a television engineer in charge of camera mixing.
2. see *technical director.*

switch pitch, *noun* an attempt on the part of a television or radio station to persuade an advertiser to place a spot announcement or schedule using funds currently employed for advertising on a competitive station.

symbiotic marketing, see *horizontal marketing system.*

symbol compatibility, compatibility between that significance of a symbol which an advertiser intends it to have and that which the public actually attributes to it.

sync, *noun* 1. (in motion pictures or television) synchronization between the sound track and action in a film, videotape, or broadcast. Also **sync sound.**
verb 2. to synchronize such elements.

syndicate, *verb* 1. to distribute a newspaper column, Sunday supplement, comic strip, etc., to a number of periodicals for simultaneous publication in exchange for payment made by the various periodicals.
2. to sell a television or radio program series as a package to a number of independent stations in the same way.
3. to sell a research service's results to contracted buyers.

syndicated art, see *standard art.*

syndicated program, a program purchased on a syndicated basis.

syndicated supplement, a newspaper supplement sold on a syndicated basis.

syndicate store, a low-price variety chain store, e.g., a five and ten.

syndicator, *noun* see *packager.*

synectics, *noun* a technique designed to encourage groups to find creative solutions to problems by uncritically using lateral or even free associations to provide new insight. Also *blue sky.*

synergy, *noun* the mutual strengthening of and by the various elements of an integrated advertising campaign or marketing effort.
synergistic, *adj.*

synopsis, *noun* see *scenario.*

synthesizer, *noun* a device for artificially producing original audio signals, especially music, whether by programming pure waveforms via a keyboard or control console, or by manipulation of other recorded material.

systematic sample, (in statistics) a sample taken by choosing a fraction of a population in a systematic way; if n is the denominator of the fraction, then every nth member of the population, which is conceived as being arranged in a meaningful series, is chosen, sometimes after a first random choice from the beginning of the series; interval sample.

T

T, *time*.

T.A., *total audience*.

T.A.B., *Traffic Audit Bureau*.

table, *noun* a printed or written presentation of data organized under and across from subject headings in a two-dimensional format, permitting interrelationships of various categories of data to be readily understood.

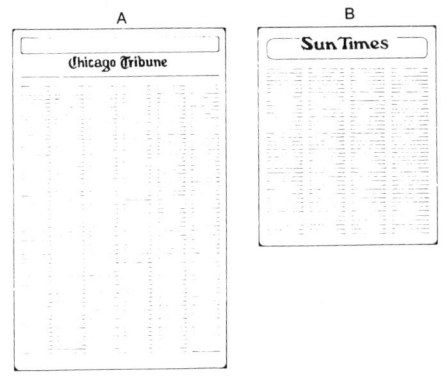

A. Standard Newspaper
B. Tabloid Newspaper

tabloid, *noun* a newspaper of less than standard page size, normally 14½" high by 12" wide, with five or six columns and between 1000 and 1200 agate lines per page.

tabulate, *verb* to organize and render information into statistical data.
tabulation, *n*.

tachistoscope, *noun* (in research) a device for the exposure of an object to respondents for a precisely measured and extremely small time interval, e.g., a tenth of a second; used in advertisement and package recognition tests. Also *T-scope*.

tactic, *noun* a vehicle or detail used to implement a strategy.
tactical, *adj*.

tag, *noun* a brief announcement at the end of a television or radio commercial, or program. Also *trailer*.

tag line, a final line of a dramatic scene or act that is treated to give point or impact to the preceding dialogue.

tail, *noun* (in radio, motion pictures or television) the last sequence of a show, commercial, or recording.

tails up, (of a reel of film) with the first frame innermost, in reverse order from that in which the film can be projected. Also **tails out**. Cf. *heads up*.

take, *noun* 1. see *shot*.
2. (in motion pictures or television) film or tape of a single shot.
3. an expression of surprise or realization made by a performer, especially through attitudes of the face or body.
4. the daily cash revenue of a store.
verb 5. to begin shooting with a specified motion picture or television camera.
6. to transmit the image from a specified television camera.

take it from the top, (in theater, motion pictures and television) *begin again;* a rehearsal instruction used by a director.

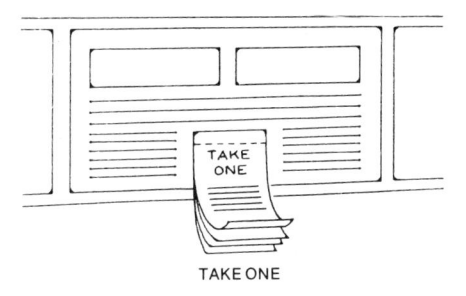

take-one, *noun* a transit car card used inside a vehicle and bearing a pouch or pad of leaflets, reply cards, etc. intended for passengers to take.

185

take-up reel, a storage reel used to hold processed film. Also **take-up spool.**

talent, *noun* (in television or radio) actors, musicians, and other performers.

talent cost, the cost for the talent of a television or radio program or commercial, including residuals. Cf. *session fee.*

talent payment, see *residuals.*

talkback, *noun* an electrical communication system used within a television or radio studio; used to permit talent to converse with producers or directors in the control room, as well as to permit control of cameramen, etc.

talk format, see *format.*

talk show, a television or radio show organized around interviews in the studio or telephone conversations with listeners conducted by the host, and often with variety entertainment.

tally light, see *camera cue.*

t and e, *travel and entertainment.* Also t & e.

tangible product, see *product.*

tape, *noun* 1. a ribbon of plastic bearing a layer of magnetizable particles and available in standard widths; used to bear recorded audio or video signals, or both together.
2. a strip of paper on which the individual charges and total charges for retail sales are printed by a cash register.

tape deck, a device used to pick up and preamplify, and sometimes to record, electrical signals on magnetic recording tape. Also *deck,* **tape recorder.**

tare, *noun* 1. the weight of an empty container.
2. the deduction for container weight, made in computing the cost of things sold by weight.

3. the weight of an unloaded vehicle.
4. a factor of shrinkage applied to the difference between the net weight of a product as shown on a package and the actual weight when sold.

target, *noun* see *target market.*

target audience, the audience intended to be reached by an advertiser in using a given communications medium or set of media.

Target Group Index, a periodic syndicated study of national media audiences and their product purchase behavior. Abbreviated *T.G.I.*

target market, an occupational, demographic, or psychographic group of consumers designated by a marketer as his best prospects for sales, and hence serving as the group at whom the marketer's most intensive sales, advertising, and promotional efforts are directed. Also *target,* **target group, target consumers.** Cf. *target audience.*

target price, a product price established by a seller who derives it by specifying a desired rate of return on costs or investment at anticipated sales volumes.

task method, a method for determining a marketing spending appropriation based on the estimated cost of attaining specific marketing goals.

T.A.T., *thematic apperception test.*

TBA, *Television Bureau of Advertising.*

T.B.A., (in television and radio) *to be announced;* said of an as yet unchosen program to fill a specific time period.

T.B.D., (in television or radio) *to be determined;* said of an as yet unchosen time period for a specific program.

T.C., *transcontinental.*

T.C.U., *tight close-up.*

T.D., *technical director.*

tearsheet, *noun* an unbound periodical page showing an article, advertisement, etc. as printed; used as a proof or as an extra copy.

tearstrip, *noun* a reinforced strip on a package which when pulled opens the package.

teaser campaign, an advertising campaign using brief announcements meant to stimulate curiosity rather than to impart information; precedes a major announcement revealing the purpose and meaning of the teaser advertisements. Also **teaser.**

technical director, the director of the technical facilities in a television studio. Abbreviated *T.D.* Also *switcher.*

teen, *noun* 1. see *daypart.*
adjective 2. noting or pertaining to a product or medium intended to appeal to adolescents.

telecast, *noun* a broadcast on television.

Telecine, *noun, trademark* an apparatus for televising films, used especially in England.

Telefex, *noun, trademark* a system of rear-screen projection used in live television performances.

telegenic, *adjective* noting or pertaining to facial or other visible personal characteristics which make for an attractive physical appearance on television. Cf. *photogenic.*
telegenity, *n.*

telephone coincidental survey, a coincidental survey conducted by means of telephone interviews. Cf. *coincidental.*

telephoto lens, a camera lens that covers a relatively smaller area of a scene and with shallower perspective than a normal lens at the same point; used for portraits or to make distant objects appear closer. Cf. *wide-angle lens.*

Teleprompter, *noun, trademark* a visual prompting device for television performers, reproducing the current portion of the script in enlarged letters.

telerecording, *noun* see *kinescope.* Abbreviated *TVR.*

teletranscription, see *television recording.*

Teletype, *noun, trademark* a remote-control typewriter reproducing business documents, news bulletins, etc., composed on a similar machine elsewhere; a leased line service of Western Union. Also *Telex, TWX.*

televiewer, *noun* see *viewer.*

television, *noun* a medium by which moving visual images and sounds are transmitted as radio or electrical waves for reconversion to moving visual images and sounds by receiving sets, usually located in consumer households. Abbreviated *TV.* Also *video.*

Television Advertisers' Report, a bimonthly report on television audience composition, program selection, and commercial sponsor identification; prepared by Trendex. Abbreviated *TVAR.*

Television Bureau of Advertising, a New York corporation sponsored by television stations and networks, station representatives, and colleges, that operates in various ways to promote the use of television as an advertising medium. Abbreviated *TvB, TBA.*

Television Code, a set of principles established for advertisers by the National Association of Broadcasters, specifying acceptable and unacceptable practices in advertising observed by member stations.

television director, 1. an advertising agency employee responsible for production management of television programs produced by the agency.
2. an advertising agency employee respon-

sible for developing and purchasing network television plans.
3. a television network or station program director.

television household, a household having at least one television set; used as the basis for most audience rating measurement units. Also **television home.** Abbreviated *TVHH.*

television recording, a kinescope or videotape of television broadcast material obtained from a station broadcast signal or receiver and intended for possible rebroadcast. Abbreviated *TVR.* Also *teletranscription.*

Telex, *noun* see *Teletype.*

telop, *noun* 1. see *telopticon.*
2. a telopticon or balopticon slide or card.

telopticon, *noun* (in television) a device for projecting small cards with messages or artwork for pickup and transmission. Also *telop.*

tempera, *noun* any of various paints using egg yolk with water or oil as a vehicle for suspension of pigments.

temporary allowance, see *allowance.*

:10, *noun* a ten-second television or radio commercial, such as an identification. Also **ten.**

10k, see *brute.*

tent card, a display card printed and folded so as to be legible from two directions.

territory, *noun* a geographical area assigned exclusively to a salesperson or sales organization by a seller.

test, *noun* an effort to minimize risk in a marketing decision by conducting a miniature simulation of the proposed conditions in order to observe results.

testimonial, *noun* a recommendation of a product by a user or supposed user for advertising purposes.

test market, a geographical area in which a test of an alternate marketing plan variable or new product is conducted. Cf. *sales area test.*
test-market, *v.*

test-market translation, 1. a conversion of a national marketing plan to test market dimensions.
2. a projection of test market results to a larger geographic area. Also *translation.*

test pattern, a pattern of lines or circles, used as an aid to the focusing of television equipment.

test-retest reliability, see *reliability.*

test store, a retail store used for tests of product movement rates, buying habits, selling practices, etc.

text, *noun* the principal verbal content of a book, document, advertisement, etc.

T.F., 1. *to fill;* an instruction to a typesetter: Set T.F. space indicated.
2. *till forbid.*

T.G.I., *Target Group Index.*

theater advertising, advertising by film in motion picture theaters, common in Canada but now rare in the United States.

theater test, (in research) an experiment conducted by simultaneously exposing a large group of respondents to a communication, in order to measure their reactions.

thematic apperception test, a projective psychological test in which a respondent, shown a series of ambiguous pictures, is asked to compose a story to fit them, the theory being that his own concerns, attitudes, and experiences will emerge. Abbreviated *T.A.T.*

theme, *noun* 1. the general subject or idea of a drama, television show, etc.

2. a musical passage that identifies a television or radio show, or theatrical personality. Cf. *signature*.

thermography, *noun* a letterpress printing process in which a powder, added to the imprinted ink while wet, is baked to create raised letters; imitates the textural effect of engraving.

thick market pattern, see *market pattern*.

thin market pattern, see *market pattern*.

thinner, *noun* an additive that promotes the flow of ink, paint, rubber cement, etc.

third cover, the inside back cover of a periodical. Abbreviated *3C*.

:30, *noun* a thirty-second television or radio commercial. Also *thirty*.

thirty, *noun* 1. an indicated ending of a news report or news release; usually printed as —30—.
2. *:30*.

35mm, see *motion picture film*.

39/13, *adjective* (obsolescent) noting or pertaining to a full year of weekly television or radio shows, 39 of which are original presentations and 13 of which are repeats. Cf. *26/26*.

30 sheet poster, an outdoor advertising space providing a copy area measuring 21 feet 7 inches by 9 feet 7 inches, usually covered with a single poster printed in sections on twelve paper sheets.

3C, 1. *third cover,* i.e., inside back cover; used in ordering magazine advertising.
2. *three-color*.

three-color, *adjective* noting or pertaining to color printing in which yellow, red, and blue are used but not black; lacks the richness of four-color printing. Abbreviated *3C*.

three-dimensional, *noun* a three-dimensional retail display.

three-sheet poster, 1. an outdoor-advertising poster 6' high by 12' wide.
2. (in transit station advertising) a poster 7' high by 3'6" wide.

Three Sigma Research, Inc., a New York marketing and media research firm; the firm's work to date has focused on use of diary panelists to study magazine readers' habits (SORTEM) and a local media and product usage study (ARMS II).

thrift shop, a retail store selling used merchandise or seconds, or remaindered items.

through-the-book method, a method used by Simmons Research Associates to determine whether a survey respondent has actually read an issue of a magazine by taking the respondent through the issue, asking questions section by section.

throw a cue, to give a hand signal as a cue.

throwaway, *noun* 1. see *handbill*.
2. a shopping newspaper.
3. a neighborhood newspaper.

thumbnail, *noun* 1. a rough layout sketch, often rendered in a smaller size than the final advertisement.
2. a brief verbal or written description or history.

Thurstone scale, a scale of degrees of agreement or disagreement with statements submitted to a respondent, intended to measure his attitudes, preferences, and opinions.

tie-in *verb* 1. to develop a cooperative marketing effort between products, brands or marketers.
noun 2. such an effort, as developed.

tie-in advertisement, 1. a periodical advertisement making reference to an advertisement in the same issue run by another

advertiser.
2. a single advertisement advertising more than one product, or service, at times involving more than one advertiser.

tie-in promotion, a single promotion event intended to encourage the sale of more than one product or brand.

tie-in sale, a sale in which, to purchase one thing, the buyer must purchase some other thing as well.

tie-up, *noun* the use of the name of a well-known person in advertising, especially in a testimonial. Cf. *spokesman.*

tight, *adjective* 1. (in motion pictures or television) noting or pertaining to a shot leaving little or no visible space around its subject.
2. (in television or radio) noting or pertaining to a show or commercial having a running time that threatens to become excessive.
3. of or pertaining to a highly detailed layout.

tight close-up, (in motion pictures or television) an exceptionally tight shot. Abbreviated *T.C.U.*

tighten up, *reduce the visible space around a subject in an image;* direction to a cameraman.

till, *noun* 1. a container for currency, especially the cash drawer of a store's cash register.
2. (informal) cash reserves, as of a company.

till forbid, until told to stop: *Run this ad till forbid.* Abbreviated *T.F.*

time, *noun* 1. broadcast occasions available or used for advertising.
2. the number of repetitions, occasions, or insertions specified in an advertising schedule or rate card. Abbreviated *T.*
verb 3. to check the number of seconds, minutes, or hours consumed by reading or playing a script, film, program, record, etc.

time bank, a reserve of television or radio station time obtained through barter.

time buyer, an employee of an advertiser or advertising agency who buys local television or radio advertising time. Cf. *television director.*

time charge, a charge to an advertiser for television or radio advertising time.

time class, see *class of time.*

time contract, an agreement between an advertising agency and a television or radio station or network, covering all time purchased by the advertiser through all agencies in order to earn the greatest possible discount.

time discount, a discount offered by periodicals if a certain number of insertions are run within a given period of time. Also *frequency discount, quantity discount.*

time sheet, 1. a daily record of agency employee job hours, prepared by the employee by account and on occasion by job number, and used for agency cost control.
2. a record of broadcast media purchases, with pertinent data. Also *buy sheet.*

time signal, 1. (in television or radio) an announcement of the time.
2. a sound giving the precise moment of the announced time.
3. an advertisement given along with an announcement of the time.

time slot, (in radio or television) a specific time period considered or planned for the broadcast of a program or commercial.

timetable, *noun* see *schedule.*

time zone, one of twenty four roughly equal longitudinal sections of the earth's surface in which a common hour of the day is conventionally observed. Four such adjacent zones cross the continental United States, with the hour in each progressively later by one than in the zone to the immediate west; moving west in order, these zones are: *Eastern, Central, Mountain,* and *Pacific.* Reference to specific times in these zones is ideally qualified by specification of whether standard time or daylight saving time (one hour earlier than standard time) is to be observed; e.g. *Eastern Daylight Time* (abbreviated *E.D.T.*), etc.

tint, *noun* a mixture of a color with white.

tint plate, a printing plate used to print a flat area of color, whether solid or textured. Also **tint block.**

tip-in, *noun* a preprinted advertising page or card, usually one, inserted into a periodical whose regular page size is larger.

tip-on, *noun* a coupon, sample, or reply card glued to a page of advertising by one edge.

tissue, *noun* 1. a sketch, as of a layout or illustration, drawn on translucent paper.
2. a translucent sheet covering finished art and mechanical elements, used to note corrections.
3. a sheet of translucent, often tinted, paper.

title, *noun* 1. see *caption.*
2. an explanatory legend beginning or terminating a motion picture or television show.
3. a name for a book, document, or motion picture.

title music, music serving as background for a motion picture or television title.

title roll, see *crawl roll.*

TM, *trademark.*

toiletries merchandiser, a rack jobber who runs a toiletries department in a grocery store.

tombstone, *noun, informal* a small print advertisement for a professional person or organization, designed to meet the legal and customary restraints observed in such advertising.

tone, *noun* 1. see *value.*
2. a musical sound, used in television and radio and over the telephone to indicate the precise moment of an announced time.

tone and manner, a phrase sometimes used to head a section of a creative strategy describing generally the executional look and feeling of advertisements executed to the strategy.

tongue, *verb* 1. to move a crane-mounted camera horizontally while aiming it at a single subject.
noun 2. a crane boom holding such a camera.

tonnage item, an item regularly supplied by a wholesaler to retailers in large volumes; so called because they form a substantial part of the load on his trucks.

tool, *verb* to work on a photoengraved plate with a hand tool, such as a shooter, beveler, etc. to improve printing fidelity.

top 40 format, see *format.*

topline, *noun* the earliest received or most important data derived from a research project.

top of mind, (in research) the first brand or advertising campaign that comes to a respondent's mind in connection with awareness and attitude research. Cf. *share of mind.*

top 100, 1. the hundred largest metropolitan market areas of the United States, as ranked by population, purchases, or other key indicators.
2. see *format.*

top order, the largest order for goods or services placed by any buyer from a source of goods or services in a given year.

total audience, 1. (in television or radio surveys) a figure reflecting the audience estimated to have tuned in to a program for at least five minutes if the program is more than ten minutes long, and for at least one

minute if the program is less than ten minutes long. Abbreviated *T.A.*
2. (in Canada) the total number of persons three years of age or older who are exposed to a television or radio program.
3. the entire readership of a periodical.

total audience impressions, the total number of exposures to a specific number of issues of a given periodical or to the issues of a given group of periodicals appearing at one time; used for survey purposes.

total audience plan, an advertising media plan for purchase of a combination of television or radio announcements intended to promote maximum audience coverage.

total circulation, the full number of copies of a publication distributed, including both copies sold to subscribers and single copy buyers, as well as complementary copies.

total distribution, 1. a situation in which an item or brand has exhausted all opportunity for enhancing its distribution in retail stores.
2. a condition of an item or brand distributed in all those retail outlets which might be expected to carry such products.

total net paid, the total number of purchasers of one issue of a periodical, whether through newsstand sales or subscriptions, according to the standards of the Audit Bureau of Circulations.

Total Prime Time, a syndicated research service of Gallup and Robinson which measures television audience recollection of paid prime-time commercials as compared with the potential audience for the programs shown. Abbreviated *T.P.T.*

total survey area, a geographical area whose counties account for 98% or more of the net weekly audience circulation of a television station, as defined by Arbitron. Abbreviated *T.S.A.*

Towne-Oller, Inc., a market research firm selling syndicated reports of periodic audits of food store deliveries of health and beauty aid products.

T.P.T., *total prime time.*

traceable expenditure, an expenditure for media space or time attributed to a specific communications medium and advertiser that is reported by published sources; given usually on a nondiscounted basis. Also *reported spending.*

track, *noun* see *sound track.*

trade advertising, advertisements for consumer products that are intended to appeal to wholesalers and retailers rather than consumers.

trade association, any organization established to promote the interests of a trade or industry, to establish and enforce standards of quality and practice, or to disseminate information among its members.

trade book, a business or trade periodical.

trade discount, a discount from an item's retail list or catalogue price made by a supplier to a professional or a retailer. Also *functional discount.*

trade magazine, a magazine edited for the interest of members of a specific trade or industry. Also *trade paper.*

trademark, *noun* 1. any symbol, piece of writing, or combination of both registered with the Federal government for exclusive use by a manufacturer, merchant, or the like in association with his goods or services. Also **trade mark.**
verb 2. to make such a registration. Abbreviated *TM.*

trade name, 1. a name applied to a type of goods or services furnished by one company that does not have the exclusive character of a trademark.
2. a name by which something is known in a trade, as opposed to its common name or technical description.
3. the name under which a company or person does business.

trade paper, 1. a newspaper edited for the interest of persons associated with a specific trade or industry.
2. see *trade magazine.*

trade-practice conference, a conference between members of the Federal Trade Commission and representatives of an industry to establish fair trading practices.

trade show, a special temporary exhibit of goods or services to trade buyers, often conducted in concert with other exhibitors at a single location. Cf. *show.*

trading area, one or more counties, usually with a central metropolitan market, in which residents transact the majority of their retail purchases.

trading stamp, any of various stamps offered as premiums with merchandise purchases, the number given being in proportion to the total sale amount; such stamps, in specific numbers, are redeemable for specific types of goods.

Traffic Audit Bureau, a New York-based nonprofit corporation, sponsored by advertisers and outdoor advertising plants, for the establishment of traffic circulation figures in order to determine the value of certain locations for outdoor advertising. Abbreviated *T.A.B.*

traffic count, a count of the traffic passing a certain point on a thoroughfare.

traffic department, a department of an advertising agency whose purpose is to keep work flowing steadily and punctually. Cf. *traffic system.*

traffic flow map, a map of traffic densities used in planning outdoor-advertising showings.

traffic management, the planning and administration of all activities concerned with the physical movement of goods being marketed.

traffic pattern, the general pattern of time and frequency of shopping established by customers.

traffic system, (in an advertising agency) any system for the coordination and continuous surveillance of the physical materials for advertisements and the processes necessary to prepare and run them. Cf. *traffic department.*

trailer, *noun* see *tag.*

transcontinental, *noun* (obsolescent) a nationwide television or radio program. Abbreviated *T.C.*

transcribe, *verb* to record sound for broadcast purposes, usually on cassettes, tapes, or 33⅓ r.p.m. phonographic discs. **transcription,** *n.*

transcribed program, a prerecorded television or radio program sold by a packager to a number of stations. Cf. *syndicated program.*

transfer, *noun* 1. merchandise passed from one chain store to another in an exchange intended to balance the stock of both.
2. see *decal.*
verb 3. to make a filmed copy, as of a broadcast or film print.

transient rate, see *one-time rate.*

transit advertising, advertising associated with public transportation, placed inside and outside vehicles and in their stations. Also *transportation advertising,* **transit.**

Transit Advertising Association, an organization of sellers of transit advertising, formed in 1942 to provide educational and promotional support for members; formerly National Association of Transportation Advertising.

transition, *noun* (in motion pictures, television, or radio) any visual or audio effect leading from one scene or shot to the next.

transition time, see *fringe time.*

193

transit radio, radio broadcasting in public transportation.

transit spectacular, an advertising display occupying all of one or both sides on the inside or outside of a public-transit vehicle.

translation, *noun* see *test-market translation*.

translator, *noun* a relay television or radio station that rebroadcasts another station's signals at a new frequency to areas the first station cannot reach. Cf. *relay station*.

translucency, *noun* a photographic or printed copy of an advertisement used in back-lighted displays.

Trans-lux, *noun, trademark* a short-focus rear-screen projector for films or slides.

transmit, *verb* 1. to send a message, signal, or communication from one place to another, especially by means of an intermediary person or device.
transmission, *noun* 2. that which is transmitted.
transmitter, *noun* 3. that person or device which transmits.

transparency, *noun* a transparent photograph, usually positive and in color.

transportation advertising, see *transit advertising*.

transportation display poster, a station or depot display poster that comes in various sizes (one-, two-, or six-sheet) viewed mainly by commuters.

transship, *verb* 1. to transfer a shipment from one means of transport to another.
2. to transfer a shipment from one geographic area of storage or inventory to another, especially when done by a wholesaler or retailer.
transshipment, *n*.

trap, *verb* (in four color wet printing) the clean superimposition of the yellow, red, blue and black inks to attain the specific hues and color density desired in the final printed image.

travel and entertainment, 1. a business expense consisting of employees' expenditure for travel, meals, lodging, and client entertainment for business purposes. Abbreviated *T and E*.
2. a budget established by an employer to pay for such expenses.

traveling display, 1. an advertising exhibit that travels from one retail store to another.
2. a display of transit advertising outside a vehicle. Cf. *car card*.

traveling matte shot, see *matte shot*.

tray pack, a carton that can be converted into a shelf-sized display unit by removing its top.

treatment, *noun* 1. the general approach to or tone of an advertising campaign or advertisement.
2. the general way in which a story is handled in converting it into a script.

Trendex, *noun* a New York firm which provides a variety of syndicated media research services.

trial, *noun* a purchase or use of a product or service by a consumer interested in personally evaluating its value, as a step preceding repurchase or regular use.

trail size, a product package of small size and consequent price, intended or serving to attract product trial.

triggyback, *noun* (in television or radio) a trio of twenty-second commercials each of whose time is sold for one-third that of a sixty-second commercial.

trim, *noun* 1. a border or molding strip used to frame an outdoor advertisement.
2. see *out-take*.
verb 3. to cut an assembled document's or publication's pages to a predetermined size.

trim flush, to trim a book cover flush with the pages.

trim size, the actual size of a book or periodical page after trimming.

trine, *noun* (in statistics) one of three equal parts into which the whole population of a sample is divided, the parts being arranged in some meaningful order.

triple associates method, a research technique in which a respondent, being given an advertising campaign theme and product type, is asked to name the brand of product or manufacturer associated with it.

triple-duty envelope, an envelope for a mailing piece so formed as to be the envelope from the advertiser, the reply envelope for the recipient, and the order form.

triple-spotting, *noun* the presentation of three commercials for a single product or service within a single station break or within a single local program. Cf. *up-cutting*.

tri-variant dimension test, a ranking order sort test for the importance or desirability, believability, and uniqueness of product features and advertising themes. Also *multivariate analysis*.

truck, *verb* to move a motion picture or television camera sideways while making a shot. Also *crab*.

tru-line rate, the milline rate of a newspaper based on the circulation in the trading area only.

T.S.A., *total survey area*.

T-scope, *noun* see *tachistoscope*.

tune, *verb* see *tune in*.

tune-in, *noun* see *sets in use*.

tune in, to calibrate a receiver so as to watch a television program or hear a radio program (sometimes followed by *to*). Also *tune*.

turnover, *noun* 1. (in television or radio) the ratio of the total number of different persons hearing a program during a specified period, to the average audience at any one time; used as a measure of the program's holding power.
2. the rate of repetition in the purchase of a product by a consumer.
3. see *stock turn*.

turntable, *noun* a motorized platform designed to bear and rotate phonographic recordings for playback.

TV, *television*.

TVAR, *Television Advertisers' Report*.

T.v.B., see *Television Bureau of Advertising*.

TVHH, *television household*.

TVR, 1. *television recording;* often followed by a number representing the number of days between the making of the recording and a given broadcast from it.
2. *telerecording*.

TVS, an independent television network specializing in sports programs.

:20, *noun* a twenty-second television or radio announcement. Also **twenty**.

24-sheet panel, see *twenty-four sheet poster panel*.

24 sheet poster, an outdoor advertising space providing a copy area measuring 8 feet 8 inches by 19 feet 6 inches, usually covered with a single poster printed in sections on ten paper sheets. Also **24 sheet**.

twenty-four-sheet poster panel, an outdoor-advertising structure 25' long and 12' high to which outdoor posters are pasted. Also *24-sheet panel*.

26/26, *adjective* noting or pertaining to a full year of weekly television shows, half of which are original presentations and half of which are repeats. Cf. *39/13.*

twin pack, a promotion event calling for two product units to be sold as one, at a discounted price; usually implemented by packaging which physically unites the two units and flags the savings offered. Cf. *bonus pack.*

2C, *second cover,* i.e., inside front cover; used in ordering magazine advertising.

two-color, *adjective* noting or pertaining to printing in black and a single color or two colors other than black. Abbreviated *2C.*

two-fold flat, see *book flat.*

two-sheet poster, a station poster not standardized in dimensions but usually 60" high by 42" wide.

two-shot, *noun* (in motion pictures or television) a shot of two subjects made from as close a position as possible.

TWX, *Teletype.*

two-step-flow theory, the hypothetical flow of information, advertising influence, etc., from a communications medium to a relatively small group of interested and informed opinion leaders, and in turn from this group to a larger group of less interested and less informed persons. Cf. *word-of-mouth advertising.*

type, *noun* 1. a piece or pieces used for printing of letters, numbers, or other standard characters.
2. a special material furnished by advertisers to periodicals, and used by the periodical to prepare its own plates.
verb 3. to compose pieces of type into an aggregate mass or printed sheet by means of a mechanical device.

type C print, see *C print.*

type face, a designed alphabet cast in metal or photographed for various photographic typesetting processes; metal versions are generally made in a range of point sizes with a complete font in each size. Cf. *type family.*

type family, a group of visually related type faces. Cf. *type face.*

type-high, *adjective* areas of a printing plate or the like flush with the printing surface of type and thus able to print.

type mechanical, see *keyline.*

type R print, see *R print.*

typo, *noun, typographical error;* used to indicate the source of a typographical flaw or mistake in typing.

typography, *noun* the art of choosing, composing, and setting type for printing.
typographical, *adj.*

U

U., *ultra high frequency.*

U.A., *urban area;* used in market surveys especially in Canada.

UC, *upper case;* used to indicate a typographical error or to give direction to a typesetter.

U & L, (in typography) *upper and lower case* type characters.

UHF, *ultra high frequency.*

ultra high frequency, noting or pertaining to any limited-range television broadcasting channel operating at from 470 to 890 megaHertz. Abbreviated *UHF, U.*

unaided recall, non-prompted answers in interviews bearing on advertising to questions regarding brands seen or heard advertised, the content of a brand's advertising, etc.

unavailable, on order, (of a television or radio station) unable to broadcast a network program at present but committed to do so as soon as possible. Abbreviated *U.O.O.*

undercut, *noun* an overetched halftone printing plate in which acid has eaten into the sides of the dots, leaving a mushroom surface dot; though usable for printing, the plate cannot be used for molding duplicate printing plates.

undisplay advertising, classified advertising without display type or artwork.

unduplicated audience, see *cumulative audience.*

unique selling proposition, the unique benefit claimed for an advertised product or service. Abbreviated *U.S.P.*

unit, *noun* 1. a sales territory, usually subdivided into several sections, each with its own salesman. Cf. *region, zone.*
2. a standard volume equivalent by which a single product item sale is measured.
3. a single copy of an advertisement or medium.

unitize, *verb* to dimension cases of merchandise so that they fit evenly into standardized warehouse space.

unit split, a division of a single television or radio commercial unit into two even parts, each with its own announcement. Cf. *piggyback commercial.*

universe, *noun* see *population.*

unload, *verb* to sell merchandise quickly through various promotional expedients.

unpaid copy, a copy of a periodical distributed free or at a price lower than the minimum prescribed by the Audit Bureau of Circulations.

unrestricted sample, see *random sample.*

U.O.O., *unavailable, on order.*

up-and-over, *adverb* (in motion pictures, television, or radio) up to a level where dialogue is obscured; a direction to a musician or sound-effects man.

up-cutting, *noun* elimination of part of a network or syndicated program by a television or radio station in order to give more time for local announcements. Cf. *triple spotting.*

upfront, *adjective, adverb* early in the buying season or planning period; as said of a purchase of advertising time or space, especially one of long duration.

upper and lower, with capitals and lower-case letters used in the normal manner; an instruction to a printer. Abbreviated *U&L, c/lc.*

upper-case, *adjective* capital; *upper-case letters.* Abbreviated *UC.*

upright, *noun* 1. a book that is taller than it is wide.
2. see *standard.*

up-scale, *adjective, adverb* at the upper end of a range in a demographic analysis in terms of education, income, etc.

upstage, *adjective, adverb* 1. (in the performing arts) away from the audience or camera.
verb 2. to lessen the effect of the performance of another performer in order to heighten the effect of one's own.

usage pull, the ability of advertising to persuade people to purchase the advertised product or service.

U.S.P., *unique selling proposition.*

V

V., *very high frequency.*

V.A.C., *Verified Audit Circulation Corporation.*

validity, *noun* (in research) the competence of a technique for measuring or sampling to perform the task for which it is intended.

value, *noun* 1. the relative lightness of a hue, white having the highest value and black the lowest. Also *tone.* Cf. *intensity, hue.*
2. the utility of a product or service to a user or prospect, as measured by the rate of sale of such products or services at varying prices.
3. the usual retail sales price of a product or service.

value analysis, a method used by purchasing agents for manufacturing companies to reduce costs by such means as use of redesigned or standardized components, or use of less costly production techniques.

vampire video, television commercial action or scenes deliberately unrelated to, or not synchronized with, the contents of the accompanying sound track.

Van Dyke, *noun, trademark* a print of offset printing work made on photosensitive paper and typically deep brown in the areas to be printed. Cf. *blueline.*

variance, *noun* (in statistics) the square of the standard deviation, used to measure the actual differences among the scores of a sample.

variance analysis, a technique used by accountants to determine the causes of a deviation from planned sales or profit goals. Cf. *analysis of variance.*

variety store, a store selling a large variety of inexpensive and usually rather small personal and household goods, with departments organized by counters.

Vari-Typer, *noun, trademark* an electric typewriter producing reproducible copy and having a large selection of interchangeable type faces.

vehicle, *noun* 1. a liquid to which pigment is added to form paint.
2. an individual advertising medium, as a magazine or television station.

velocity, *noun* the relative speed with which a specific retail item is sold. Cf. *stock turn.*

Velox, *noun, trademark* a photographic print that is sometimes screened so that it can be rephotographed and reproduced as line copy.

vending machine, a device designed to dispense products to purchasers in exchange for established amounts of currency per item. Also *automatic vending machine.*

vendor, *noun* any person or organization with products to sell. Cf. *supplier.*

venie, *noun* a Venetian blindlike pattern created with a cucalorus.

venture team, a group of a corporation's managers responsible for developing and implementing plans to enter new markets, whether by new product entries, expansion of existing products, or acquisitions.

verbatim, *noun* (in research) a word-for-word report of an interview.

**Verified Audit Circulation Corpora-

tion, a corporation that audits periodical circulations. Abbreviated *V.A.C.*

vertical arrangement, a shelf arrangement in a retail store in which all similar or related items are placed from top to bottom of a relatively limited section. Cf. *horizontal arrangement.*

vertical case, a retail display case higher than it is wide.

vertical contiguity, see *contiguity.*

vertical cume, a cumulative rating for two or more programs broadcast on the same day.

vertical discount, a discount for purchase of television or radio time at a given frequency during a limited time period, e.g., a week.

vertical half-page, half the entire width of the full height of a periodical page purchased for an advertisement.

vertical integration, the common ownership of more than one level in the traditional multilevel supply and distribution chain of autonomous businesses which create and distribute products to consumers. Cf. *vertical marketing systems.*

vertical marketing systems, means used by organizations to diminish the traditional autonomy of their suppliers, dealers, or customers; such techniques include vertical integration, franchises, cooperatives, or leveraged application of scalar advantages. Cf. *vertical integration.*

vertical publication, a publication intended for persons in a specific trade, profession, interest group, life style, etc. Cf. *horizontal publication.*

vertical saturation, concentrated television or radio advertising by a single advertiser during a single broadcast day.

vertical selling, selling to buyers in a limited range of industries.

vertigrate, *verb* to vertically integrate the advertising and promotion efforts of a retail dealer, franchiser, or licensee into the broader advertising and promotion plans of a manufacturer or licensor, to permit greater impact and efficiency.
vertigration, *n.*

very high frequency, noting or pertaining to relatively long-range television channels operating at from 54 to 216 megaHertz. Abbreviated *VHF, V.*

VHF, *very high frequency.*

V.I., *volume indicator.*

video, *noun* 1. the visual, as opposed to the audio, part of television.
2. see *television.*

videocassette, *noun* a magnetic tape unit which can be used for video recordings, permanently housed within a case which includes takeup reels; eliminates the need for several time-consuming set-up operations.

videodisc, *noun* a disc of phonograph record size on which video and audio signals are recorded for playback only in consumer's homes. Two major such systems are currently under development, one by RCA, and one by MCA and Phillips.

video engineer, a studio engineer responsible for the video portion of a television program.

videotape, *noun* a magnetic tape for recording both the video and audio elements of a television commercial or program.

videotape transfer, a videotape recording of a filmed sequence; used on occasion to provide air-ready commercials or the like on an accelerated timetable.
Cf. *film transfer.*

viewer, *noun* a person who watches television. Also *televiewer.* Cf. *listener.*

viewer impression study, a study conducted by the research firm of Daniel

Starch and Associates to obtain qualitative data about television commercials through interviews on the messages and significance of the commercials to viewers.

Viewers in Profile, see *Nielsen Station Index.* Abbreviated *V.I.P.*

viewers per household, the average number of persons viewing a television program in both viewing and nonviewing households. Abbreviated *V.P.H.*

viewers per set, see *viewers per viewing household.*

viewers per viewing houshold, the average number of persons viewing a television program per viewing household. Abbreviated *V/VH.* Also *viewers per set.*

viewfinder, *noun* an optical device on a camera showing the operator that area of the scene being covered by the camera.

viewpoint, *noun* see *camera angle.*

vignette, *noun* 1. an illustration or photograph with an indefinite outer edge that blends into the surrounding blank area through shading, increasingly open hatching, etc.
2. a mask for the lens of a motion-picture or television camera that gives a vignettelike effect to a shot.
3. see *spot drawing.*
verb 4. to fade or blur the edges of a photograph, camera shot, etc. to give a vignettelike effect.

V.I.P., *Viewers in Profile.*

visible distribution, the measured extent to which a given product is visible and readily accessible to the customers of retail stores. Also **visual distribution.** Cf. *visual inventory.*

visual, *noun* 1. (in motion pictures or television) a visible element comprising an image in a sequence of shots.
2. a rough sketch depicting an advertising layout or illustration.

visual inventory, the measured amount of a given product visible and readily accessible to the customers of retail stores; specifically excludes storeroom inventory. Cf. *visible distribution.*

visualization, *noun* (in psychology) the formation of a mental image of a situation as a whole on the basis of partial verbal or pictorial information; used as the basis of projective techniques.

V.M.A., *volume merchandising allowance.*

V.M.A.—C, *volume merchandising allowance—contract.*

V.O., *voice over.*

voice over, (in motion pictures or television) the voice of a narrator or commentator who is not seen. Abbreviated *V.O.*

voice track, a film sound track for voices.

volume discount, 1. a discount offered for the purchase of a certain amount of advertising in a medium.
2. a discount offered by a seller for the purchase of a certain amount of merchandise.

volume indicator, a meter for measuring the sound volume of a television or radio performance. Abbreviated *V.I.*

volume merchandising allowance, an allowance offered to a retailer for the purchase of large volumes of wholesale goods; offered as an encouragement to the retailer to merchandise the goods aggressively. Abbreviated *V.M.A.*

volume merchandising allowance — contract, a volume merchandising allowance made in consideration of a contract obligating a retailer to merchandise the goods in question aggressively. Abbreviated *V.M.A. — C.*

voluntary chain, a group of independent stores that combine under a common trade name for merchandising purposes, often under the sponsorship of a wholesaler. Also **voluntary association, voluntary group, voluntary.**

voluntary store, an independent retailer who belongs to a voluntary chain.

V.P.H., *viewers per household.*

V.P.S., *viewers per set.*

VTR, *videotape recording;* used as a notation or direction on commercial production material.

V/VH, *viewers per viewing household.*

W

waist shot, (in motion pictures or television) a shot of a person from the waist up.

wait order, an order to a periodical to hold an advertisement until told to run it.

walk-through, *noun* an early rehearsal for the purpose of allowing a show's performers to become acquainted with dialogue, motions, etc. Cf. *dry run.*

wall banner, a hanging advertisement in a retail store.

wall-to-wall, *adjective, informal* (of motion picture, radio, or television productions) without space or time for additional material.

warehouse, *noun* 1. a storage point for merchandise; can be owned by a manufacturer, wholesaler, or retailer.
verb 2. to place merchandise into such storage.

warehouse delivery, delivery directly from a manufacturer's or wholesaler's warehouse to a customer. Cf. *store-door delivery.*

warehouse store, a retail store, usually of large size, offering discount prices by means of reducing such services as carryouts, deliveries, price marking of items, shelf stocking, etc. Cf. *hypermarché.*

warm-up, *noun* a brief period before actual broadcasting or program recording in which the studio audience for a television or radio show is put in a responsive mood.

warning light, see *camera cue.*

warranty, *noun* a supplier's commitment to retail purchasers of a product or service that it will perform as specified, or the supplier will provide a limited compensation or service of a corrective nature. Cf. *guarantee.*

wash drawing, an ink or water-color drawing done mainly in tints or shaded tones, by use of diluted vehicles. Also **wash.**

waste circulation, a figure reflecting the readers of a periodical who are unlikely to purchase a certain product or service advertised in it.

water color, 1. any water-soluble paint, especially one intended for use on paper. 2. a painting made with such paint.

watermark, *noun* a faint design integrated into paper, appearing as a lighter area against the darker main area of the paper when held to the light; used as a papermaker's trademark, a symbol of the purchaser of the paper, etc.

wax-mold electrotype, a duplicate printing plate made from a wax mold of an original.

wearout, *noun* the point at which an advertisement loses its sales effectiveness due to excessive exposure and consequent disregard. Cf. *life.*

web, *noun* a roll of printing paper that allows continuous and repeated printing on a rotary press; used especially for newspapers, magazines and long run collateral pieces.

web-fed press, a rotary printing press using curved plates to print on a continuous roll of paper at high speeds. Also **web press.**

weekend special, a type of retail merchan-

203

dise given special displays or sold at a special price from Thursday through Saturday.

weight, *noun* 1. the relative darkness of the impression of a type face.
2. a description of paper stock weight based on weight of a ream (500 sheets) of predetermined size; e.g. 500 sheets, 25 by 38 inches, of enamel stock weighing 60 lbs. is called 60 lb. enamel.
3. the amount of advertising in support of an effort; expressed in terms of gross rating points, reach and frequency, impressions, spending levels, etc.

weighted mean, (in statistics) a mean attained by dividing a total distribution into steps, multiplying the midpoint for each step by the frequency scored for each step, adding the products together, and dividing by the total number of cases represented.

West Coast feed, 1. a television or radio program rebroadcast at a convenient hour on the West Coast that originates in New York or some other easterly point.
2. any broadcast material fed by a network to the West Coast.

Westinghouse Rule, a modification of the Prime Time Access Rule made in 1972 on an appeal by the Westinghouse Corporation, which included network film reruns among the network material restricted.

wet printing, a printing process, usually four color, in which each ink color is immediately laid over the previous color printed before it has dried.

w.f., *wrong font.*

Wheeler-Lea Amendment, an amendment of 1938 to the Federal Trade Commission Act forbidding false advertising of food, drugs, cosmetics, and health devices.

whip pan, (in motion pictures or television) a very rapid panning shot. Also *swish, zip pan.*

white audit, see *audit report.*

white coat rule, the restriction which prohibits advertisers from using spokesmen who purport or appear to be medical professionals (doctors, dentists, etc.) in advertisements, especially commercials.

white goods, (in retailing) major household appliances, such as refrigerators, stoves, washing machines, dishwashers, dryers, etc.

white space, an area or amount of unprinted space in or surrounding an advertisement.

whodunit, *noun* a mystery story presented via motion pictures, television, or radio.

wholesale broker, a broker who maintains a warehouse for resale of goods to wholesalers or retailers.

wholesaler, *noun* 1. a person or organization that sells to retailers only.
2. a person or organization that sells at wholesale prices.

wide-angle lens, a camera lens that covers a relatively larger area of a scene, with deeper perspective, than a normal lens at the same point. Cf. *telephoto lens.*

widow, *noun* (in typesetting) an objectionable short line, usually one word, or the end of a hyphenated word in a column of type.

wild recording, a recording of motion picture or television sound that is not syncronized with action shown, e.g., background noises.

wild shot, a motion picture or television camera shot without an accompanying recording of sound.

wild spot, (in television or radio) a spot commercial announcement for a national or regional advertiser used on local station breaks. Also *spot announcement.*

wild track, (in motion pictures or television) a sound track recorded separately from visual images it will accompany, hence not synchronized.

window, *noun* a transparent paper panel on an envelope that allows an address printed on a bill, form letter, etc. inside, to become the address of the envelope.

WINDOW STREAMER

A. Orange Festival Week

B. Special of the Day APPLES

A. Window Streamer
B. Window Poster

window streamer, a strip of advertising posted in a store window. Also **window banner.**

wing flat, see *book flat.*

wipe, *noun* 1. (in motion pictures or television) a transition between shots in the form of a moving line, expanding or contracting circle, etc. that forms a boundary between the preceding shot and the following shot.
verb 2. to remove recorded signals from magnetic tape.

wire recording, a magnetic audio recording made on wire.

withholding, *noun* (in Canada) preemption of television or radio time for the presentation of programs of special interest but not of any emergency or nationally important nature.

women's service magazine, a magazine largely of interest to homemakers and to women generally. Also *service magazine,* **women's service book.**

woodcut, *noun* 1. an engraving or carving on the face of a wooden block.
2. a print made from such a block.

Wool Products Labeling Act, a Federal law, effective in 1941, requiring truthful labeling of products purporting to contain wool.

word association test, a test used for evaluating attitudes, in which a respondent is asked to reply to a word spoken to him with the first word that comes to mind.

word-of-mouth advertising, advocacy of action regarding a product or service which is passed from one person to another without a sponsor's paid support (hence, not truly advertising). Cf. *two-step-flow theory.*

word space, to justify a line of type to a required measure by using more or less than normal spacing between words. Cf. *letterspace.*

work and turn, *adjective* noting or pertaining to the printing of sheets in such a way that the front side of a printed sheet and the back side of that sheet are printed side by side on the first pass through the press; turning the sheet over and feeding it through the press again completes the printing for both sides; the front backs up the back and the back backs up the front. Done to save the cost of an extra printing plate for each side and for each color. (If both fronts were printed two up and then backed up with two backs, an extra printing plate would be necessary). Cf. *sheetwise.*

work-back calculation, a calculation of a manufacturer's feasible price for a product, working back from the competitive retail price and the retailer's and wholesaler's markups.

work picture, (in motion pictures) a picture on an edited film, with optical effects to be added.

work print, a film print used for final editing in order to produce the answer print.

wove paper, a paper showing a faint textilelike mesh when held to the light.

wrap, *noun* 1. (in motion pictures and television) an end to a film or videotape recording sequence, when all shots necessary for the production are completed.
verb 2. to reach such an end.

wraparound, *noun* a decorative or promotional printed sheet wrapped around a case of retail items for display purposes.

wrapper, *noun* 1. see *dust jacket*.
2. a paper enclosure for a product, used as a package or label.

wrong font, a designation for a character from a different font set in place of one from the font specified. Abbreviated *w.f.*

X

x-axis, *noun* see *abscissa*.

xerography, *noun* a duplicating process in which pigment is attracted to the printing areas of a page by electric charges and baked on.

x-height, (in typography) the standard height of lower-case letters in a given font, measured by the height of the letter x.

X's, *crosses stage;* used as a stage direction.

Y

y-axis, *noun* see *ordinate.*

yellow goods, goods that are seldom consumed and replaced; usually require relatively high levels of service, are not broadly distributed, and have a relatively high gross margin (e.g., washing machines). Cf. *red goods, orange goods.*

Z

zero correlation, see *correlation.*

zinc etching, (obsolete) a line or halftone etching on zinc by means of nitric acid.

zinc halftone, (obsolete) a halftone etching on zinc.

Zip-A-Tone, *noun, trademark* a shading medium applied to artwork to create gray values without the use of a standard halftone screen.

zip pan, see *whip pan.*

zone, *noun* a geographical sub-area, used to define sales territories, mailing areas, etc. Cf. *unit, region.*

zone plan, (obsolescent) a plan for a nationwide advertising campaign beginning with an experimental campaign in one sales zone; test market. Cf. *test market, sales area test.*

zoomar lens, see *zoom lens.*

zoom in, (of a motion picture or television camera) to move swiftly from a long or medium camera position, to a close-up, without changing shots.

zoom lens, a camera lens capable of rapid changes of magnification and range, and hence, scene scale. Also *zoomar lens.*

zoom out, (of a motion picture or television camera) to move rapidly from a close-up or medium camera position to a long position, without changing shots.